the unbeatable Squirrel Girl

the unbeatab

COLLECTION EDITOR: **JENNIFER GRÜNWALD**
ASSISTANT EDITOR: **SARAH BRUNSTAD**
ASSOCIATE MANAGING EDITOR: **ALEX STARBUCK**
EDITOR, SPECIAL PROJECTS: **MARK D. BEAZLEY**
SENIOR EDITOR, SPECIAL PROJECTS: **JEFF YOUNGQUIST**
SVP PRINT, SALES & MARKETING: **DAVID GABRIEL**
BOOK DESIGNER: **JAY BOWEN**

EDITOR IN CHIEF: **AXEL ALONSO**
CHIEF CREATIVE OFFICER: **JOE QUESADA**
PUBLISHER: **DAN BUCKLEY**
EXECUTIVE PRODUCER: **ALAN FINE**

THE UNBEATABLE SQUIRREL GIRL VOL. 1: SQUIRREL POWER. Contains material originally published in magazine form as THE UNBEATABLE SQUIRREL GIRL #1-4 and MARVEL SUPER-HEROES #8. First printing 2015. ISBN# 978-0-7851-9702-7. Published by MARVEL WORLDWIDE, INC., a subsidiary of MARVEL ENTERTAINMENT, LLC. OFFICE OF PUBLICATION: 135 West 50th Street, New York, NY 10020. Copyright © 2015 MARVEL No similarity between any of the names, characters, persons, and/or institutions in this magazine with those of any living or dead person or institution is intended, and any such similarity which may exist is purely coincidental. **Printed in Canada. ALAN FINE,** President, Marvel Entertainment; DAN BUCKLEY, President, TV, Publishing and Brand Management; JOE QUESADA, Chief Creative Officer; TOM BREVOORT, SVP of Publishing; DAVID BOGART, SVP of Operations & Procurement, Publishing; C.B. CEBULSKI, VP of International Development & Brand Management; DAVID GABRIEL, SVP Print, Sales & Marketing; JIM O'KEEFE, VP of Operations & Logistics; DAN CARR, Executive Director of Publishing Technology; SUSAN CRESPI, Editorial Operations Manager; ALEX MORALES, Publishing Operations Manager; STAN LEE, Chairman Emeritus. For information regarding advertising in Marvel Comics or on Marvel.com, please contact Jonathan Rheingold, VP of Custom Solutions & Ad Sales, at jrheingold@marvel.com. For Marvel subscription inquiries, please call 800-217-9158. **Manufactured between** 6/26/2015 and 8/3/2015 by SOLISCO PRINTERS, SCOTT, QC, CANADA.

10 9 8 7 6 5 4 3 2 1

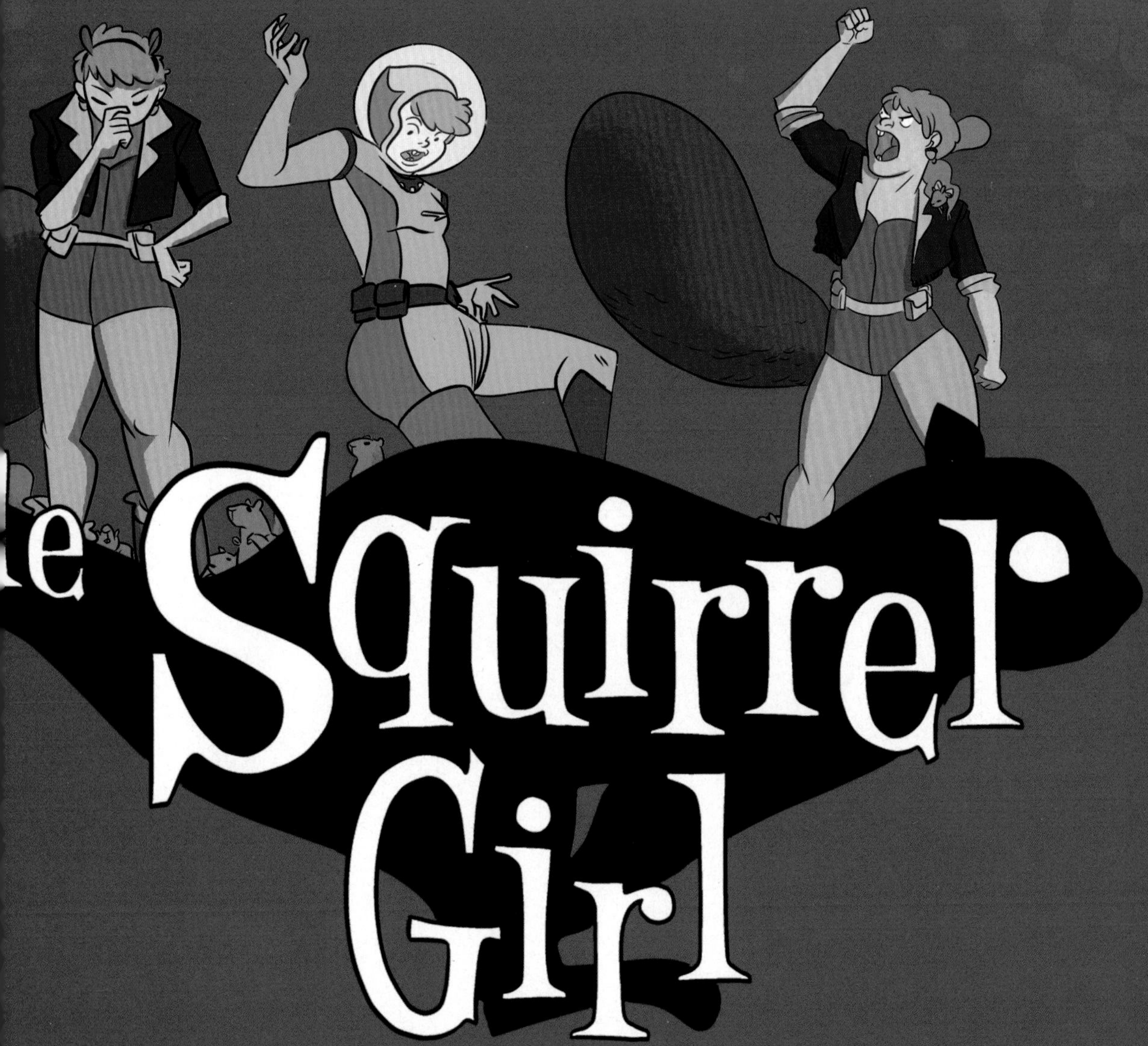
Squirrel
Girl

Ryan North
WRITER

Erica Henderson
ARTIST

Maris Wicks *(#1)*, ***Kyle Starks*** *(#3)* & ***Chris Giarrusso*** *(#4)*
TRADING CARD ART

Rico Renzi
COLOR ARTIST

VC's Clayton Cowles
LETTERER

Erica Henderson
COVER ART

Jon Moisan & Jake Thomas
ASSISTANT EDITORS

Wil Moss
EDITOR

Tom Brevoort
EXECUTIVE EDITOR

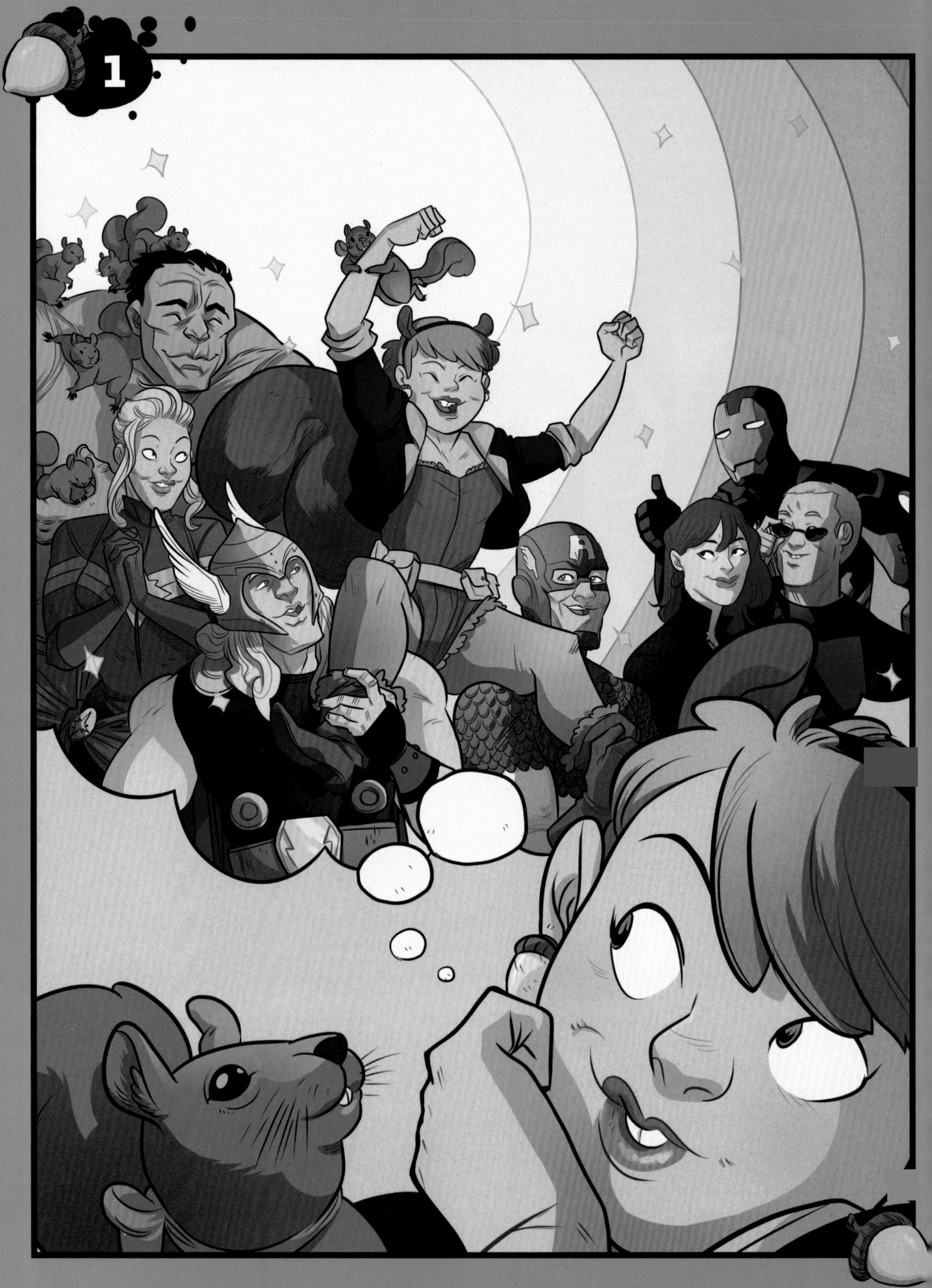
1

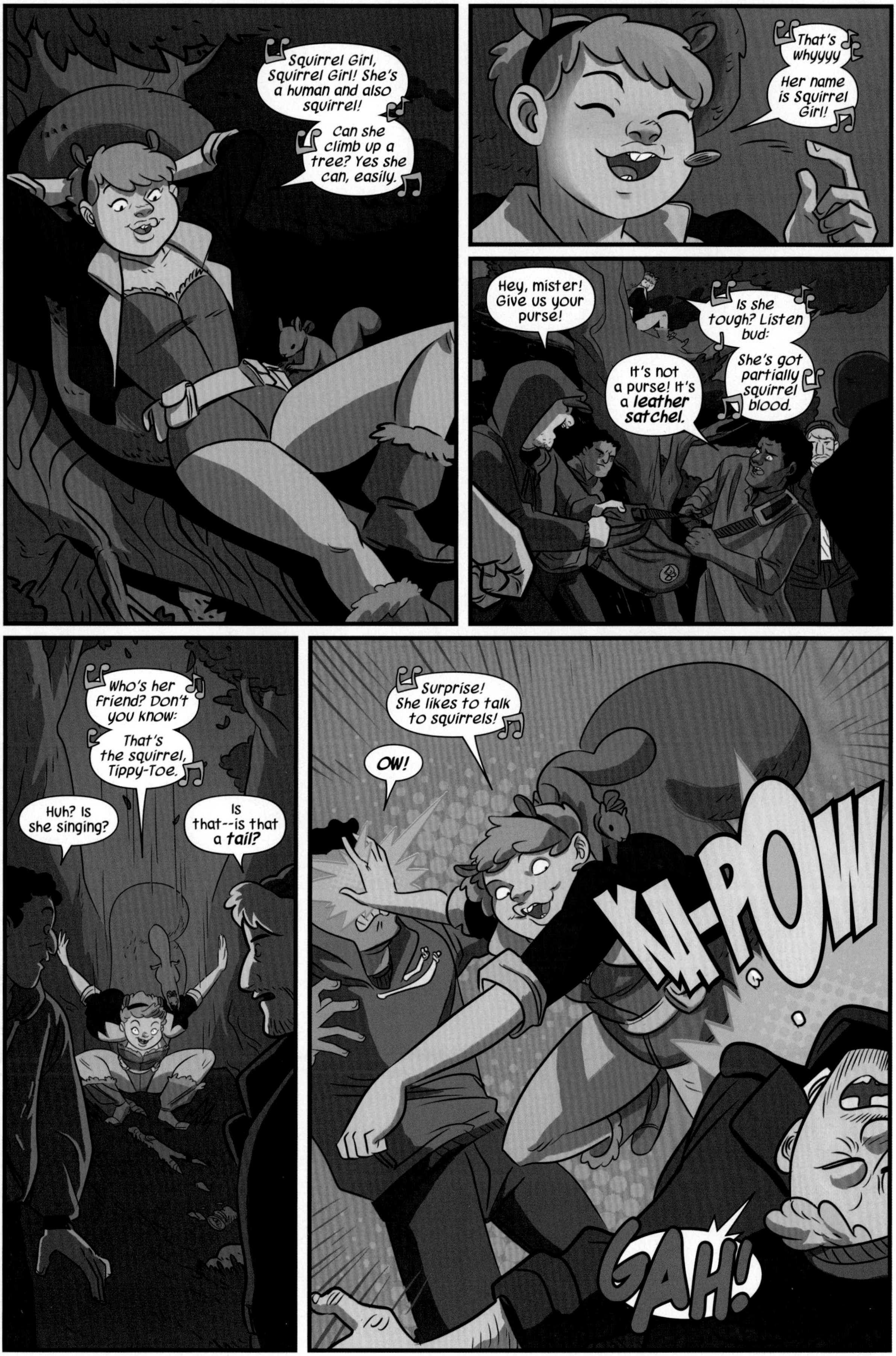
Squirrel Girl, Squirrel Girl! She's a human and also squirrel!
Can she climb up a tree? Yes she can, easily.
That's whyyyy
Her name is Squirrel Girl!
Hey, mister! Give us your purse!
Is she tough? Listen bud:
It's not a purse! It's a leather satchel.
She's got partially squirrel blood.
Who's her friend? Don't you know:
That's the squirrel, Tippy-Toe.
Huh? Is she singing?
Is that--is that a tail?
Surprise! She likes to talk to squirrels!
OW!
KA-POW
GAH!

At the top of trees, is where she spends her time

Like a huuuuman squirrel

She enjoys

Fighting crime!!

AHHHHHH!

I am currently reevaluating the choices that led me to a criminal liiiiiife!!

Squirrel Girl, Squirrel Girl! Powers of both squirrel and girl!

Finds some nuts, eats some nuts! Kicks bad guuuuuys' evil butts!

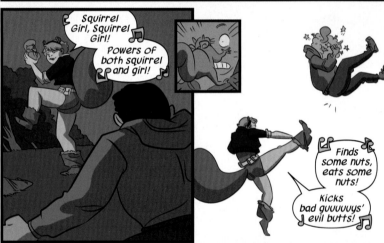

To her, life is a great big acorn!

Where there's a city crime-torn,

You'll find the **Squirrel Girl!!!**

Now if we could just get anyone **else** to sing that song, we'd be set.

I know, right??

You now have the Spider-Man theme song stuck in your head for the rest of this issue. *You're welcome.*

AR

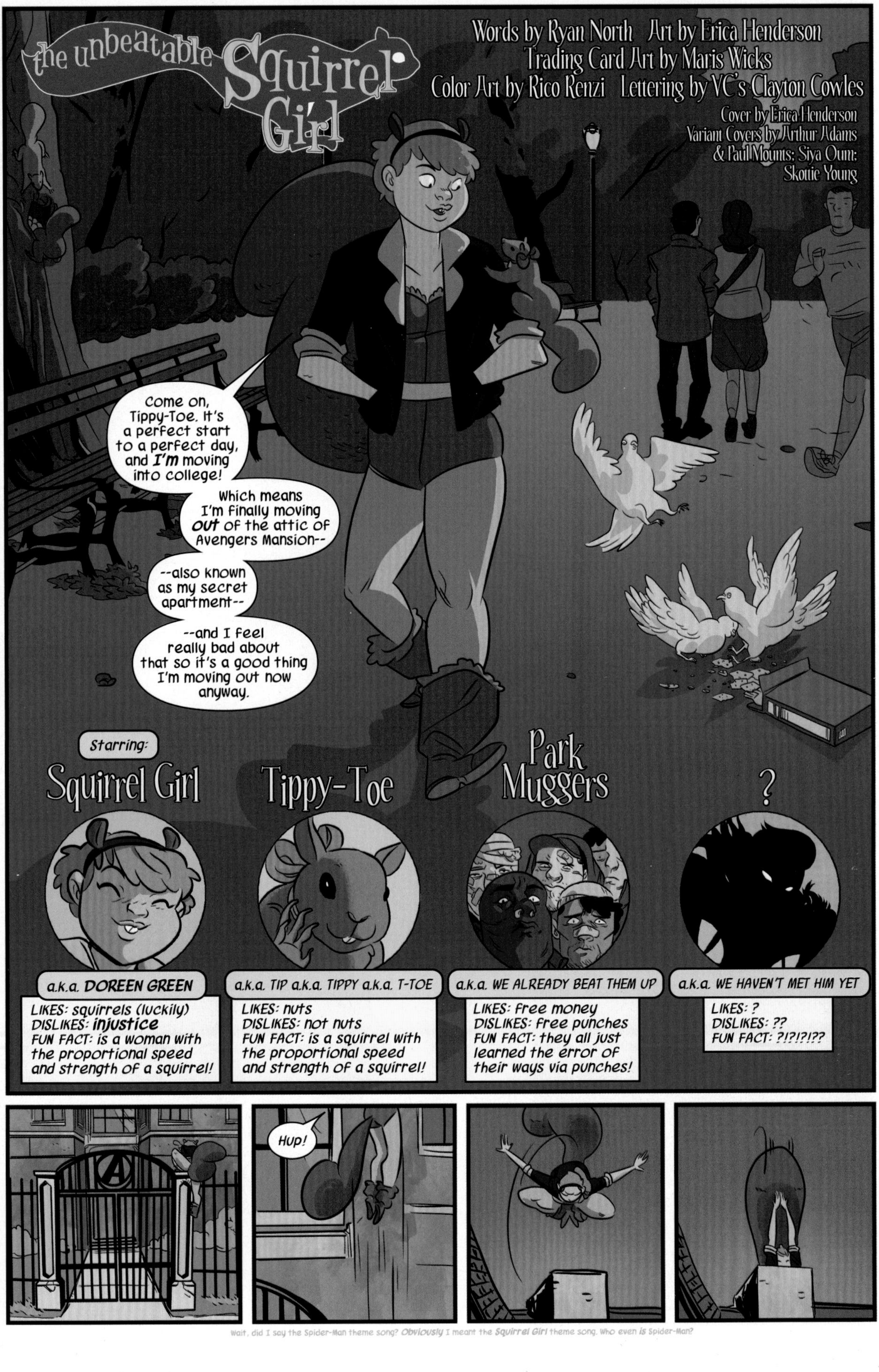
the unbeatable Squirrel Girl
Words by Ryan North Art by Erica Henderson
Trading Card Art by Maris Wicks
Color Art by Rico Renzi Lettering by VC's Clayton Cowles
Cover by Erica Henderson
Variant Covers by Arthur Adams & Paul Mounts; Siya Oum; Skottie Young
Come on, Tippy-Toe. It's a perfect start to a perfect day, and *I'm* moving into college!
Which means I'm finally moving *out* of the attic of Avengers Mansion--
--also known as my secret apartment--
--and I feel really bad about that so it's a good thing I'm moving out now anyway.
Starring:
Squirrel Girl
a.k.a. DOREEN GREEN
LIKES: squirrels (luckily)
DISLIKES: injustice
FUN FACT: is a woman with the proportional speed and strength of a squirrel!
Tippy-Toe
a.k.a. TIP a.k.a. TIPPY a.k.a. T-TOE
LIKES: nuts
DISLIKES: not nuts
FUN FACT: is a squirrel with the proportional speed and strength of a squirrel!
Park Muggers
a.k.a. WE ALREADY BEAT THEM UP
LIKES: free money
DISLIKES: free punches
FUN FACT: they all just learned the error of their ways via punches!
?
a.k.a. WE HAVEN'T MET HIM YET
LIKES: ?
DISLIKES: ??
FUN FACT: ?!?!?!??
Hup!

Wait, did I say the Spider-Man theme song? *Obviously* I meant the *Squirrel Girl* theme song. Who even *is* Spider-Man?

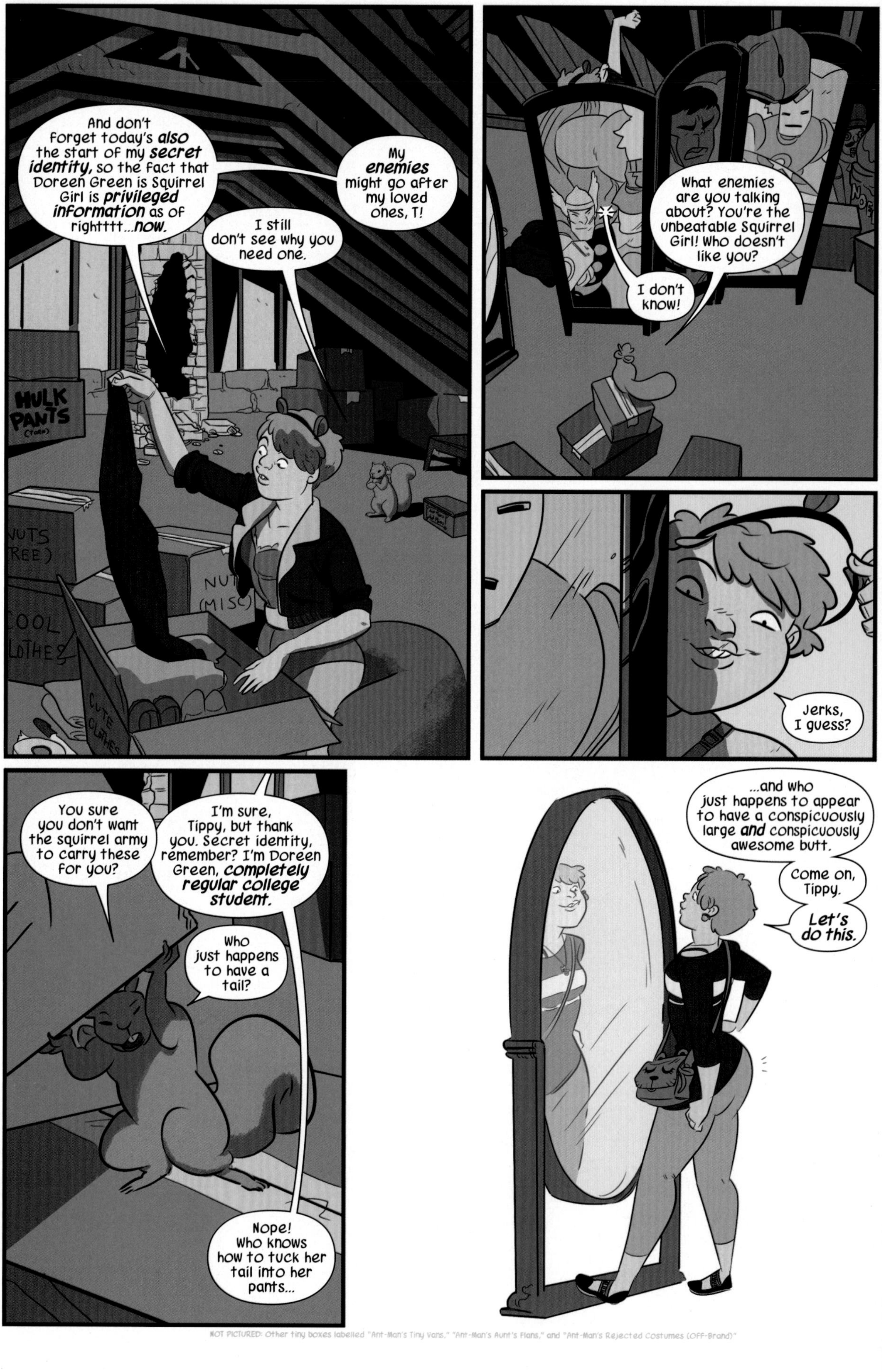
And don't forget today's also the start of my secret identity, so the fact that Doreen Green is Squirrel Girl is privileged information as of righttttt...now.
My enemies might go after my loved ones, T!
I still don't see why you need one.
HULK PANTS
NUTS (TREE)
NUTS (MISC)
COOL CLOTHES
CUTE CLOTHES
What enemies are you talking about? You're the unbeatable Squirrel Girl! Who doesn't like you?
I don't know!
Jerks, I guess?
You sure you don't want the squirrel army to carry these for you?
I'm sure, Tippy, but thank you. Secret identity, remember? I'm Doreen Green, completely regular college student.
Who just happens to have a tail?
Nope! Who knows how to tuck her tail into her pants...
...and who just happens to appear to have a conspicuously large and conspicuously awesome butt.
Come on, Tippy.
Let's do this.

NOT PICTURED: Other tiny boxes labelled "Ant-Man's Tiny Vans," "Ant-Man's Aunt's Flans," and "Ant-Man's Rejected Costumes (OFF-Brand)"

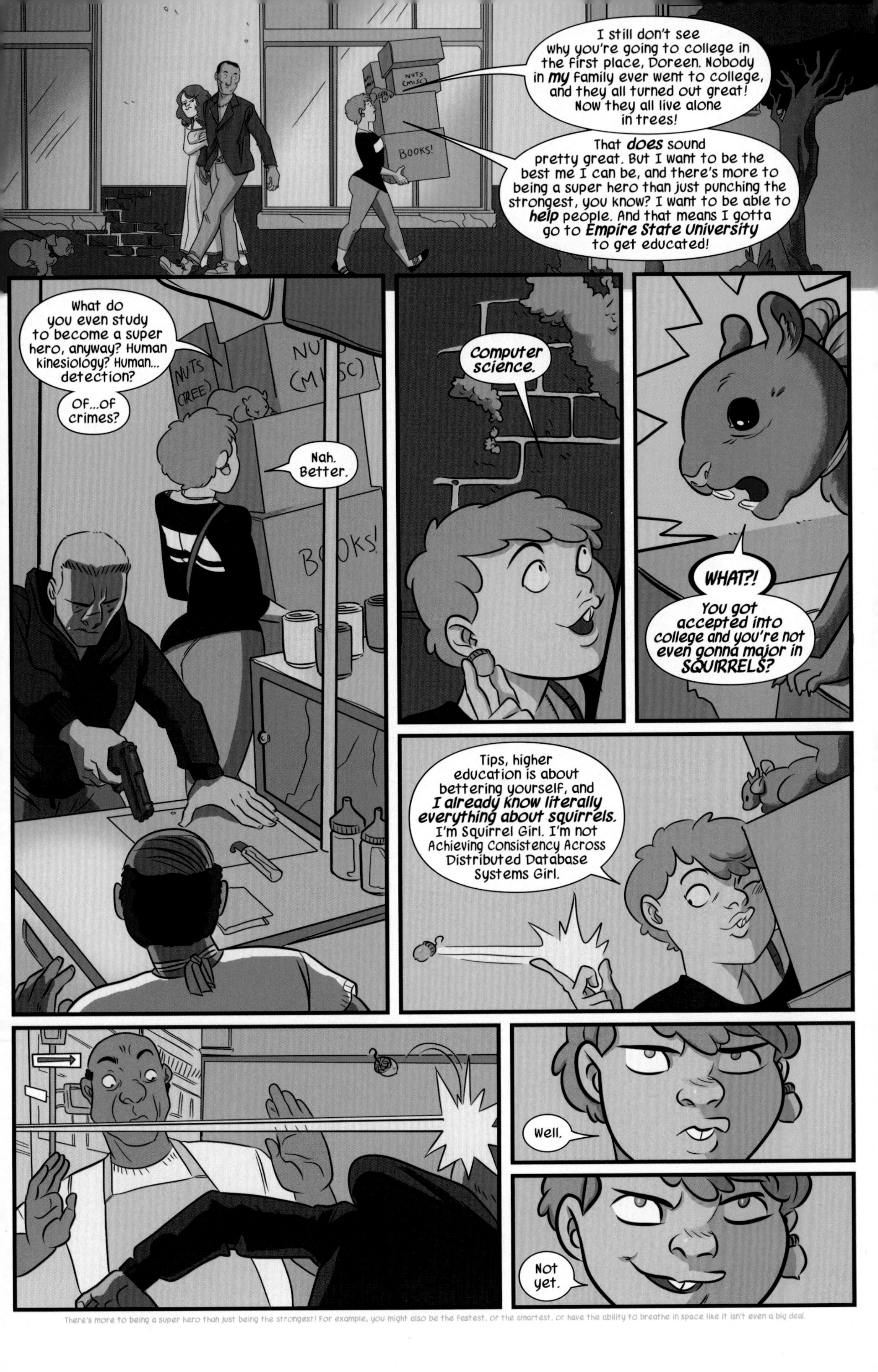
I still don't see why you're going to college in the first place, Doreen. Nobody in my family ever went to college, and they all turned out great! Now they all live alone in trees!
NUTS (MISC)
BOOKS!
That does sound pretty great. But I want to be the best me I can be, and there's more to being a super hero than just punching the strongest, you know? I want to be able to help people. And that means I gotta go to Empire State University to get educated!
What do you even study to become a super hero, anyway? Human kinesiology? Human... detection?
Of...of crimes?
NUTS (TREE)
NUTS (MISC)
BOOKS!
Nah. Better.
Computer science.
WHAT?!
You got accepted into college and you're not even gonna major in SQUIRRELS?
Tips, higher education is about bettering yourself, and I already know literally everything about squirrels. I'm Squirrel Girl. I'm not Achieving Consistency Across Distributed Database Systems Girl.
Well.
Not yet.

There's more to being a super hero than just being the strongest! For example, you might also be the fastest, or the smartest, or have the ability to breathe in space like it isn't even a big deal.

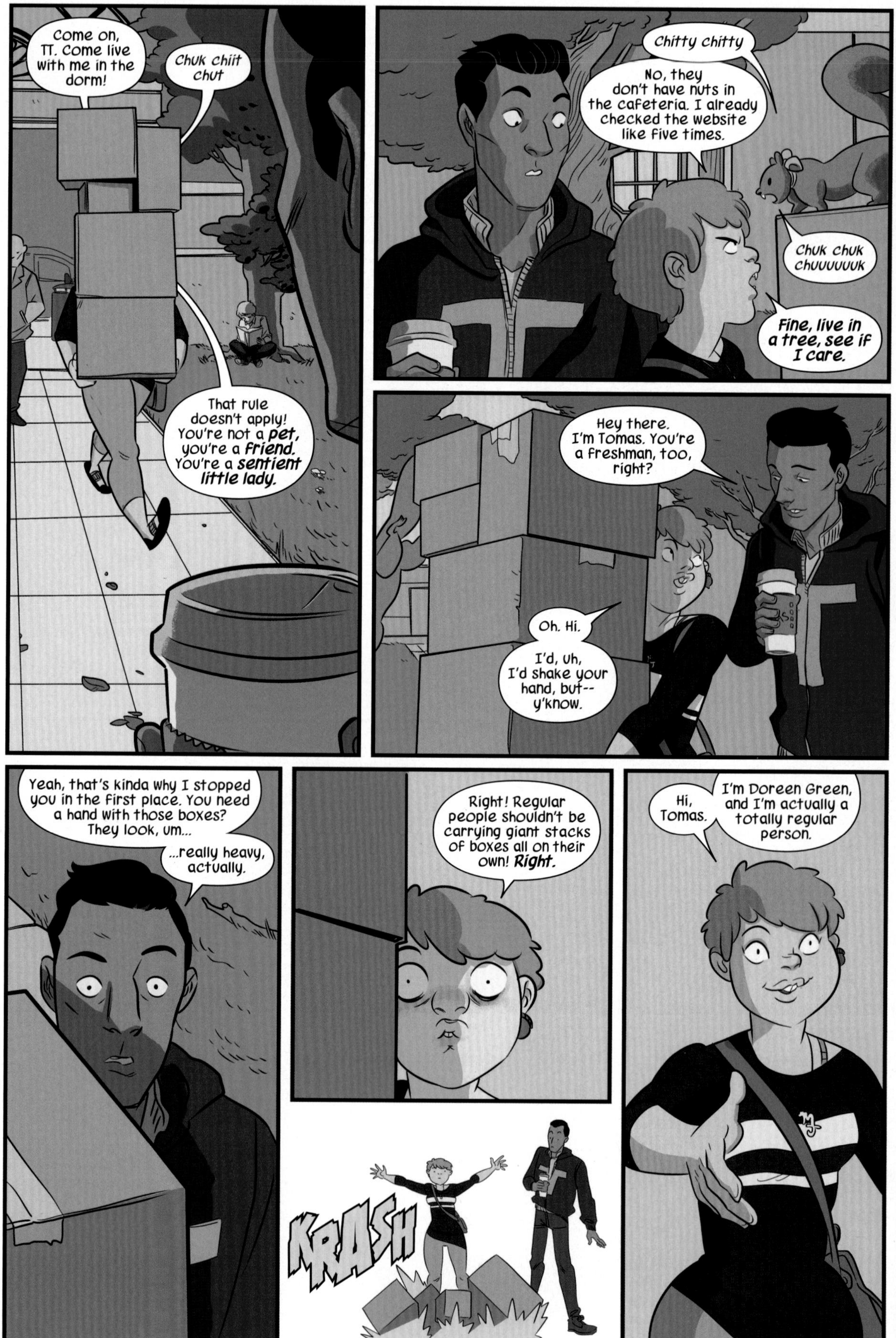
Come on, TT. Come live with me in the dorm!
Chuk chiit chut
That rule doesn't apply! You're not a **pet**, you're a **friend**. You're a **sentient little lady.**
Chitty chitty
No, they don't have nuts in the cafeteria. I already checked the website like five times.
Chuk chuk chuuuuuuk
Fine, live in a tree, see if I care.
Hey there. I'm Tomas. You're a freshman, too, right?
Oh. Hi.
I'd, uh, I'd shake your hand, but-- y'know.
Yeah, that's kinda why I stopped you in the first place. You need a hand with those boxes? They look, um...
...really heavy, actually.
Right! Regular people shouldn't be carrying giant stacks of boxes all on their own! **Right.**
KRASH
Hi, Tomas.
I'm Doreen Green, and I'm actually a totally regular person.

Also, my name rhymes. Yes, that too is but one of the ***several*** ways in which I am totally regular.

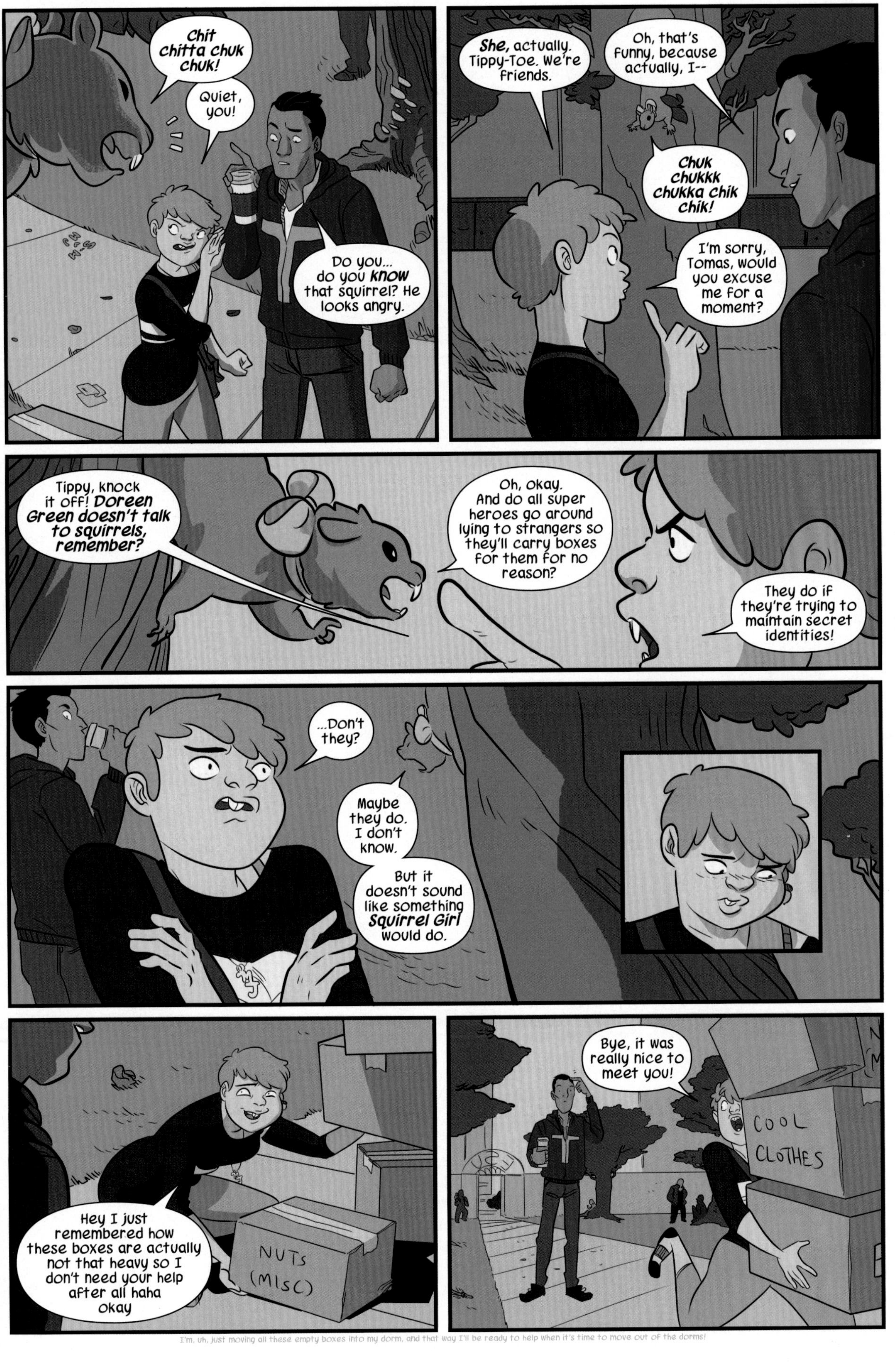
Chit chitta chuk chuk!
Quiet, you!
Do you... do you know that squirrel? He looks angry.
She, actually. Tippy-Toe. We're friends.
Oh, that's funny, because actually, I--
Chuk chukkk chukka chik chik!
I'm sorry, Tomas, would you excuse me for a moment?
Tippy, knock it off! Doreen Green doesn't talk to squirrels, remember?
Oh, okay. And do all super heroes go around lying to strangers so they'll carry boxes for them for no reason?
They do if they're trying to maintain secret identities!
...Don't they?
Maybe they do. I don't know.
But it doesn't sound like something Squirrel Girl would do.
Hey I just remembered how these boxes are actually not that heavy so I don't need your help after all haha okay
NUTs (MISC)
Bye, it was really nice to meet you!
COOL CLOTHES

I'm, uh, just moving all these empty boxes into my dorm, and that way I'll be ready to help when it's time to move out of the dorms!

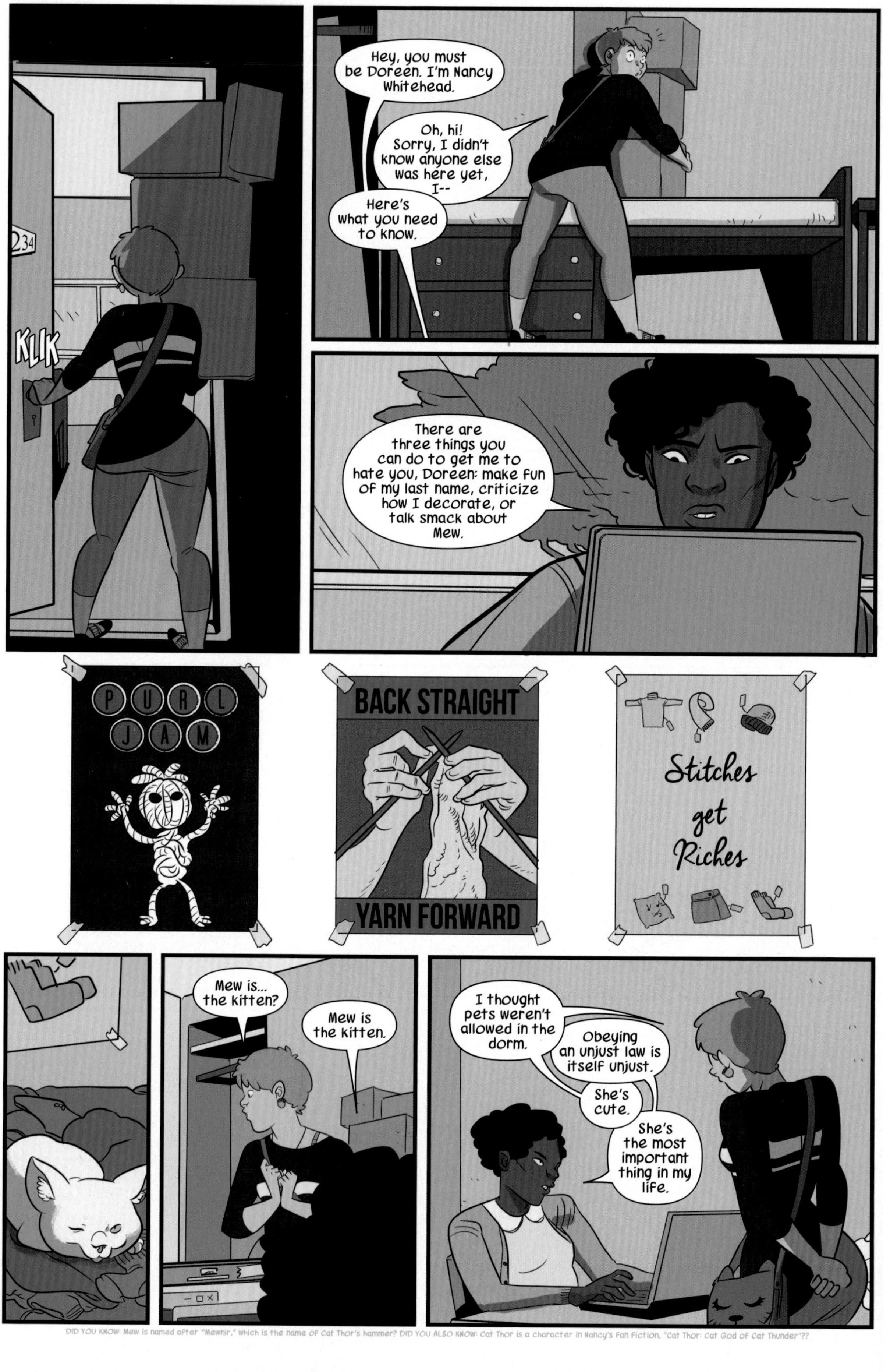
KLIK
234
Hey, you must be Doreen. I'm Nancy Whitehead.
Oh, hi! Sorry, I didn't know anyone else was here yet, I--
Here's what you need to know.
There are three things you can do to get me to hate you, Doreen: make fun of my last name, criticize how I decorate, or talk smack about Mew.
PURL JAM
BACK STRAIGHT
YARN FORWARD
Stitches get Riches
Mew is... the kitten?
Mew is the kitten.
I thought pets weren't allowed in the dorm.
Obeying an unjust law is itself unjust.
She's cute.
She's the most important thing in my life.

DID YOU KNOW: Mew is named after "Mewnir," which is the name of Cat Thor's hammer? DID YOU ALSO KNOW: Cat Thor is a character in Nancy's Fan Fiction, "Cat Thor: Cat God of Cat Thunder"??

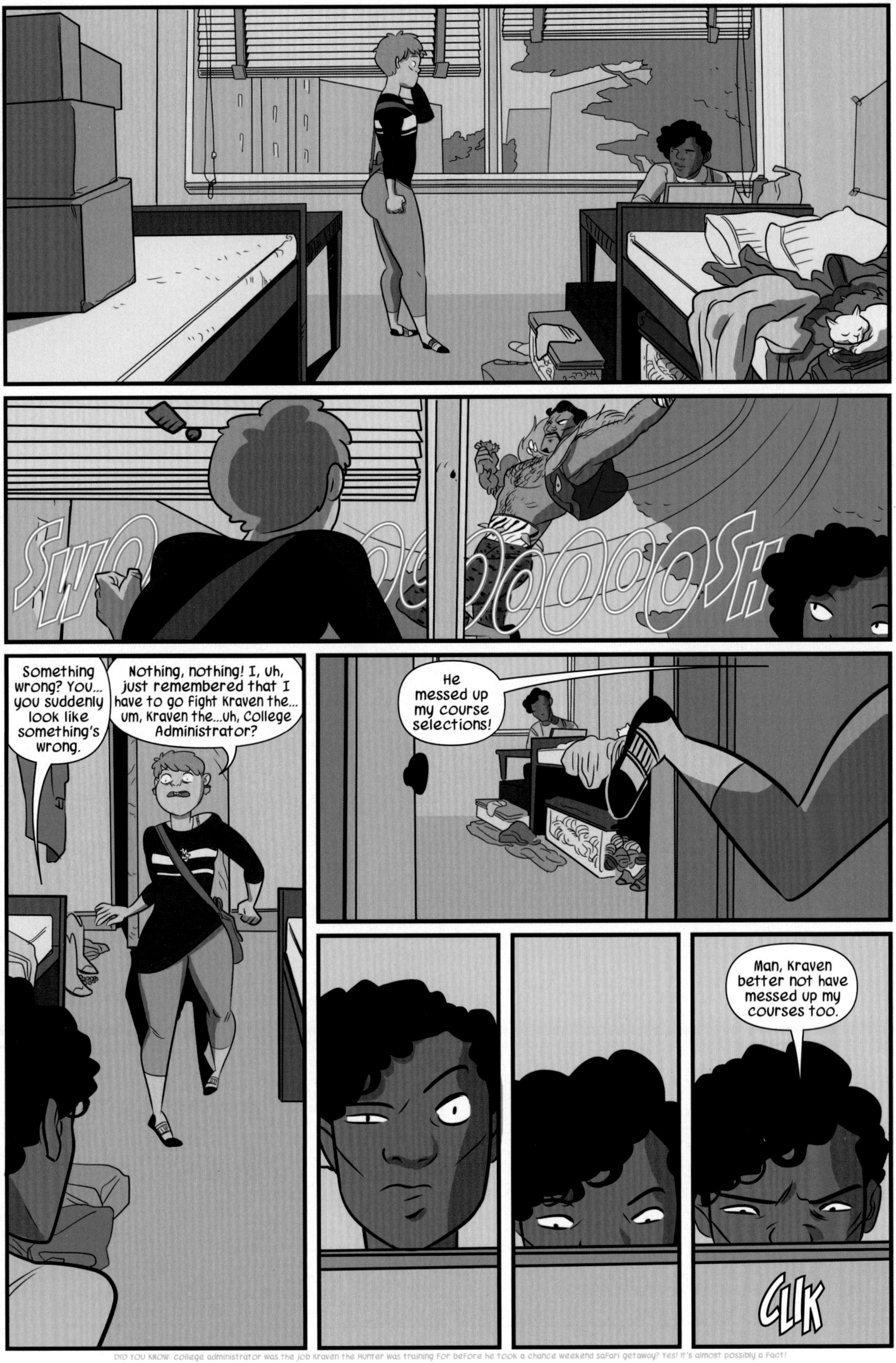
SWOOOOOOOOOSH
Something wrong? You... you suddenly look like something's wrong.
Nothing, nothing! I, uh, just remembered that I have to go fight Kraven the... um, Kraven the...uh, College Administrator?
He messed up my course selections!
Man, Kraven better not have messed up my courses too.
CLIK

DID YOU KNOW: college administrator was the job Kraven the Hunter was training for before he took a chance weekend safari getaway? Yes! It's almost possibly a fact!

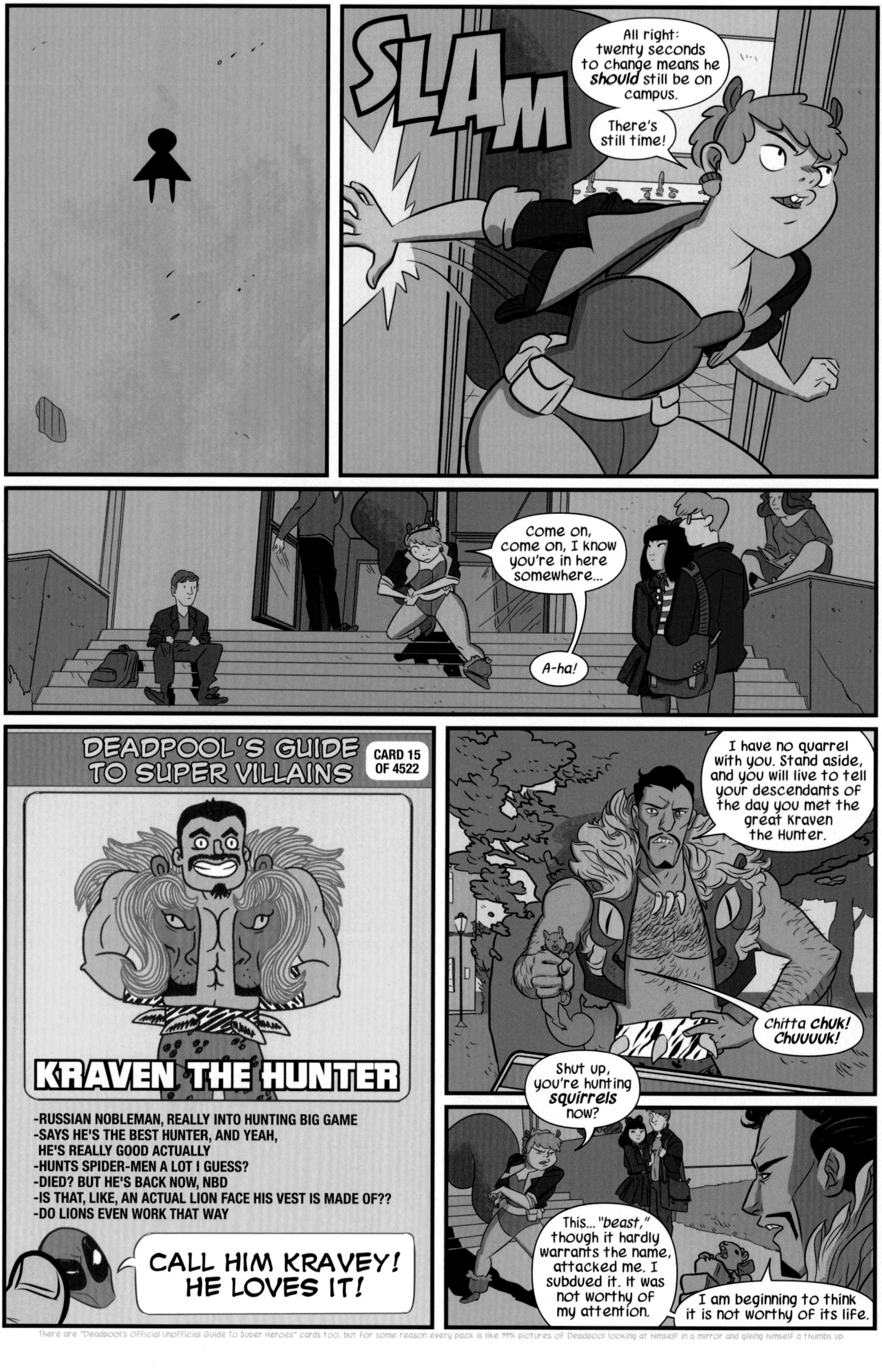
SLAM
All right: twenty seconds to change means he *should* still be on campus.
There's still time!
Come on, come on, I know you're in here somewhere...
A-ha!
DEADPOOL'S GUIDE TO SUPER VILLAINS
CARD 15 OF 4522
KRAVEN THE HUNTER
-RUSSIAN NOBLEMAN, REALLY INTO HUNTING BIG GAME
-SAYS HE'S THE BEST HUNTER, AND YEAH, HE'S REALLY GOOD ACTUALLY
-HUNTS SPIDER-MEN A LOT I GUESS?
-DIED? BUT HE'S BACK NOW, NBD
-IS THAT, LIKE, AN ACTUAL LION FACE HIS VEST IS MADE OF??
-DO LIONS EVEN WORK THAT WAY
CALL HIM KRAVEY! HE LOVES IT!
I have no quarrel with you. Stand aside, and you will live to tell your descendants of the day you met the great Kraven the Hunter.
Chitta **CHUK! CHUUUUK!**
Shut up, you're hunting **squirrels** now?
This... *"beast,"* though it hardly warrants the name, attacked me. I subdued it. It was not worthy of my attention.
I am beginning to think it is not worthy of its life.

There are "Deadpool's Official Unofficial Guide To Super Heroes" cards too, but for some reason every pack is like 99% pictures of Deadpool looking at himself in a mirror and giving himself a thumbs up.

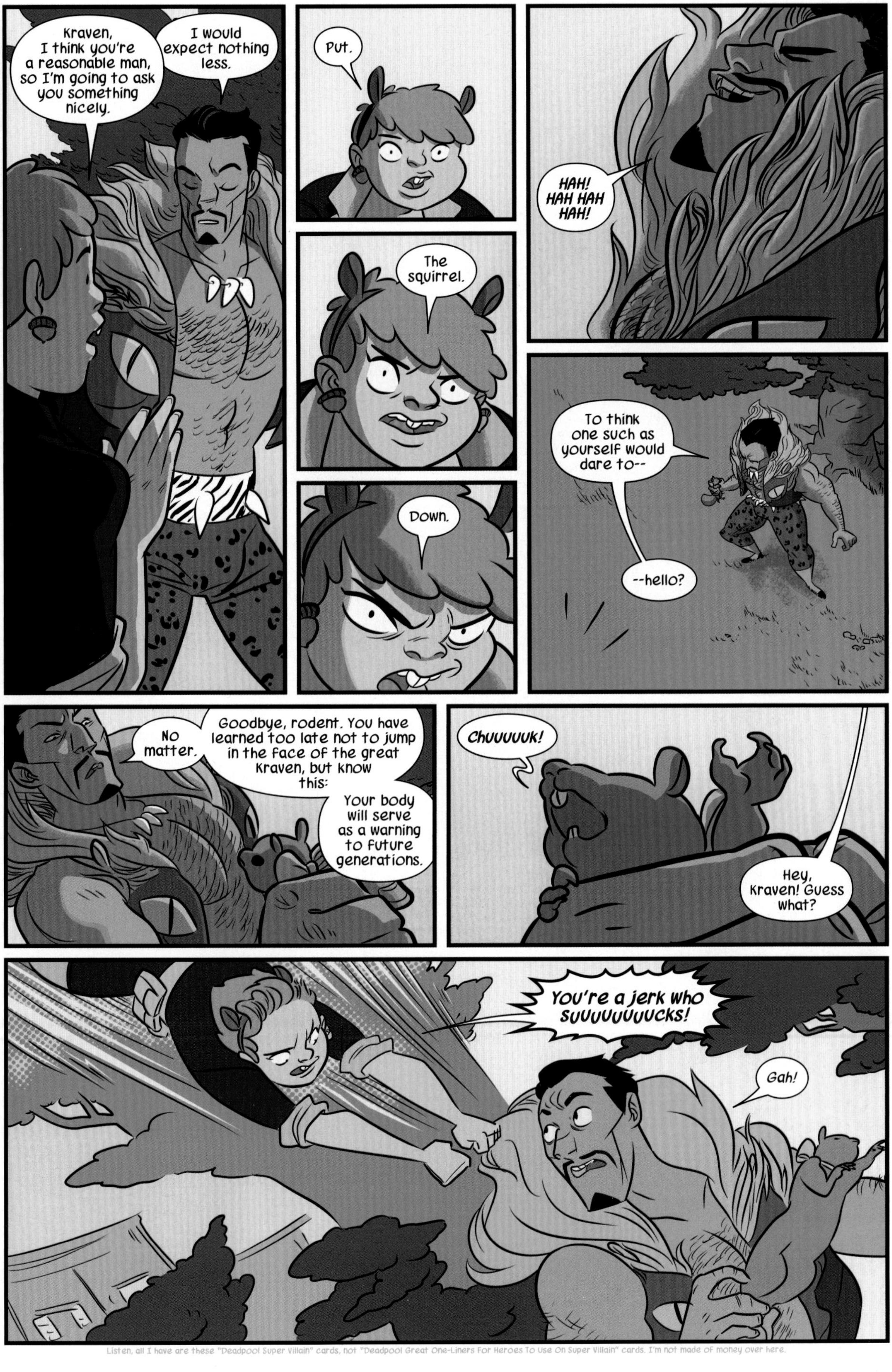
Kraven, I think you're a reasonable man, so I'm going to ask you something nicely.
I would expect nothing less.
Put.
The squirrel.
Down.
HAH! HAH HAH HAH!
To think one such as yourself would dare to--
--hello?
No matter.
Goodbye, rodent. You have learned too late not to jump in the face of the great Kraven, but know this:
Your body will serve as a warning to future generations.
Chuuuuuk!
Hey, Kraven! Guess what?
You're a jerk who SUUUUUUUUCKS!
Gah!

Listen, all I have are these "Deadpool Super Villain" cards, not "Deadpool Great One-Liners For Heroes To Use On Super Villain" cards. I'm not made of money over here.

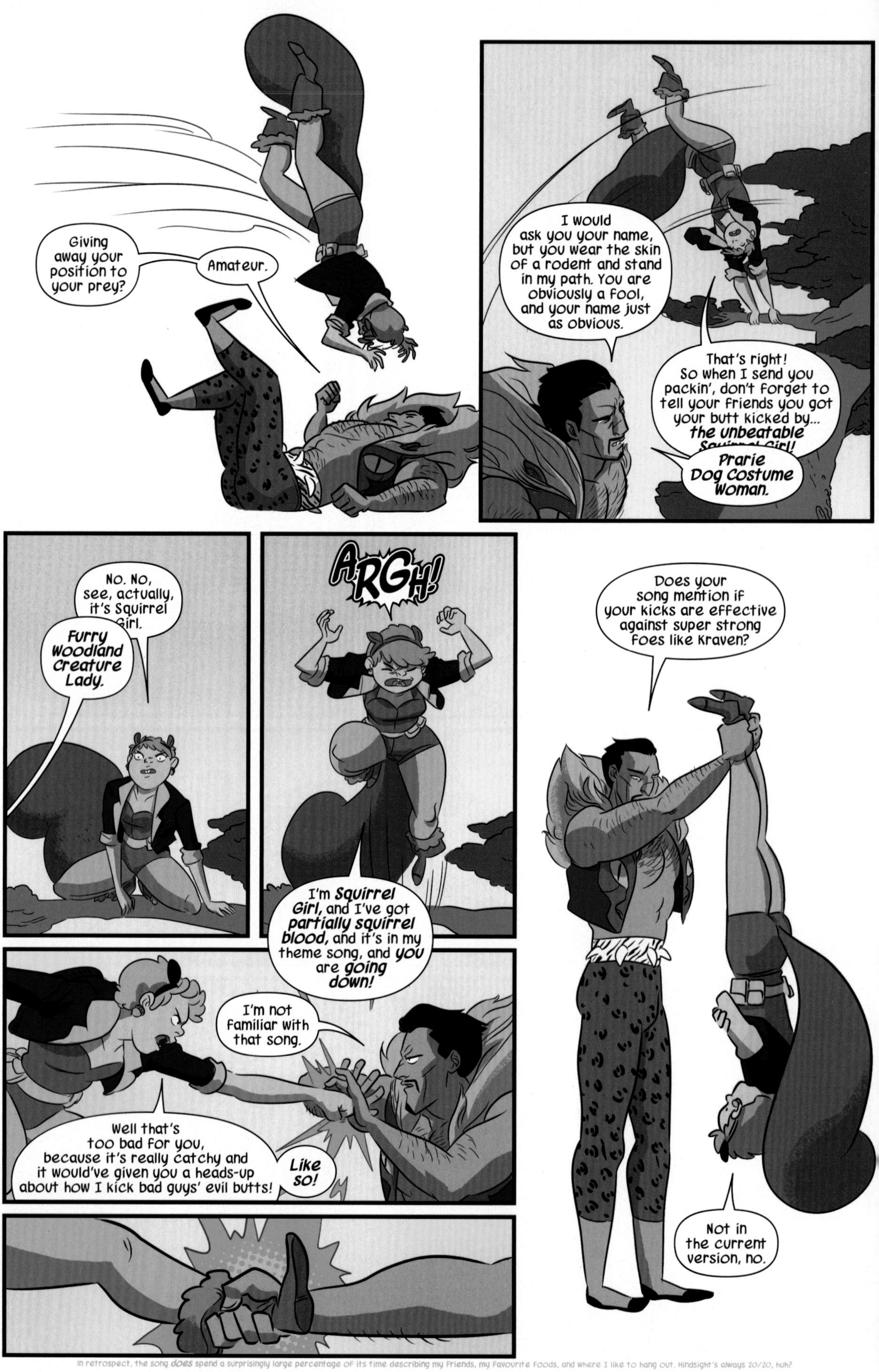
Giving away your position to your prey?
Amateur.
I would ask you your name, but you wear the skin of a rodent and stand in my path. You are obviously a fool, and your name just as obvious.
That's right! So when I send you packin', don't forget to tell your friends you got your butt kicked by... ***the unbeatable***
Prarie Dog Costume Woman.
No. No, see, actually, it's Squirrel Girl.
Furry Woodland Creature Lady.
ARGH!
I'm ***Squirrel Girl,*** and I've got ***partially squirrel blood,*** and it's in my theme song, and ***you*** are ***going down!***
I'm not familiar with that song.
Well that's too bad for you, because it's really catchy and it would've given you a heads-up about how I kick bad guys' evil butts!
Like so!
Does your song mention if your kicks are effective against super strong foes like Kraven?
Not in the current version, no.

In retrospect, the song *does* spend a surprisingly large percentage of its time describing my friends, my favourite foods, and where I like to hang out. Hindsight's always 20/20, huh?

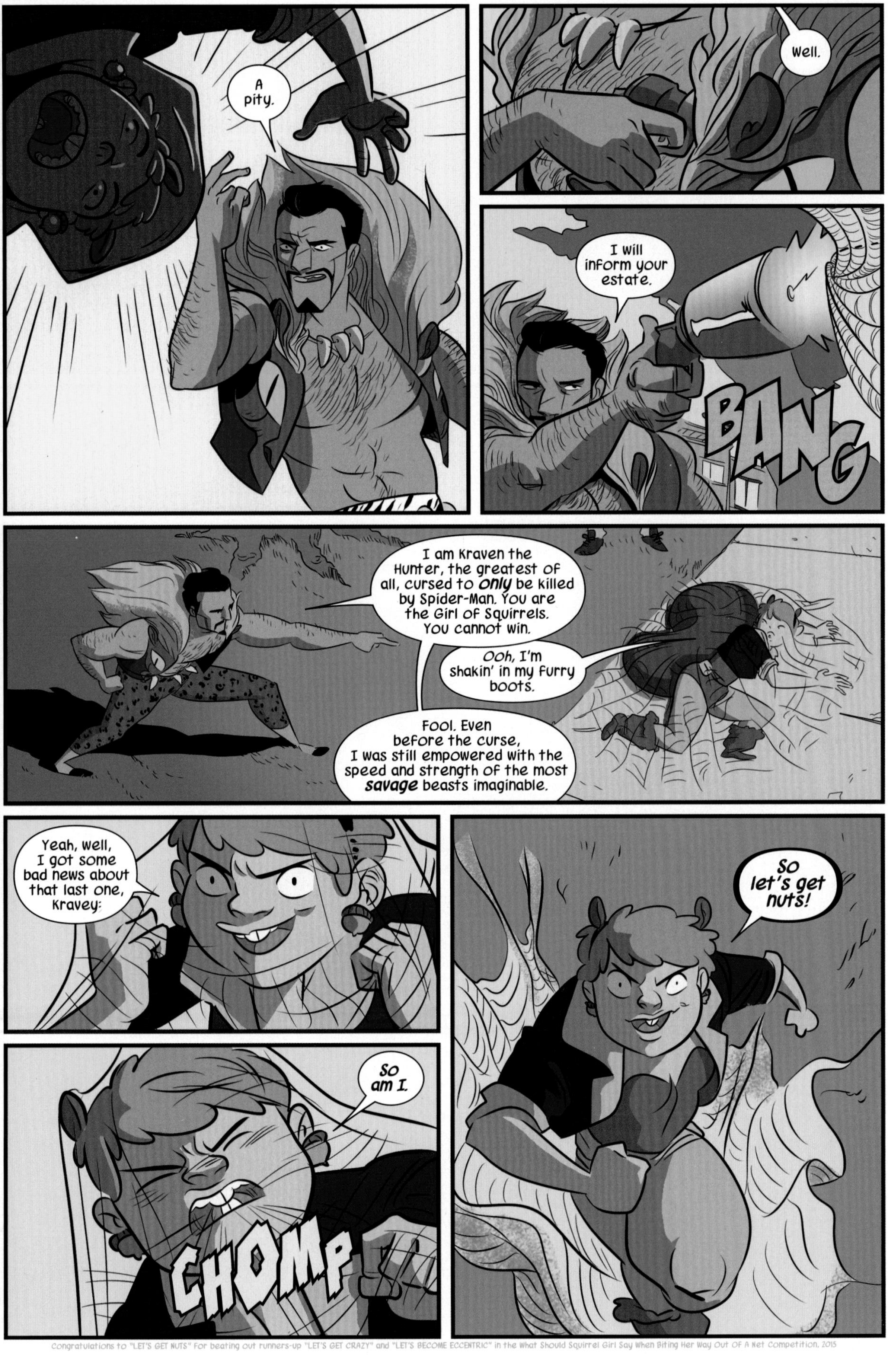
A pity.
Well.
I will inform your estate.
BANG
I am Kraven the Hunter, the greatest of all, cursed to *only* be killed by Spider-Man. You are the Girl of Squirrels. You cannot win.
Ooh, I'm shakin' in my furry boots.
Fool. Even before the curse, I was still empowered with the speed and strength of the most *savage* beasts imaginable.
Yeah, well, I got some bad news about that last one, Kravey:
So am I.
CHOMP
So let's get nuts!

Congratulations to "LET'S GET NUTS" for beating out runners-up "LET'S GET CRAZY" and "LET'S BECOME ECCENTRIC" in the What Should Squirrel Girl Say When Biting Her Way Out Of A Net Competition, 2015

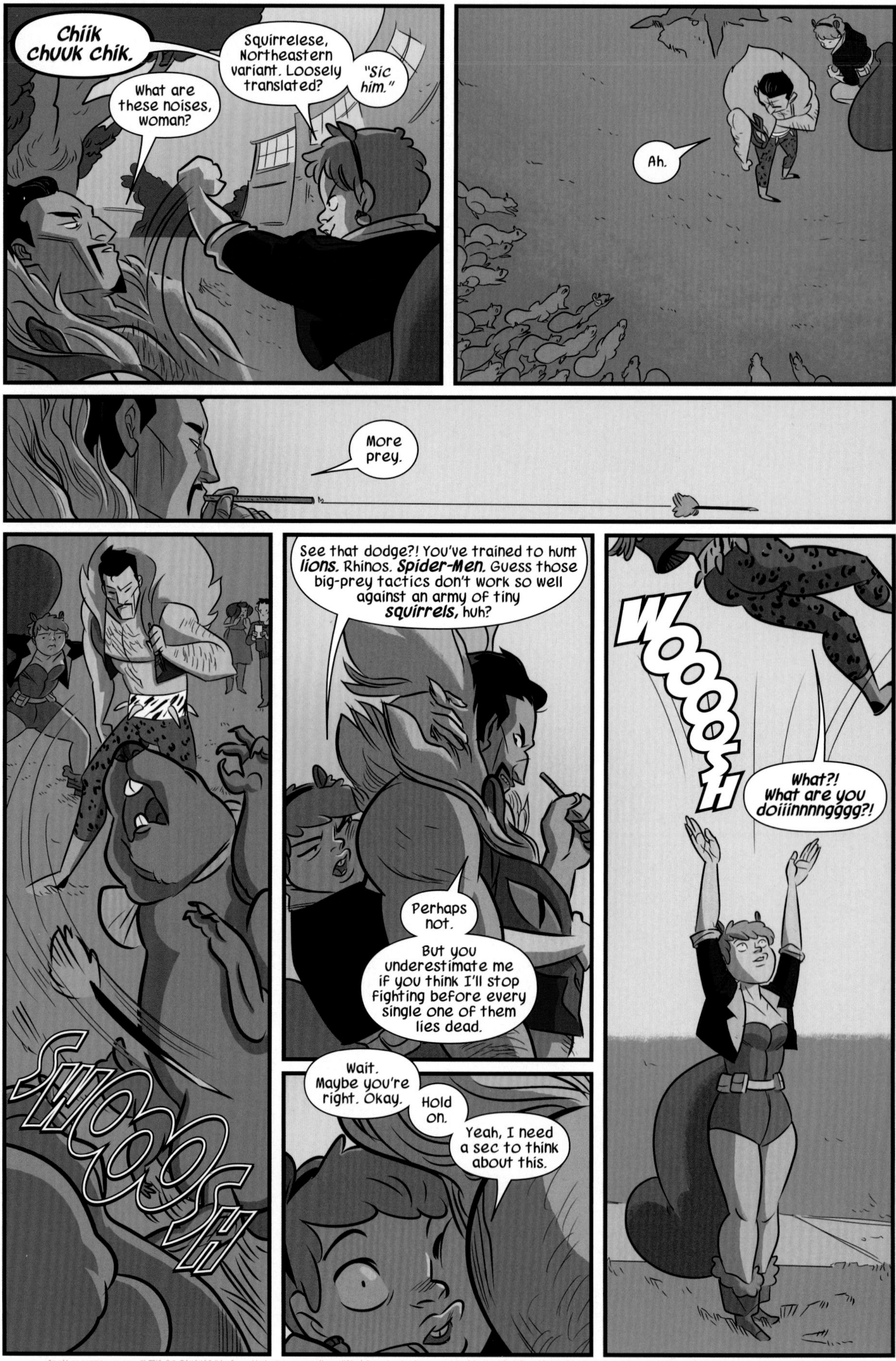
Chiik chuuk chik.
What are these noises, woman?
Squirrelese, Northeastern variant. Loosely translated?
"Sic him."
Ah.
More prey.
WOOOOOSH
See that dodge?! You've trained to hunt lions. Rhinos. Spider-Men. Guess those big-prey tactics don't work so well against an army of tiny squirrels, huh?
Perhaps not.
But you underestimate me if you think I'll stop fighting before every single one of them lies dead.
Wait. Maybe you're right. Okay.
Hold on.
Yeah, I need a sec to think about this.
WOOOOOSH
What?! What are you doiiinnnngggg?!

Another runner-up was "LET'S GO BANANAS," before that phrase was disqualified for also having competed in the What Should Man-Ape Say When Biting into A Banana Really Intensely Competition, 2015.

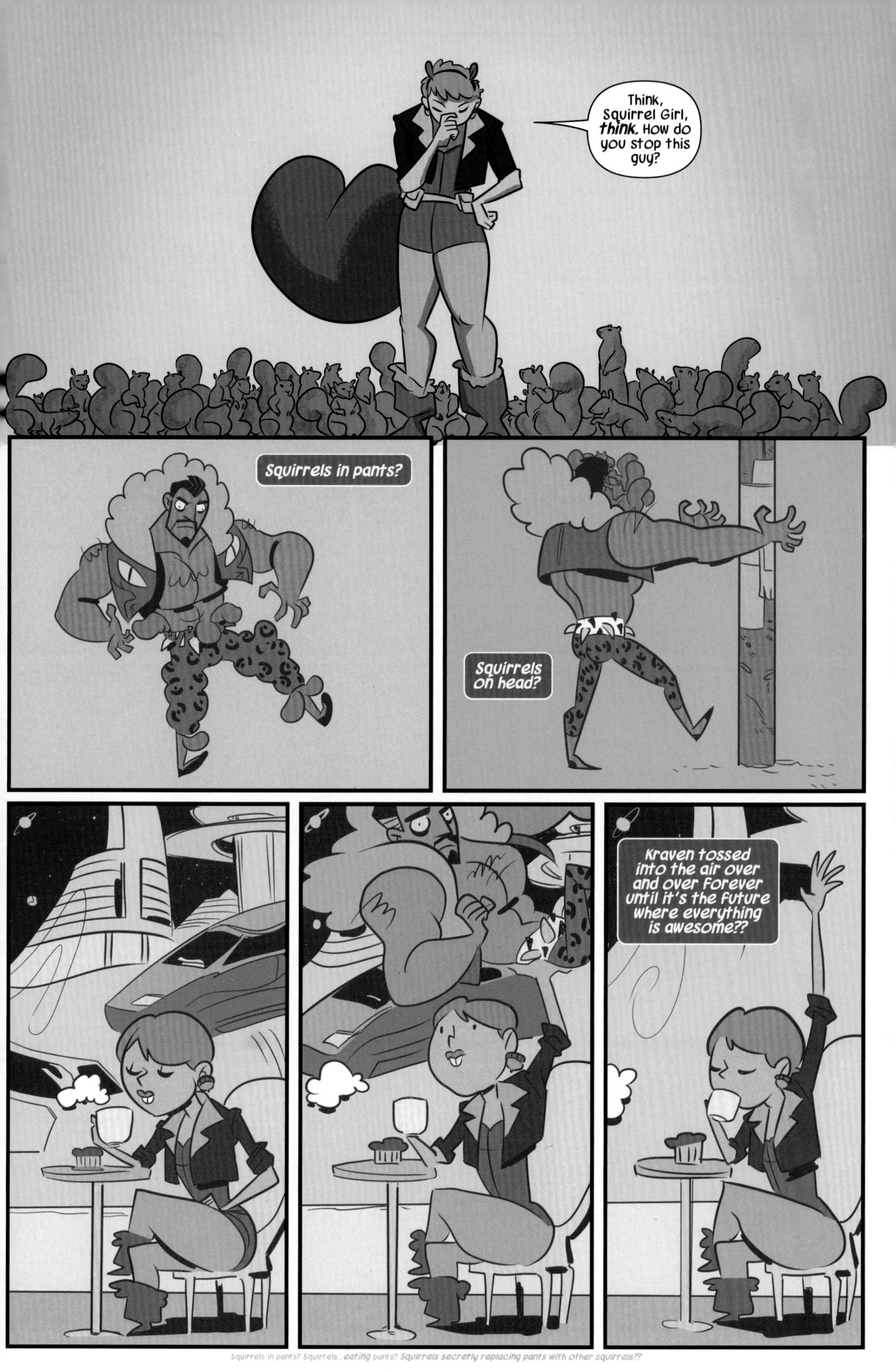
Think, Squirrel Girl, *think.* How do you stop this guy?
Squirrels in pants?
Squirrels on head?
Kraven tossed into the air over and over forever until it's the future where everything is awesome??

Squirrels in pants? Squirrels...*eating* pants? *Squirrels secretly replacing pants with other squirrels??*

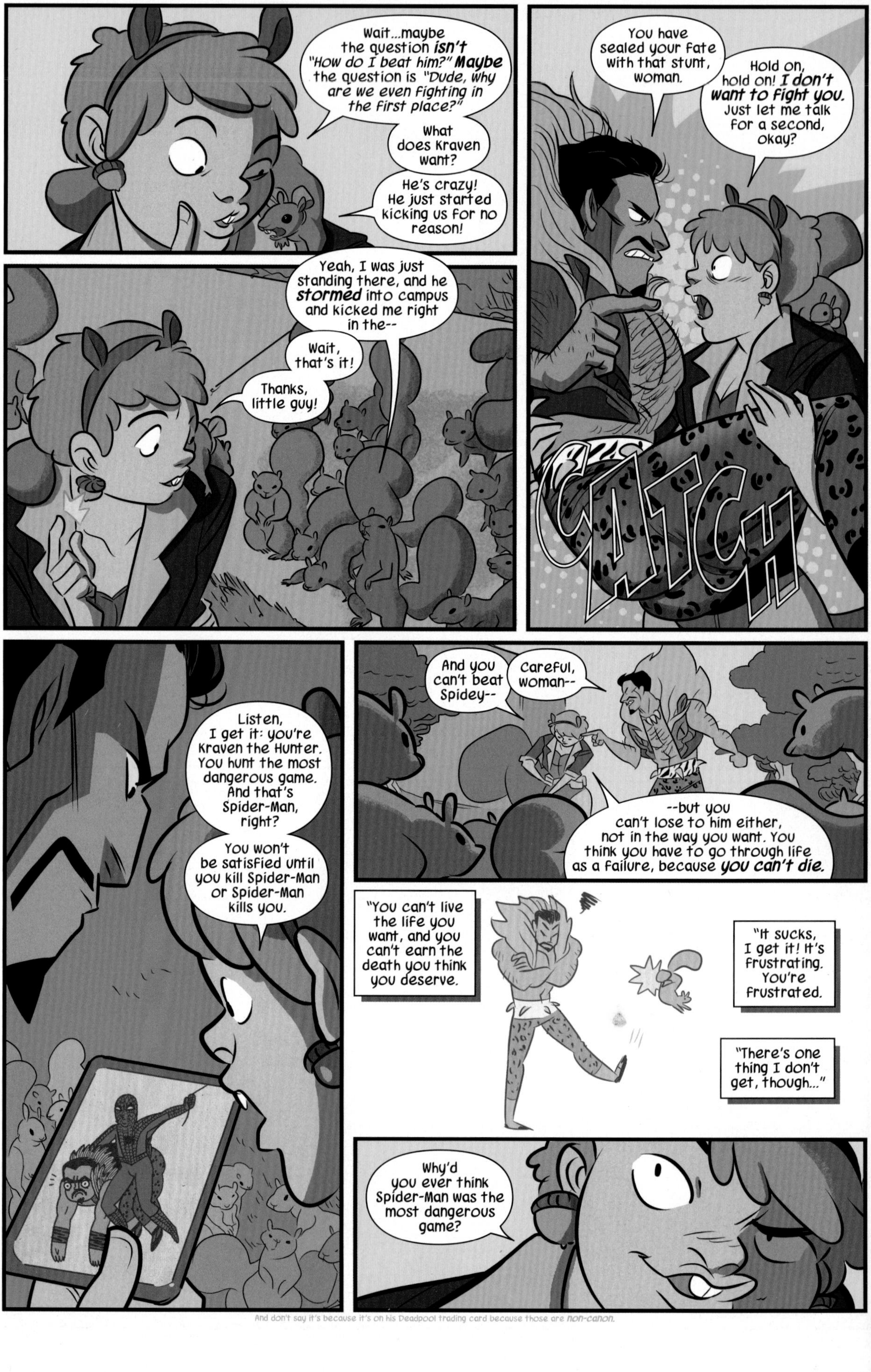
Wait...maybe the question isn't "How do I beat him?" Maybe the question is "Dude, why are we even fighting in the first place?"
What does Kraven want?
He's crazy! He just started kicking us for no reason!
Yeah, I was just standing there, and he stormed into campus and kicked me right in the--
Wait, that's it!
Thanks, little guy!
You have sealed your fate with that stunt, woman.
Hold on, hold on! I don't want to fight you. Just let me talk for a second, okay?
CATCH
Listen, I get it: you're Kraven the Hunter. You hunt the most dangerous game. And that's Spider-Man, right?
You won't be satisfied until you kill Spider-Man or Spider-Man kills you.
And you can't beat Spidey--
Careful, woman--
--but you can't lose to him either, not in the way you want. You think you have to go through life as a failure, because you can't die.
"You can't live the life you want, and you can't earn the death you think you deserve.
"It sucks, I get it! It's frustrating. You're frustrated.
"There's one thing I don't get, though..."
Why'd you ever think Spider-Man was the most dangerous game?

And don't say it's because it's on his Deadpool trading card because those are *non-canon.*

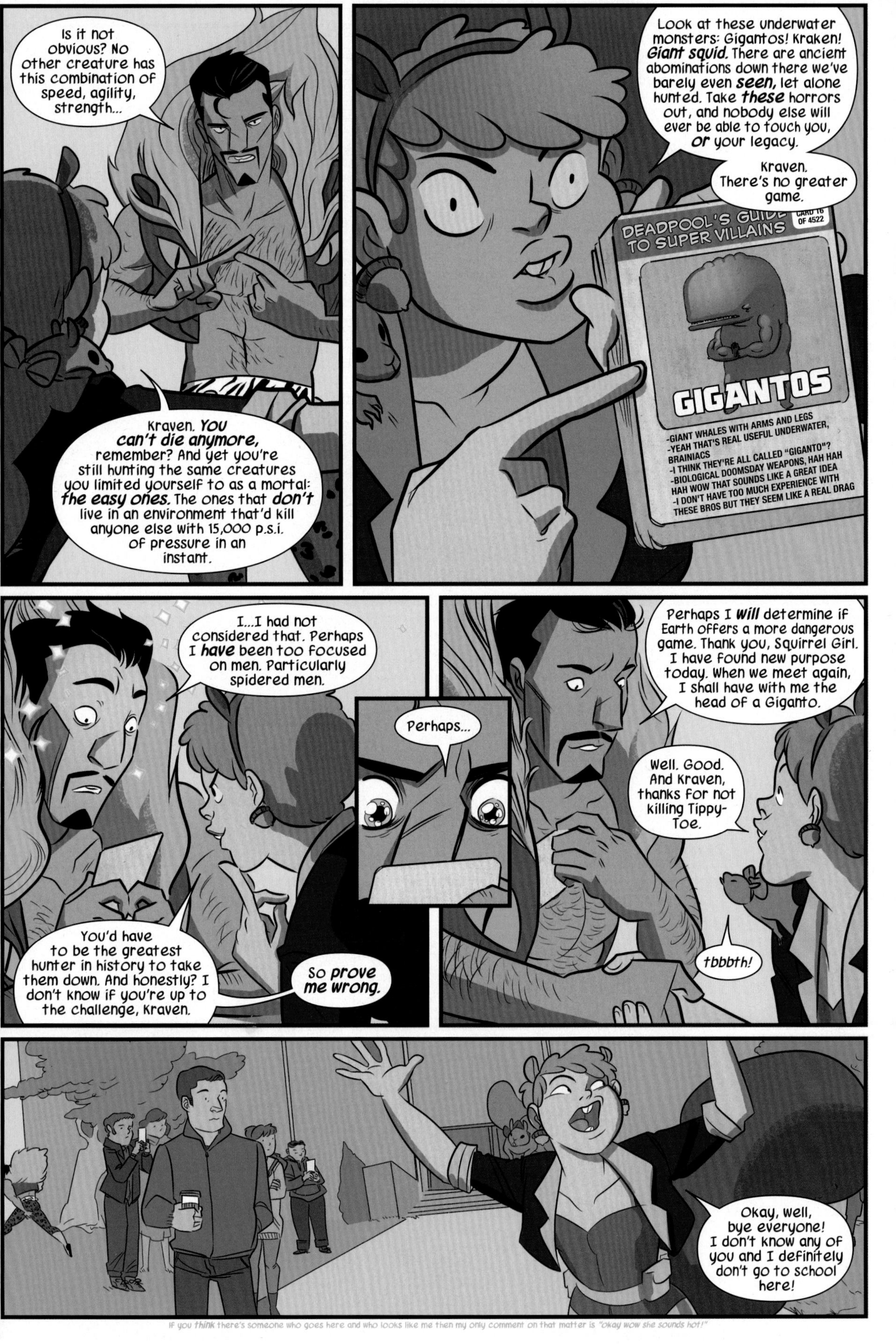
Is it not obvious? No other creature has this combination of speed, agility, strength...
Kraven. You can't die anymore, remember? And yet you're still hunting the same creatures you limited yourself to as a mortal: the easy ones. The ones that don't live in an environment that'd kill anyone else with 15,000 p.s.i. of pressure in an instant.
Look at these underwater monsters: Gigantos! Kraken! Giant squid. There are ancient abominations down there we've barely even seen, let alone hunted. Take these horrors out, and nobody else will ever be able to touch you, or your legacy.
Kraven. There's no greater game.
DEADPOOL'S GUIDE TO SUPER VILLAINS
CARD 16 OF 4522
GIGANTOS
-GIANT WHALES WITH ARMS AND LEGS
-YEAH THAT'S REAL USEFUL UNDERWATER, BRAINIACS
-I THINK THEY'RE ALL CALLED "GIGANTO"?
-BIOLOGICAL DOOMSDAY WEAPONS, HAH HAH HAH WOW THAT SOUNDS LIKE A GREAT IDEA
-I DON'T HAVE TOO MUCH EXPERIENCE WITH THESE BROS BUT THEY SEEM LIKE A REAL DRAG
I...I had not considered that. Perhaps I have been too focused on men. Particularly spidered men.
You'd have to be the greatest hunter in history to take them down. And honestly? I don't know if you're up to the challenge, Kraven.
So prove me wrong.
Perhaps...
Perhaps I will determine if Earth offers a more dangerous game. Thank you, Squirrel Girl. I have found new purpose today. When we meet again, I shall have with me the head of a Giganto.
Well. Good. And Kraven, thanks for not killing Tippy-Toe.
tbbbth!
Okay, well, bye everyone! I don't know any of you and I definitely don't go to school here!

If you *think* there's someone who goes here and who looks like me then my only comment on that matter is *"okay wow she sounds hot!"*

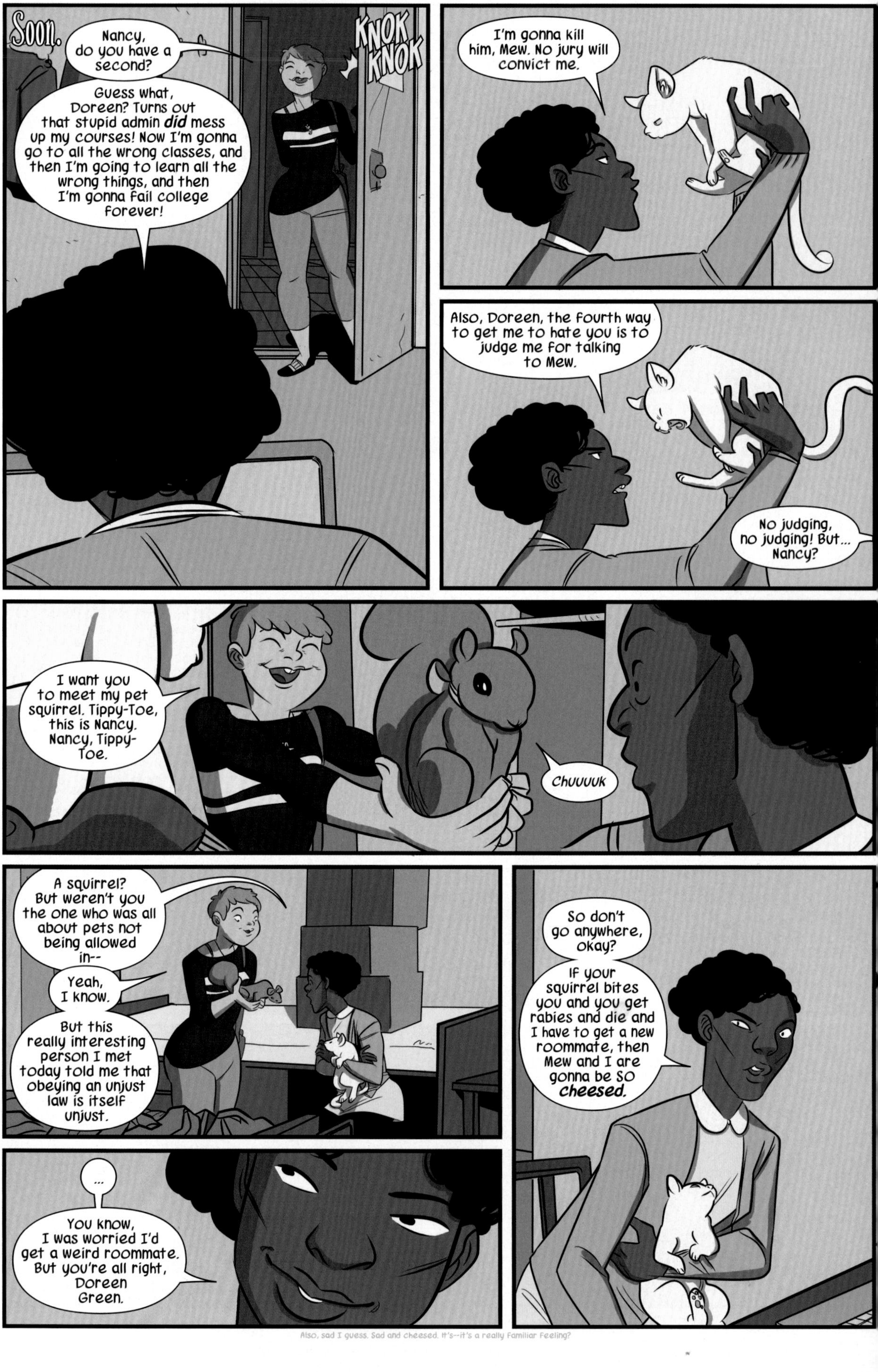
Soon.
Nancy, do you have a second?
KNOK KNOK
Guess what, Doreen? Turns out that stupid admin *did* mess up my courses! Now I'm gonna go to all the wrong classes, and then I'm going to learn all the wrong things, and then I'm gonna fail college forever!
I'm gonna kill him, Mew. No jury will convict me.
Also, Doreen, the fourth way to get me to hate you is to judge me for talking to Mew.
No judging, no judging! But... Nancy?
I want you to meet my pet squirrel. Tippy-Toe, this is Nancy. Nancy, Tippy-Toe.
Chuuuuk
A squirrel? But weren't you the one who was all about pets not being allowed in--
Yeah, I know.
But this really interesting person I met today told me that obeying an unjust law is itself unjust.
...
You know, I was worried I'd get a weird roommate. But you're all right, Doreen Green.
So don't go anywhere, okay?
If your squirrel bites you and you get rabies and die and I have to get a new roommate, then Mew and I are gonna be SO ***cheesed.***

Also, sad I guess. Sad and cheesed. It's--it's a really familiar feeling?

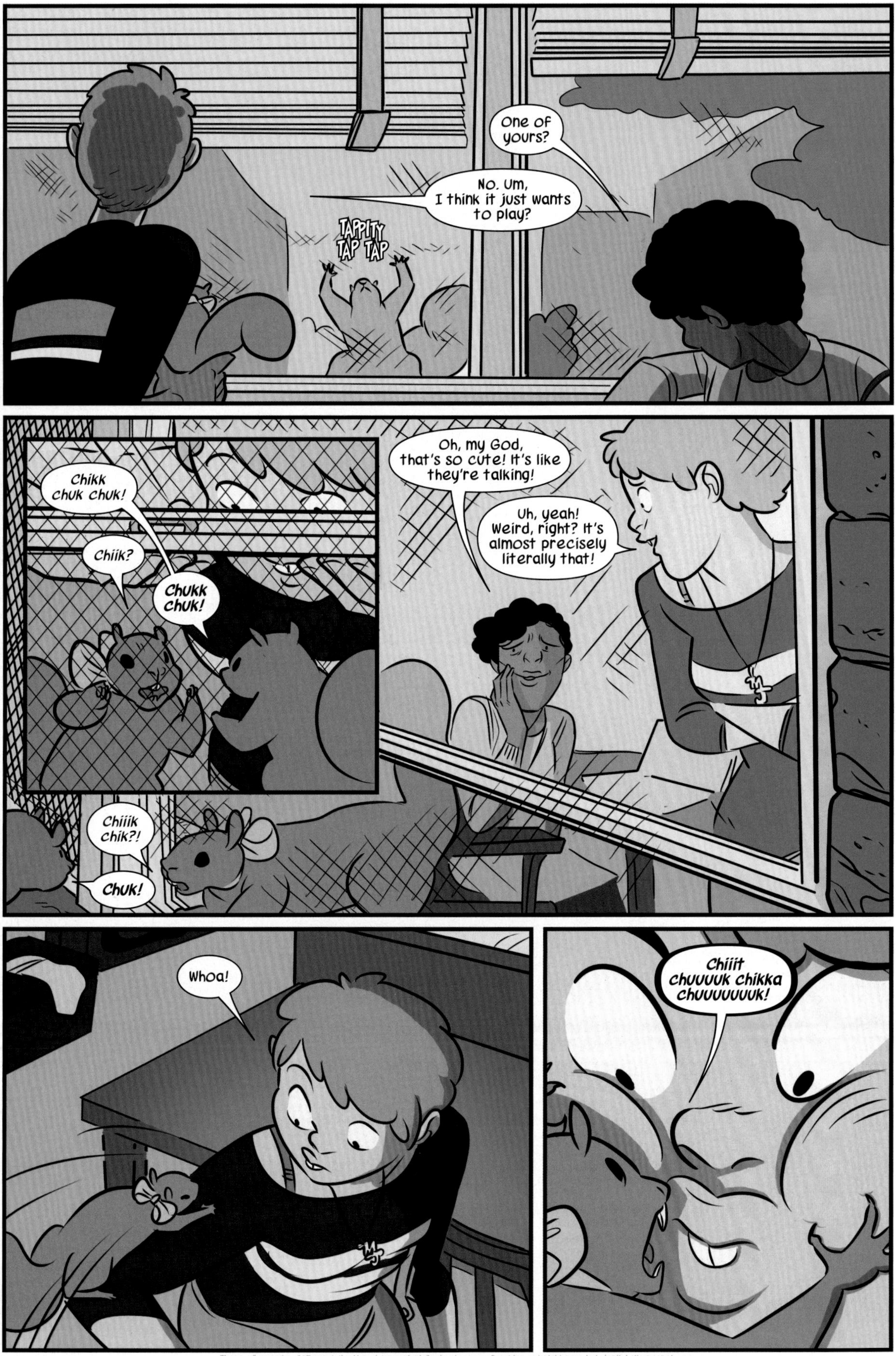
One of yours?
No. Um, I think it just wants to play?
TAPPITY TAP TAP
Oh, my God, that's so cute! It's like they're talking!
Uh, yeah! Weird, right? It's almost precisely literally that!
Chikk chuk chuk!
Chiik?
Chukk chuk!
Chiiik chik?!
Chuk!
Whoa!
Chiiit chuuuuk chikka chuuuuuuuk!

Those of you who *can* speak Northeastern variant Squirrelese are freaking out right now, but don't tell anyone!
Keep it a surprise for the rest of us who have to read the next page to find out what the deal is, okay?

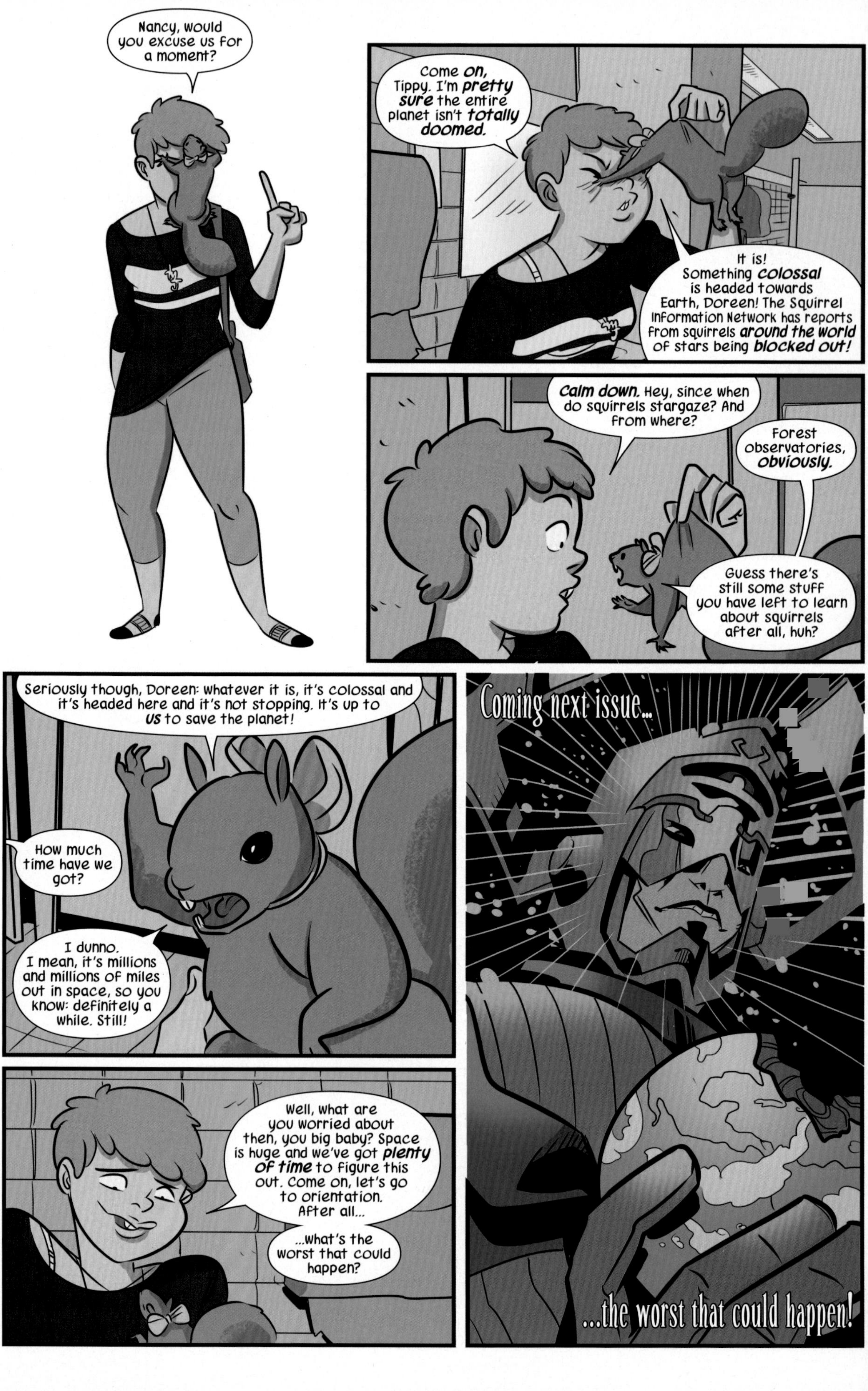
Nancy, would you excuse us for a moment?
Come on, Tippy. I'm pretty sure the entire planet isn't totally doomed.
It is! Something colossal is headed towards Earth, Doreen! The Squirrel Information Network has reports from squirrels around the world of stars being blocked out!
Calm down. Hey, since when do squirrels stargaze? And from where?
Forest observatories, obviously.
Guess there's still some stuff you have left to learn about squirrels after all, huh?
Seriously though, Doreen: whatever it is, it's colossal and it's headed here and it's not stopping. It's up to US to save the planet!
How much time have we got?
I dunno. I mean, it's millions and millions of miles out in space, so you know: definitely a while. Still!
Well, what are you worried about then, you big baby? Space is huge and we've got plenty of time to figure this out. Come on, let's go to orientation. After all...
...what's the worst that could happen?
Coming next issue...
...the worst that could happen!

Letters From Nuts

Ryan!

Erica!

Send letters to mheroes@marvel.com or 135 W 50th St, 7th Floor, New York, NY 10020 (Please mark "OKAY TO PRINT")

Hello! We're Erica and Ryan and Rico, we're writing and drawing and coloring a comic about a woman with squirrel powers. We've actually been writing and drawing and coloring this comic for YEARS, decades really, and last month Marvel came to us and asked if they could publish it, and we said "YES!" and then went on to say "Also we've been kinda using your character so you don't really have to ask, also thanks for not suing us."

OKAY NO that's nut true. We only started this comic recently! But we ARE following in the footsteps of the people who have made Squirrel Girl comics before: great guys like Will Murray, Steve Ditko, Dan Slott, Paul Pelletier, Brian Michael Bendis and Mike Deodato!

This book is an experiment: can a book like this find an audience? Will people TRULY read a comic about someone who dresses up like a rodent-like animal and fights crime in a major metropolitan area, even if that animal ISN'T a bat?? We hope they will. If you liked this comic, share it! Tell your friends! Tell the WHOLE WORLD you liked it, because then they might like it too, and then we'll all get more comics like this: fun, funny, awesome books about a crime-fighter with a utility belt and animal-themed gadgets (again, NOT a bat). And if you've got a computer, you can check out unbeatablesquirrelgirl.tumblr. com where we post SNEAK PEEKS at upcoming issues and behind-the-scenes art!

We thought we'd start here with your letters. You can send them to MHEROES@ MARVEL.COM, and don't forget to mark them "OKAY TO PRINT" so we know your letter is cool to print. But since this is our first issue all we've gotten so far are some TOTALLY FAKE LETTERS we'll use to get the ball rolling! Can YOU send us something better? I'd sincerely like to see that!!

Q: Excuse me, but how are you following me, how are you getting all this information??

- D. Green

A: Erica is really good at sketching quickly AND at being discreet. A winning combination!

Q: Who wrote Squirrel Girl's theme song?
- Pat W.

A: The song was composed by Academy Award winner Paul Francis Webster and Robert "Bob" Harris in 1967, but at the time it was accidentally applied to another obscure Marvel character named "Spider-Man." Several decades later we detected this error and corrected it, restoring the song to its originally intended glory, and now it's totally about a woman who talks to squirrels.

Q: Who would win in a fight, Squirrel Girl or the Hulk?

- Jenn K.

A: If you ask the Hulk team, they might say something different, which is frankly ADORABLE, but clearly it's Squirrel Girl. Is their character called "The Unbeatable Hulk"? No, they call him "The Incredible Hulk," as in "Incredible! The Hulk just got beat up by Squirrel Girl, she's the greatest and I love her forever!!"

Q: Who would win in a fight, Squirrel Girl or Ms. Marvel?

- Emily H.

A: Yo, why are they fighting? Doreen and Kamala are on the same side here, so it's LITERALLY CRAZY that they're fighting. A better question is who would Squirrel Girl and Ms. Marvel fight FIRST?? My money is on EVERYONE WHO STANDS IN THEIR WAY.

Q: Who would win in a fight, Tippy-Toe the Squirrel or Howard the Duck?

- Chip Z.

A: Tippy-Toe is a regular squirrel with zero super powers, and Howard the Duck is a sentient duck who is approximately as smart as the average human! That said, Tippy-Toe. PROVE ME WRONG, HOWARD.

Q: Who would YOU rather fight, one squirrel-sized Hulk or a hundred Hulk-sized squirrels?

- Lucy W.

A: Doreen would obviously take the squirrel-sized Hulk, seeing as she'd never want to fight squirrels since they are ULTIMATE PALS. Personally, I'd take the squirrel-sized Hulk too, because while I wouldn't like the Hulk when he's angry, I would LOVE him when ADORABLY-SIZED, super-cute, and could fit inside a bottle of pop.

I don't know why I apparently keep trying to pick a fight with the Hulk team here. Send us some letters! DO IT!!

Thanks everyone, and we'll see you next month!

Next: Suit Up!

When you see this: **AR** , open up the MARVEL AR APP (available on applicable Apple ® iOS or Android ™ devices) and use your camera-enabled device to unlock extra-special exclusive features!

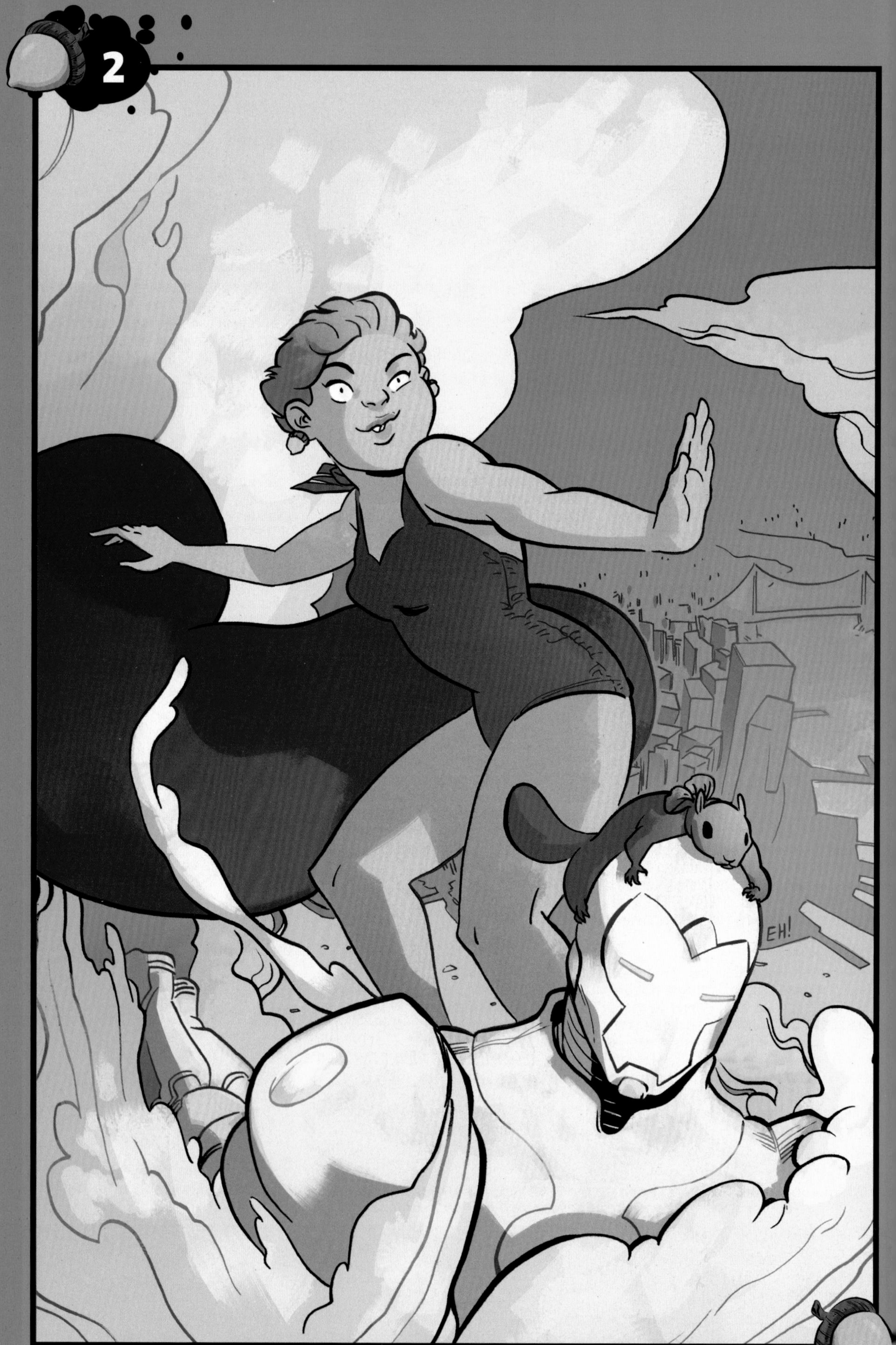
2
EH!

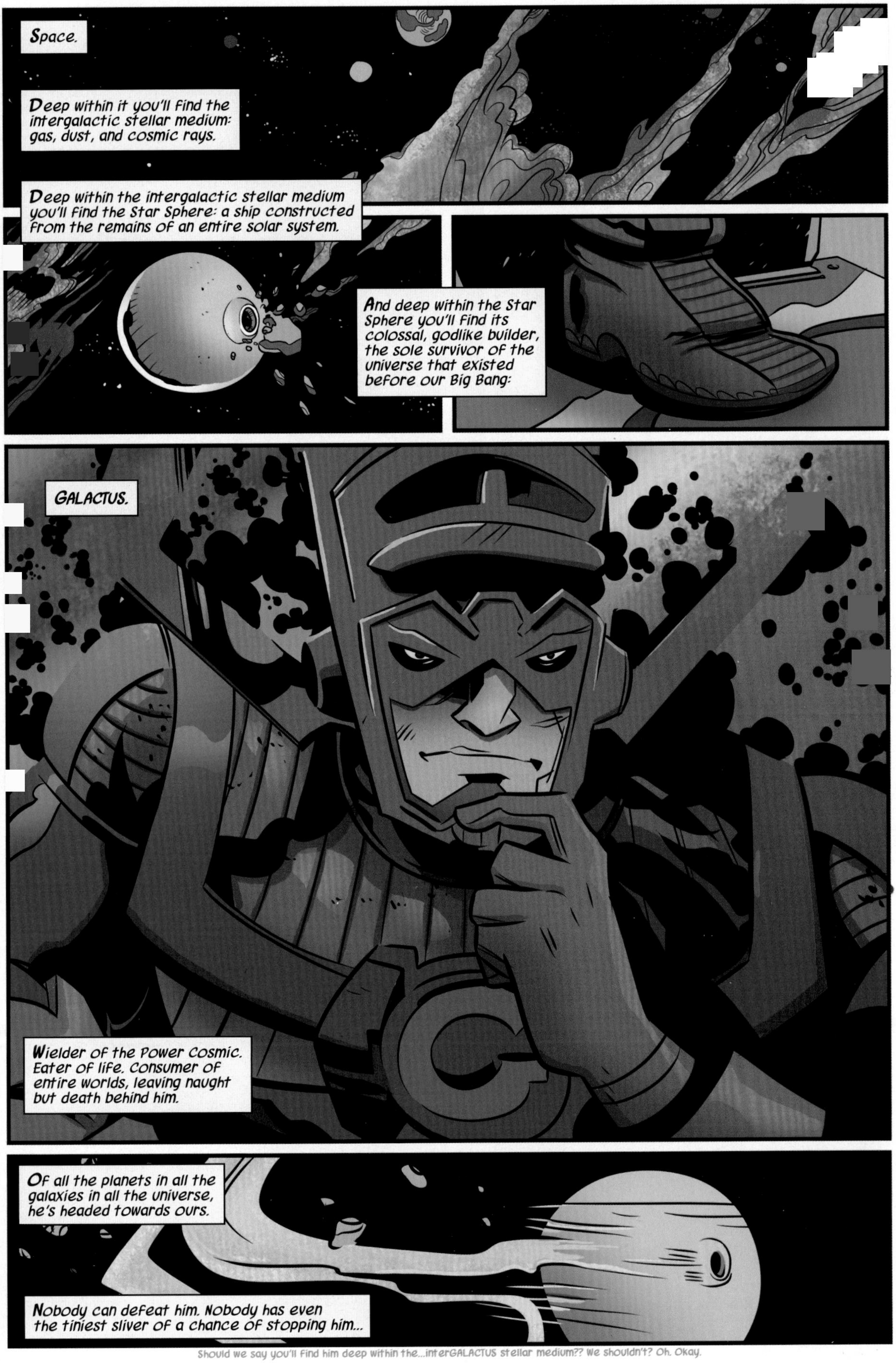
Space.
Deep within it you'll find the intergalactic stellar medium: gas, dust, and cosmic rays.
Deep within the intergalactic stellar medium you'll find the Star Sphere: a ship constructed from the remains of an entire solar system.
And deep within the Star Sphere you'll find its colossal, godlike builder, the sole survivor of the universe that existed before our Big Bang:
GALACTUS.
Wielder of the Power Cosmic. Eater of life. Consumer of entire worlds, leaving naught but death behind him.
Of all the planets in all the galaxies in all the universe, he's headed towards ours.
Nobody can defeat him. Nobody has even the tiniest sliver of a chance of stopping him...

Should we say you'll find him deep within the...interGALACTUS stellar medium?? We shouldn't? Oh. Okay.

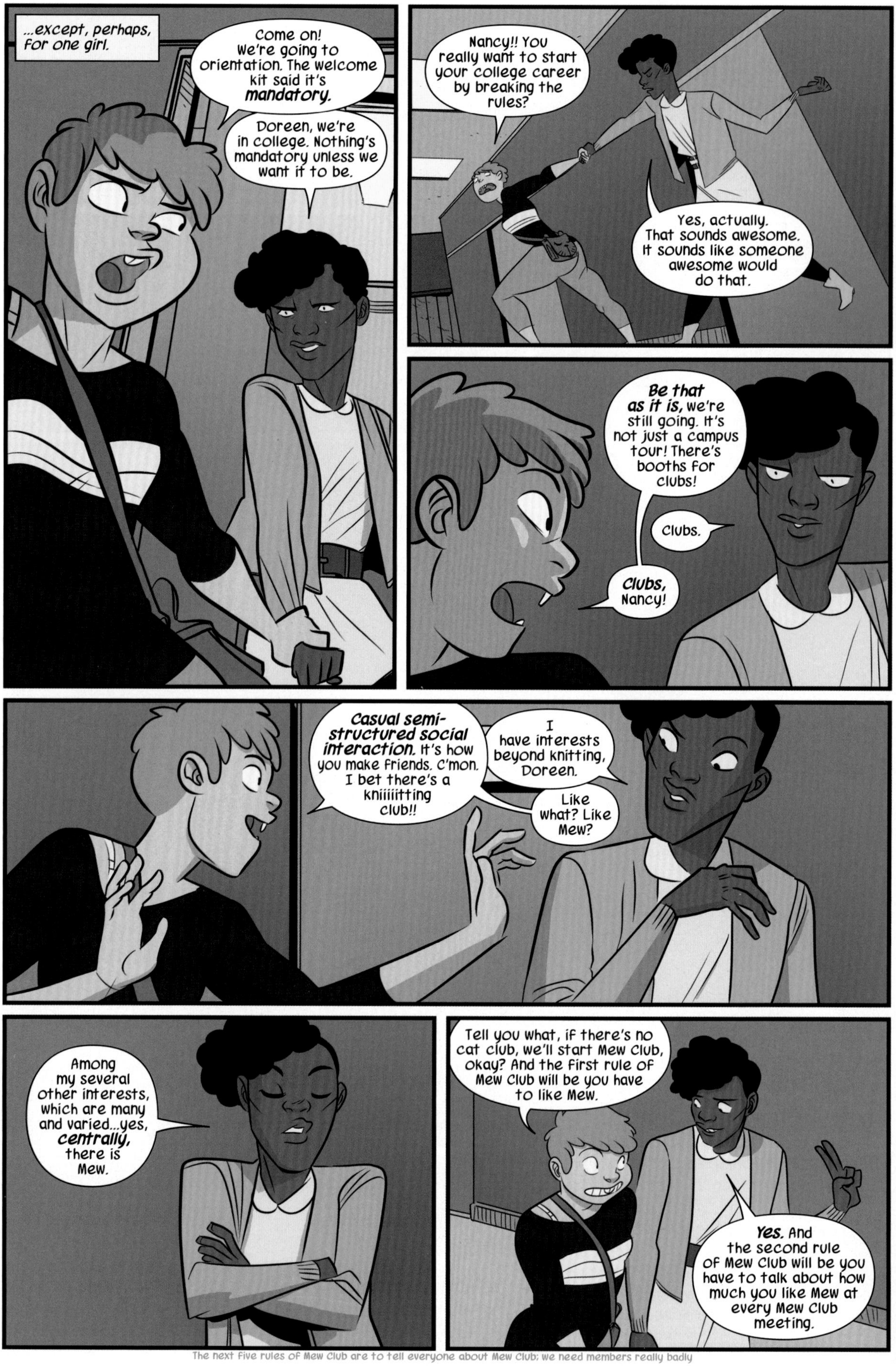
...except, perhaps, for one girl.
Come on! We're going to orientation. The welcome kit said it's *mandatory.*
Doreen, we're in college. Nothing's mandatory unless we want it to be.
Nancy!! You really want to start your college career by breaking the rules?
Yes, actually. That sounds awesome. It sounds like someone awesome would do that.
Be that as it is, we're still going. It's not just a campus tour! There's booths for clubs!
Clubs.
Clubs, Nancy!
Casual semi-structured social interaction. It's how you make friends. C'mon. I bet there's a kniiiiitting club!!
I have interests beyond knitting, Doreen.
Like what? Like Mew?
Among my several other interests, which are many and varied...yes, *centrally,* there is Mew.
Tell you what, if there's no cat club, we'll start Mew Club, okay? And the first rule of Mew Club will be you have to like Mew.
Yes. And the second rule of Mew Club will be you have to talk about how much you like Mew at every Mew Club meeting.

The next five rules of Mew Club are to tell everyone about Mew Club; we need members really badly

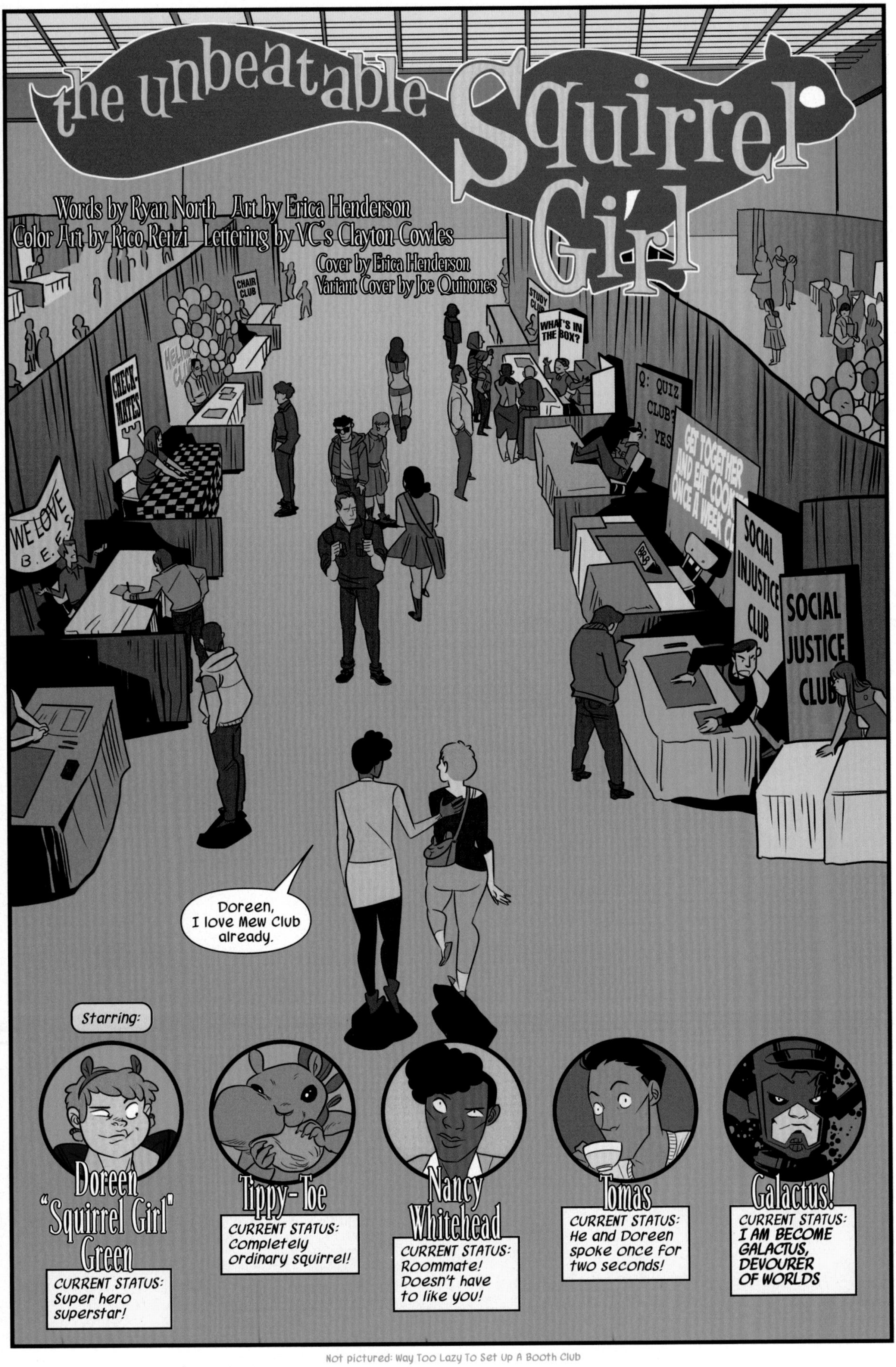
the unbeatable Squirrel Girl
Words by Ryan North Art by Erica Henderson
Color Art by Rico Renzi Lettering by VC's Clayton Cowles
Cover by Erica Henderson
Variant Cover by Joe Quinones
CHAIR CLUB
STUDY CLUB
WHAT'S IN THE BOX?
CHECK-MATES
Q: QUIZ CLUB? A: YES
GET TOGETHER AND EAT COOKIES ONCE A WEEK CL
WE LOVE B.E.E.S.
SOCIAL INJUSTICE CLUB
SOCIAL JUSTICE CLUB
Doreen, I love Mew Club already.
Starring:
Doreen "Squirrel Girl" Green
CURRENT STATUS: Super hero superstar!
Tippy-Toe
CURRENT STATUS: Completely ordinary squirrel!
Nancy Whitehead
CURRENT STATUS: Roommate! Doesn't have to like you!
Tomas
CURRENT STATUS: He and Doreen spoke once for two seconds!
Galactus!
CURRENT STATUS: I AM BECOME GALACTUS, DEVOURER OF WORLDS

Not pictured: Way Too Lazy To Set Up A Booth Club

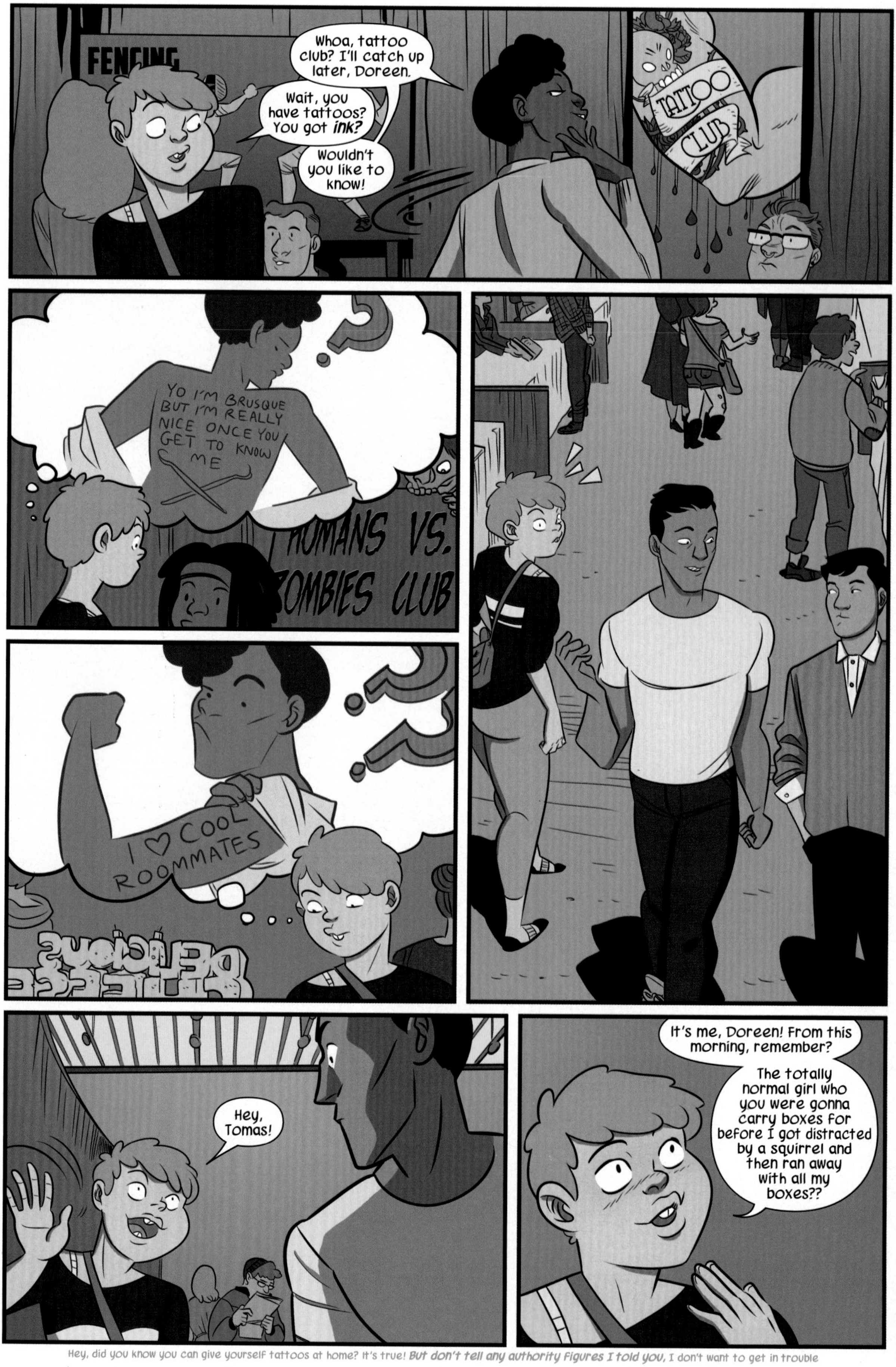
FENCING
Whoa, tattoo club? I'll catch up later, Doreen.
Wait, you have tattoos? You got *ink?*
Wouldn't you like to know!
TATTOO CLUB
YO I'M BRUSQUE BUT I'M REALLY NICE ONCE YOU GET TO KNOW ME
HUMANS VS. ZOMBIES CLUB
I ♡ COOL ROOMMATES
Hey, Tomas!
It's me, Doreen! From this morning, remember?
The totally normal girl who you were gonna carry boxes for before I got distracted by a squirrel and then ran away with all my boxes??

Hey, did you know you can give yourself tattoos at home? It's true! ***But don't tell any authority figures I told you,*** I don't want to get in trouble

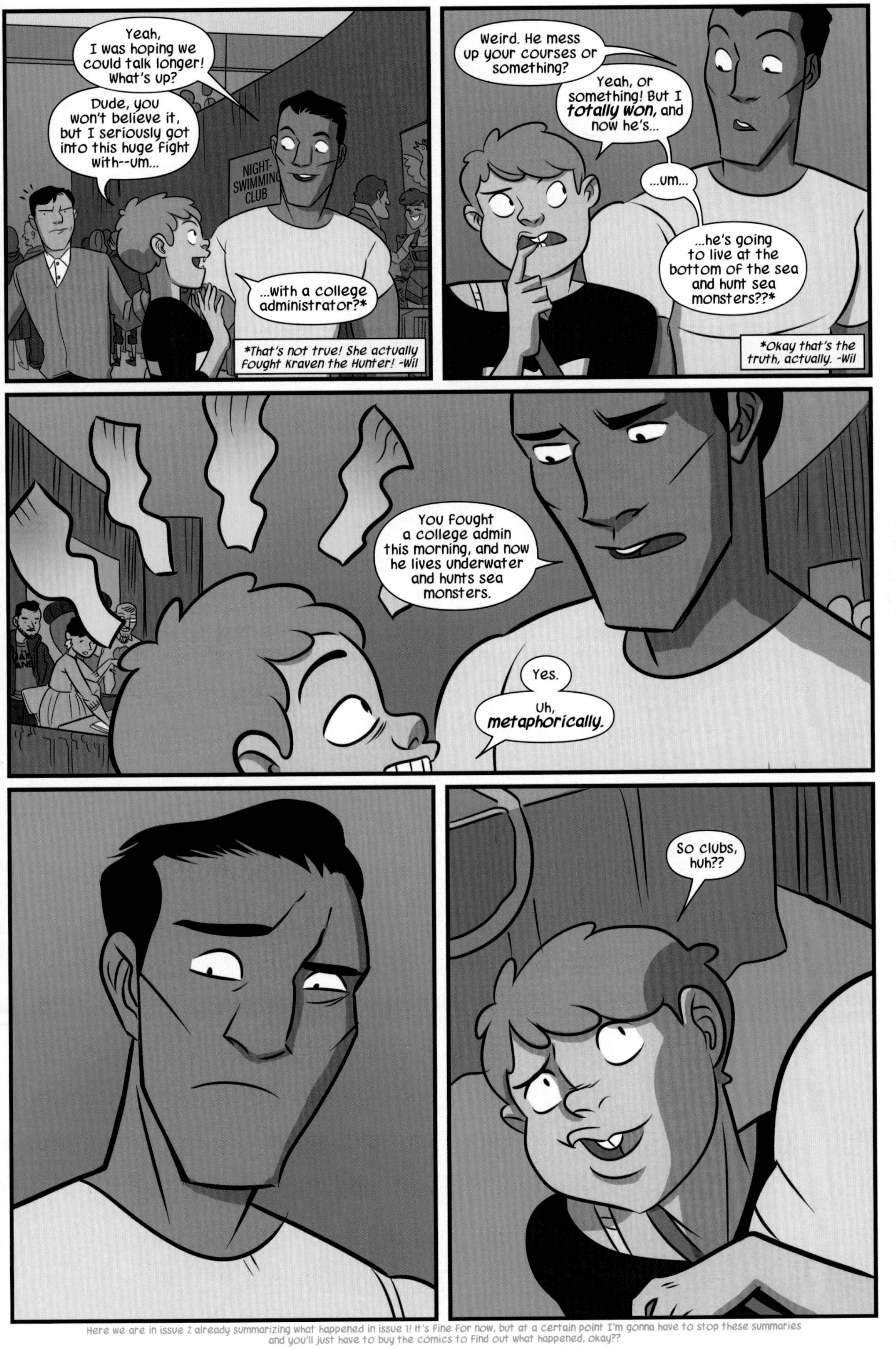
Yeah, I was hoping we could talk longer! What's up?
Dude, you won't believe it, but I seriously got into this huge fight with--um...
NIGHT-SWIMMING CLUB
...with a college administrator?*
*That's not true! She actually fought Kraven the Hunter! -Wil
Weird. He mess up your courses or something?
Yeah, or something! But I totally won, and now he's...
...um...
...he's going to live at the bottom of the sea and hunt sea monsters??*
*Okay that's the truth, actually. -Wil
You fought a college admin this morning, and now he lives underwater and hunts sea monsters.
Yes.
Uh, metaphorically.
So clubs, huh??

Here we are in issue 2 already summarizing what happened in issue 1! It's fine for now, but at a certain point I'm gonna have to stop these summaries and you'll just have to buy the comics to find out what happened, okay??

Yeah, I thought I'd check it out. There's a fencing club I was looking at, but I dunno. I've never thought of fencing before; it just looks fun.

Well, I mean, they'd teach you, right?

COMEDY CLUB

Doreen! You've barely been here a day and *already* you're making friends with people who haven't been assigned to live with you. You're awesome!

I guess! I mainly just want to be ready in case I find myself in a swordfight where I have to swing from chandeliers and roguishly smile as swords clash, saying things like *"Let's get right to the point!"*

Hah!

SHORT BLUDGEONING STAFF CLUB aka CLUB CLUB

Although this Tomas guy doesn't *really* know who I am. What if I tell him I'm Squirrel Girl and he *flips out* or something?

So I'm there in front of their table, looking up *"fencing"* on my phone because I'm suddenly not sure if what I have in mind is even called that, you know?

Like he's all *"Oh no, the fact that you're so awesome and dress up in an awesome outfit and fight crime awesomely is terrible to me!"*

Uh-huh.

Anyway, it turns out there's three kinds of fencing: foil, sabre, and epee, and what I had in mind is none of those. Mine imaginary swashbuckler turns out the actual *really* what they do.

Though, if he *did* say that, that at least tells me he's a jerk and saves me the time of getting to know him any more.

Dang, though. He sure is handsome.

Uh-huh.

And they'll challenge you ... it's

Look at me, chatting up a megahunk like it isn't even a big deal!! Not bad, self, *not bad.*

Uh-huh.

Doreen? Did my fencing club story lose you?

Uh...

...huh?

Hello. I, uh, need Doreen to join me in the ladies' room for a second.

Whoa!!

I believe the canonical attractiveness hierarchy runs--when going from most to least hunky--from hyperhunk, to megahunk, to hunk, to minihunk, and, finally, to nanohunk.

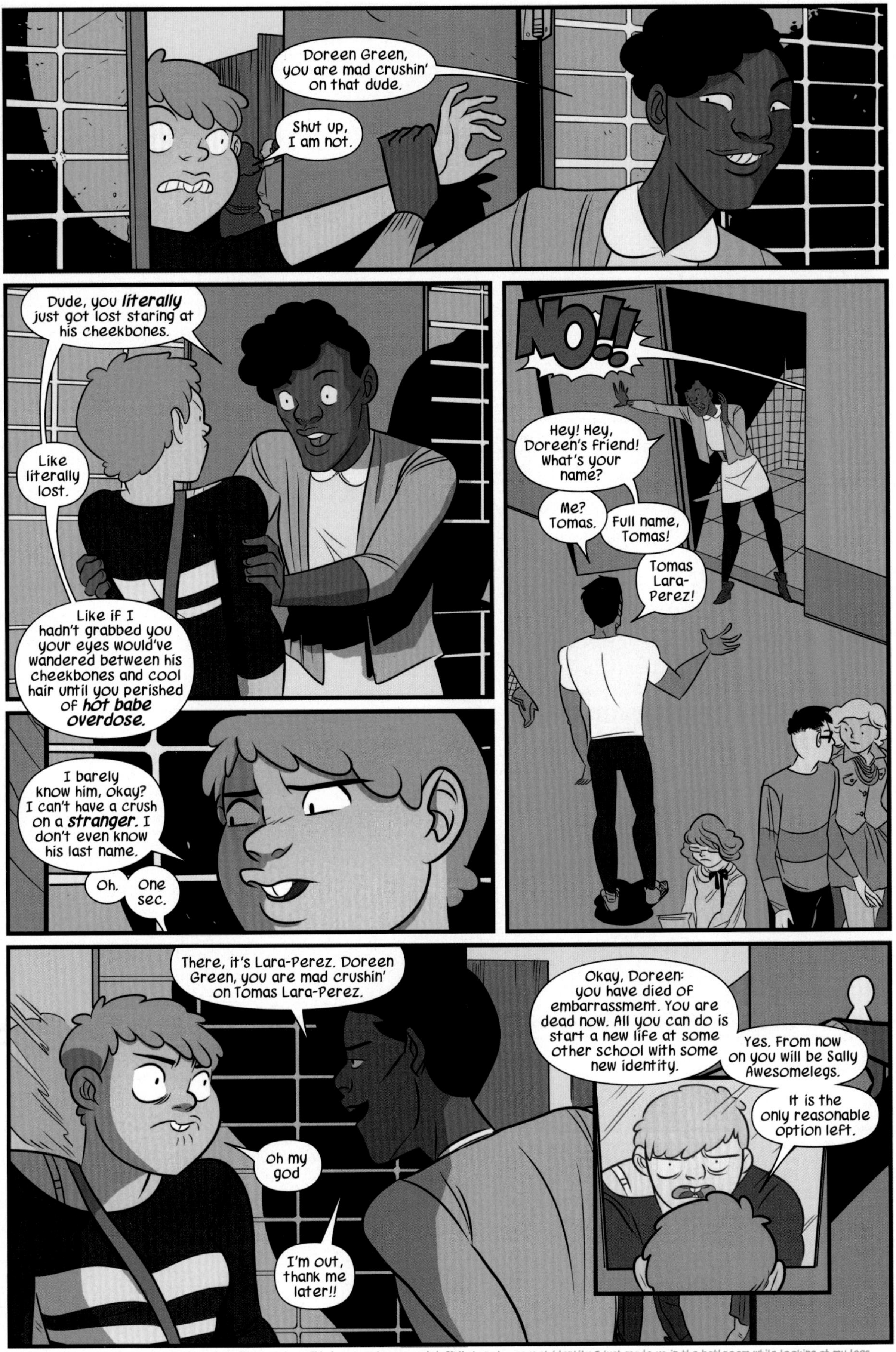
Doreen Green, you are mad crushin' on that dude.
Shut up, I am not.
Dude, you *literally* just got lost staring at his cheekbones.
Like literally lost.
Like if I hadn't grabbed you your eyes would've wandered between his cheekbones and cool hair until you perished of ***hot babe overdose.***
I barely know him, okay? I can't have a crush on a ***stranger.*** I don't even know his last name.
Oh.
One sec.
NO!!
Hey! Hey, Doreen's friend! What's your name?
Me? Tomas.
Full name, Tomas!
Tomas Lara-Perez!
There, it's Lara-Perez. Doreen Green, you are mad crushin' on Tomas Lara-Perez.
Oh my god
I'm out, thank me later!!
Okay, Doreen: you have died of embarrassment. You are dead now. All you can do is start a new life at some other school with some new identity.
Yes. From now on you will be Sally Awesomelegs.
It is the only reasonable option left.

Hello, I'm the new exchange student, Sally Awesomelegs. This is my real name and definitely not a secret identity I just made up in the bathroom while looking at my legs.

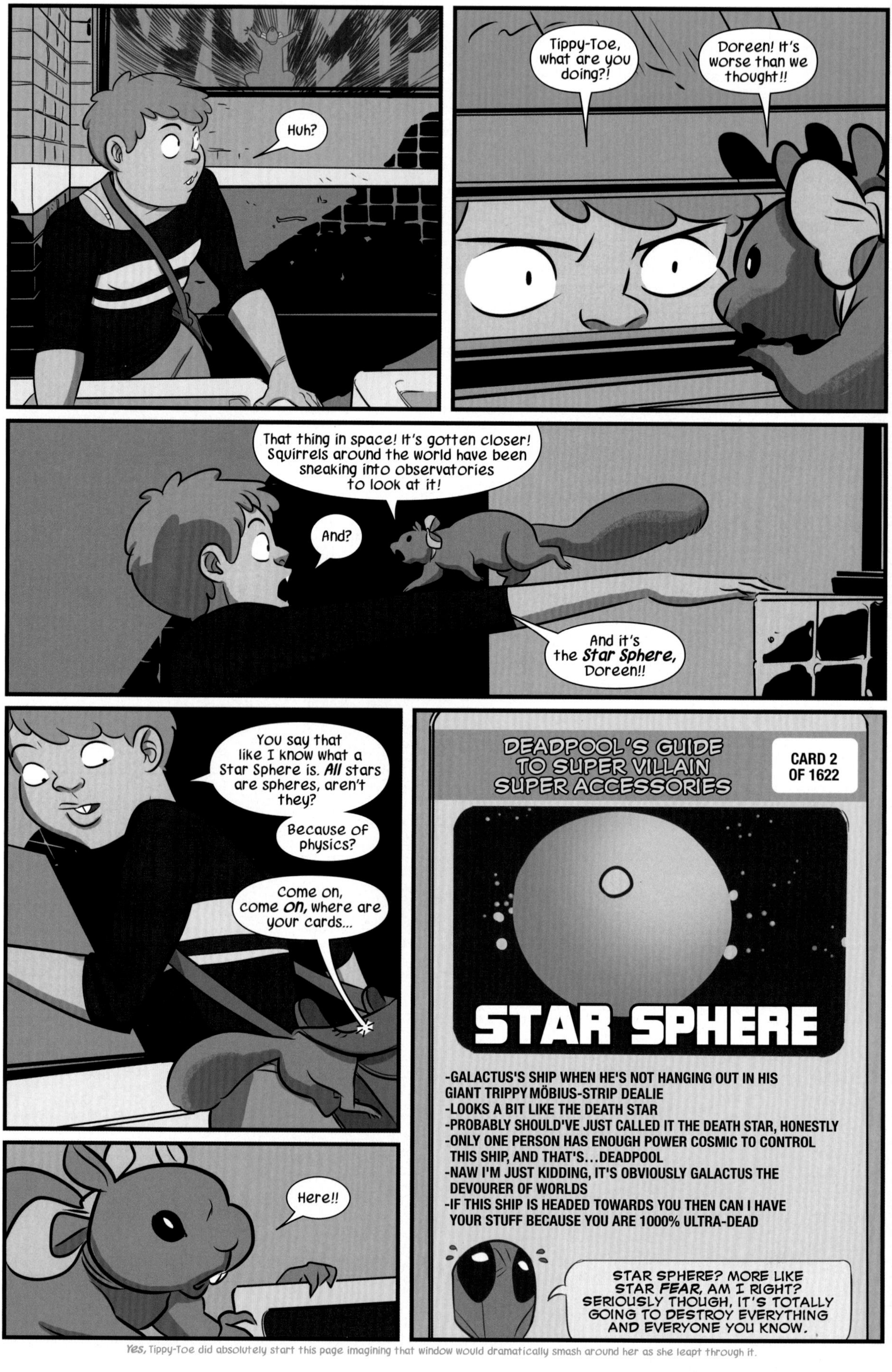
Huh?
Tippy-Toe, what are you doing?!
Doreen! It's worse than we thought!!
That thing in space! It's gotten closer! Squirrels around the world have been sneaking into observatories to look at it!
And?
And it's the Star Sphere, Doreen!!
You say that like I know what a Star Sphere is. All stars are spheres, aren't they?
Because of physics?
Come on, come on, where are your cards...
Here!!
DEADPOOL'S GUIDE TO SUPER VILLAIN SUPER ACCESSORIES
CARD 2 OF 1622
STAR SPHERE
-GALACTUS'S SHIP WHEN HE'S NOT HANGING OUT IN HIS GIANT TRIPPY MÖBIUS-STRIP DEALIE
-LOOKS A BIT LIKE THE DEATH STAR
-PROBABLY SHOULD'VE JUST CALLED IT THE DEATH STAR, HONESTLY
-ONLY ONE PERSON HAS ENOUGH POWER COSMIC TO CONTROL THIS SHIP, AND THAT'S...DEADPOOL
-NAW I'M JUST KIDDING, IT'S OBVIOUSLY GALACTUS THE DEVOURER OF WORLDS
-IF THIS SHIP IS HEADED TOWARDS YOU THEN CAN I HAVE YOUR STUFF BECAUSE YOU ARE 1000% ULTRA-DEAD
STAR SPHERE? MORE LIKE STAR FEAR, AM I RIGHT? SERIOUSLY THOUGH, IT'S TOTALLY GOING TO DESTROY EVERYTHING AND EVERYONE YOU KNOW.

Yes, Tippy-Toe did absolutely start this page imagining that window would dramatically smash around her as she leapt through it.

Wait, why hasn't anyone else noticed this ship? Shouldn't everyone on Earth be freaking out right now?

We're the only ones who know he's coming!!

Near as we can figure out, he's coming in with some stealth field around the ship, so everyone else just sees the stars they're expecting.

But he forgot to make it work on squirrels!

And it's like, hello? We're everywhere, *and we're always watching.* Nobody ever thinks of the squirrels!

Okay, dude, don't get mad at me, obviously I think about squirrels *all the time.*

You need to stop him, Doreen! We don't have time to convince others to help us, and they'd want evidence that we don't have anyway. You alone must stop *Galactus.*

What?

Aaaaaaand our best estimates kinda put him arriving at Earth in *two hours.*

ARRIVAL COUNTER

02:00

WHAT?? I've got *two hours* to stop GALACTUS??

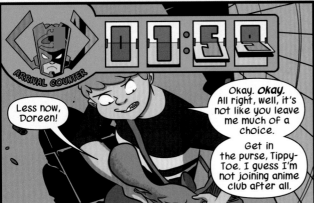

ARRIVAL COUNTER

01:59

Less now, Doreen!

Okay. *Okay.* All right, well, it's not like you leave me much of a choice.

Get in the purse, Tippy-Toe. I guess I'm not joining anime club after all.

I guess I'm just gonna have to go *kick* Galactus's butt instead.

Honestly I wish there was time to do both, but there's not, and a girl has to make choices sometimes. Someone else join anime club for me, I'll catch up later.

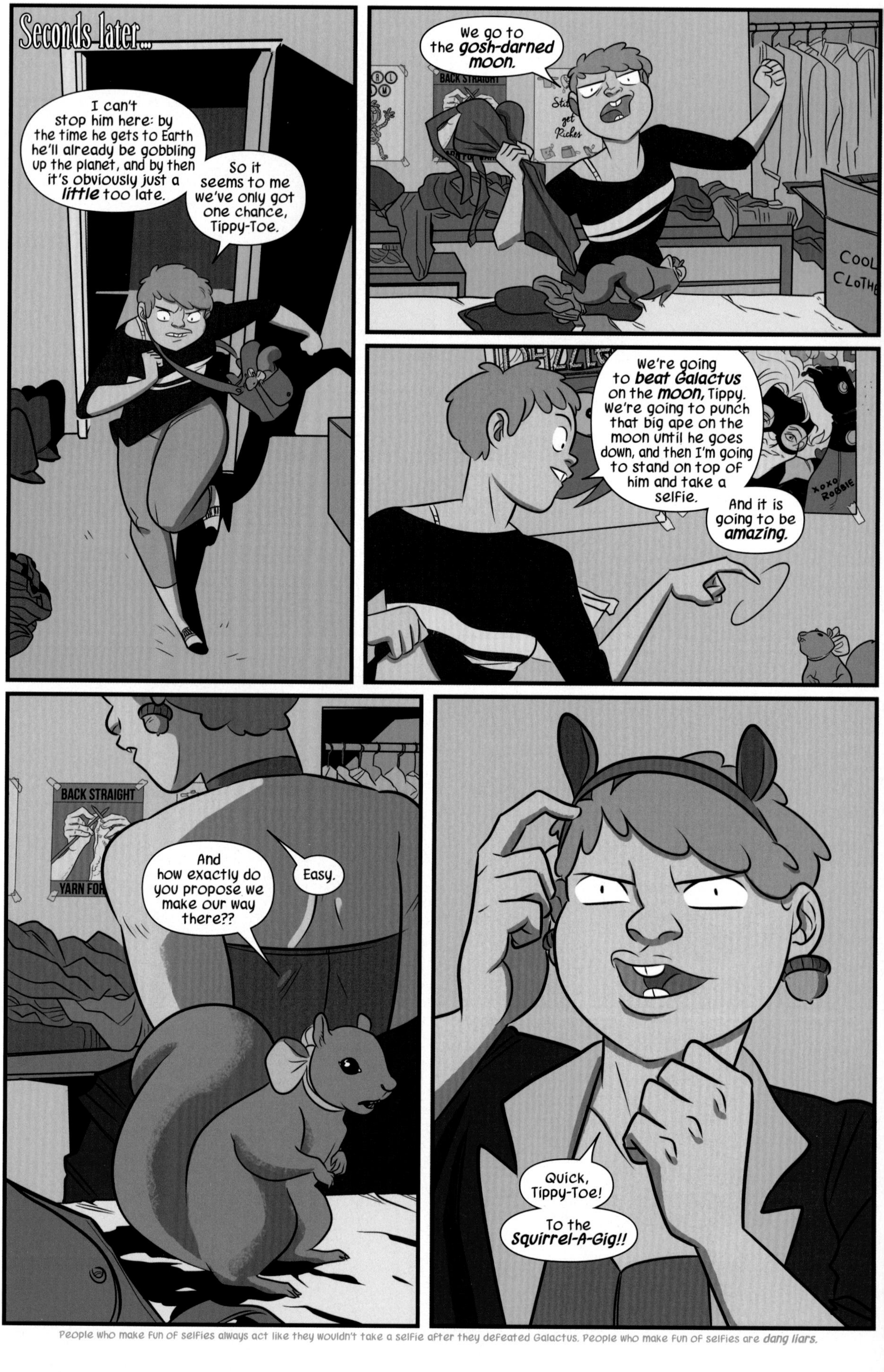
Seconds later...
I can't stop him here: by the time he gets to Earth he'll already be gobbling up the planet, and by then it's obviously just a *little* too late.
So it seems to me we've only got one chance, Tippy-Toe.
We go to the *gosh-darned moon.*
BACK STRAIGHT
YARN FOR
get Riches
COOL CLOTHE
We're going to *beat Galactus* on the *moon,* Tippy. We're going to punch that big ape on the moon until he goes down, and then I'm going to stand on top of him and take a selfie.
And it is going to be *amazing.*
XOXO ROBBIE
BACK STRAIGHT
YARN FOR
And how exactly do you propose we make our way there??
Easy.
Quick, Tippy-Toe!
To the *Squirrel-A-Gig!!*

People who make fun of selfies always act like they wouldn't take a selfie after they defeated Galactus. People who make fun of selfies are *dang liars.*

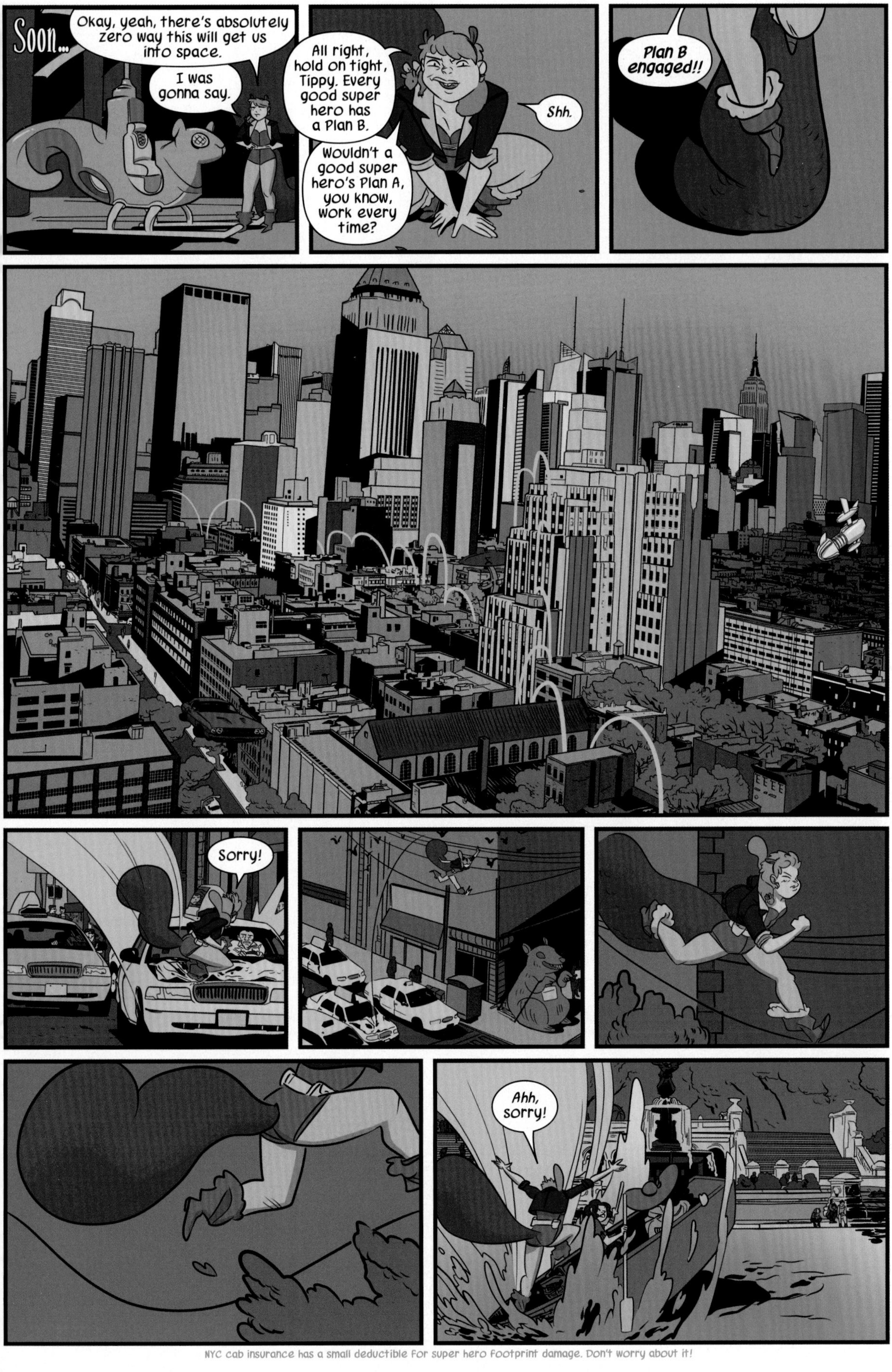
Soon...
Okay, yeah, there's absolutely zero way this will get us into space.
I was gonna say.
All right, hold on tight, Tippy. Every good super hero has a Plan B.
Shh.
Wouldn't a good super hero's Plan A, you know, work every time?
Plan B engaged!!
Sorry!
Ahh, sorry!

NYC cab insurance has a small deductible for super hero footprint damage. Don't worry about it!

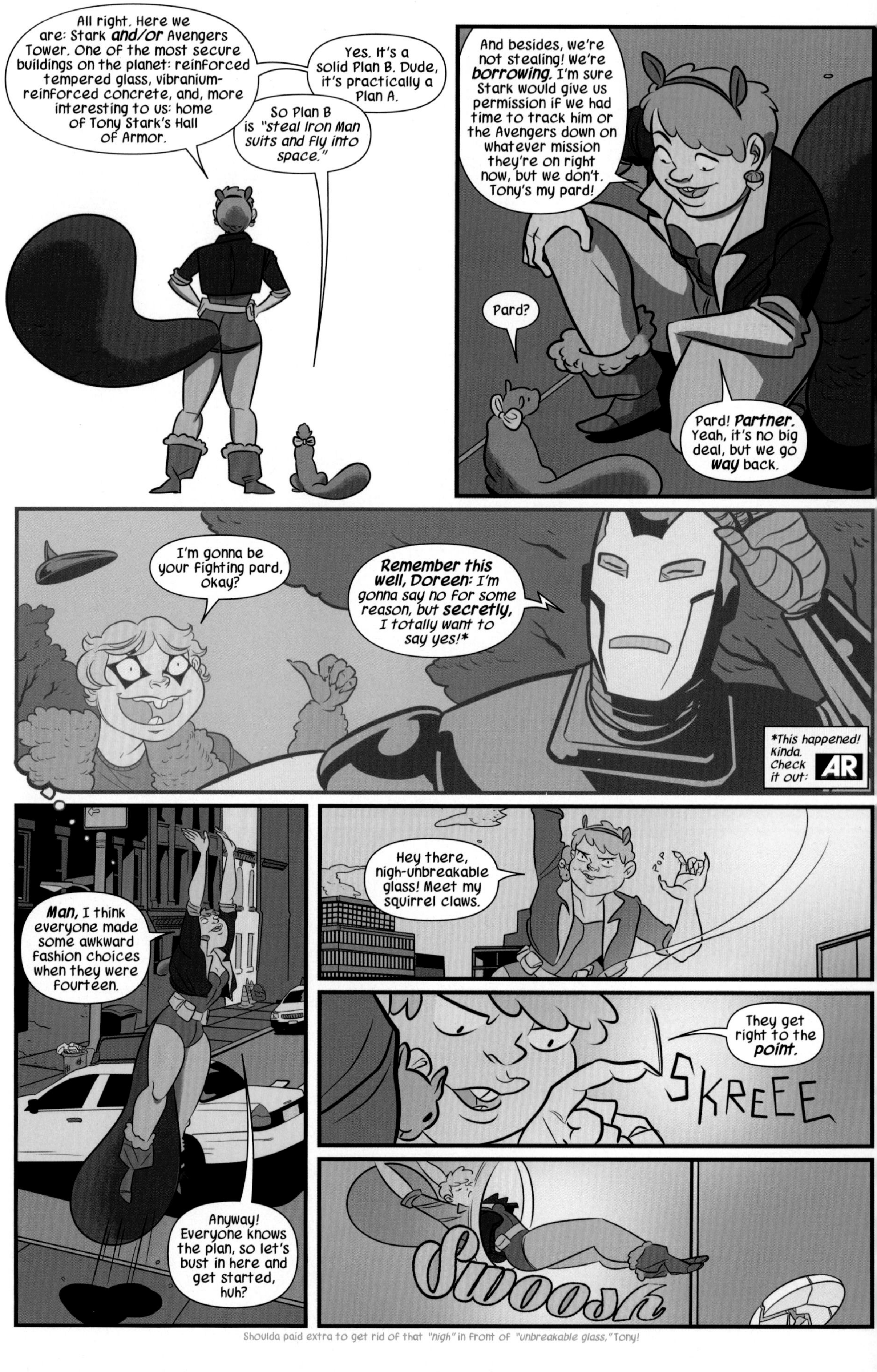
All right. Here we are: Stark **and/or** Avengers Tower. One of the most secure buildings on the planet: reinforced tempered glass, vibranium-reinforced concrete, and, more interesting to us: home of Tony Stark's Hall of Armor.
Yes. It's a solid Plan B. Dude, it's practically a Plan A.
So Plan B is *"steal Iron Man suits and fly into space."*
And besides, we're not stealing! We're ***borrowing.*** I'm sure Stark would give us permission if we had time to track him or the Avengers down on whatever mission they're on right now, but we don't. Tony's my pard!
Pard?
Pard! ***Partner.*** Yeah, it's no big deal, but we go ***way*** back.
I'm gonna be your fighting pard, okay?
Remember this well, Doreen: *I'm gonna say no for some reason, but* ***secretly,*** *I totally want to say yes!**
**This happened! Kinda. Check it out:* AR
Man, I think everyone made some awkward fashion choices when they were fourteen.
Anyway! Everyone knows the plan, so let's bust in here and get started, huh?
Hey there, nigh-unbreakable glass! Meet my squirrel claws.
POP
They get right to the ***point.***
SKREEE
SWOOSH

Shoulda paid extra to get rid of that *"nigh"* in front of *"unbreakable glass,"* Tony!

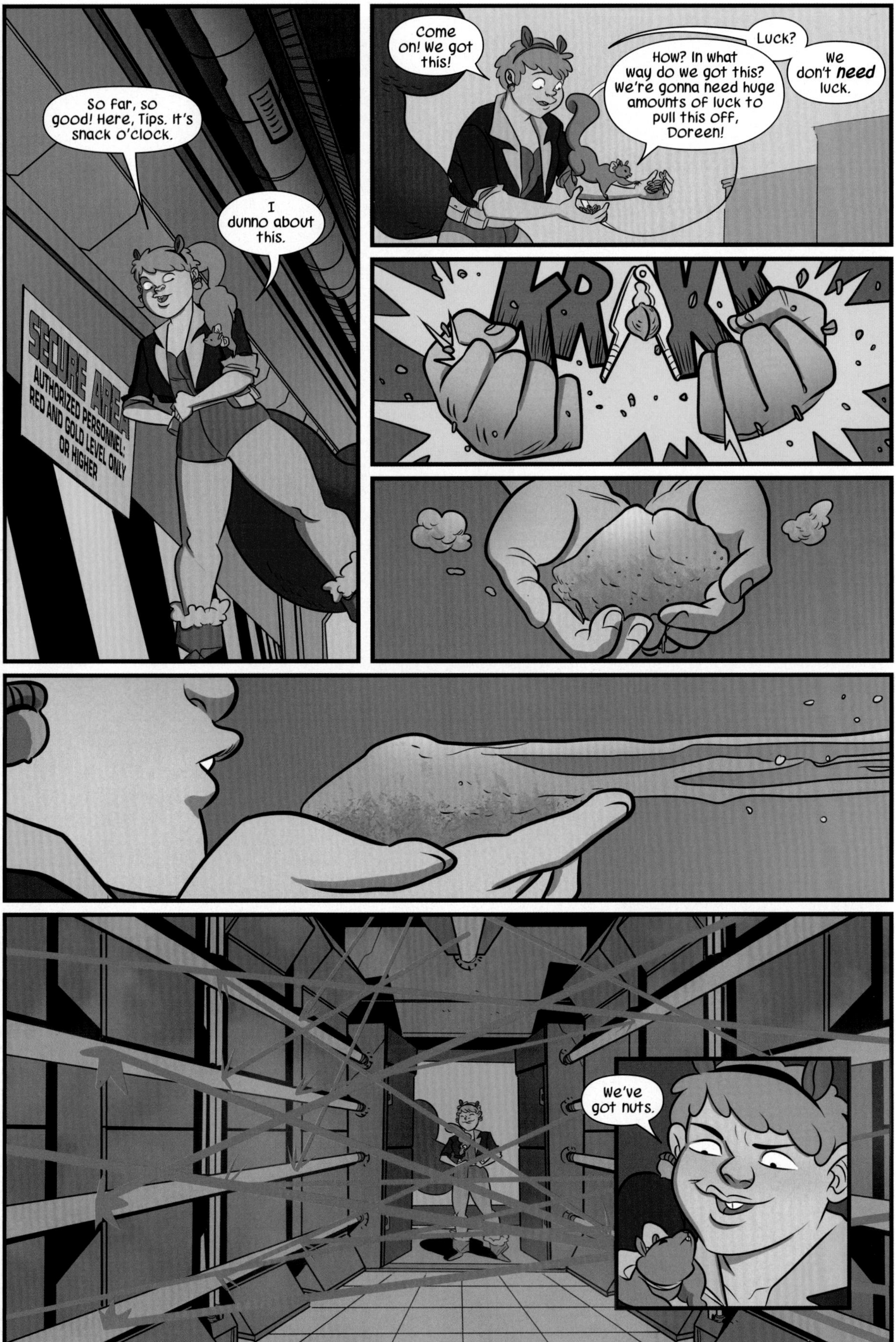
So far, so good! Here, Tips. It's snack o'clock.
I dunno about this.
SECURE AREA
AUTHORIZED PERSONNEL: RED AND GOLD LEVEL ONLY OR HIGHER
Come on! We got this!
How? In what way do we got this? We're gonna need huge amounts of luck to pull this off, Doreen!
Luck?
We don't **need** luck.
KRAK
We've got nuts.

Okay, now breathe through your mouth! That way we can still taste them, so we're not wasting these delicious nuts.

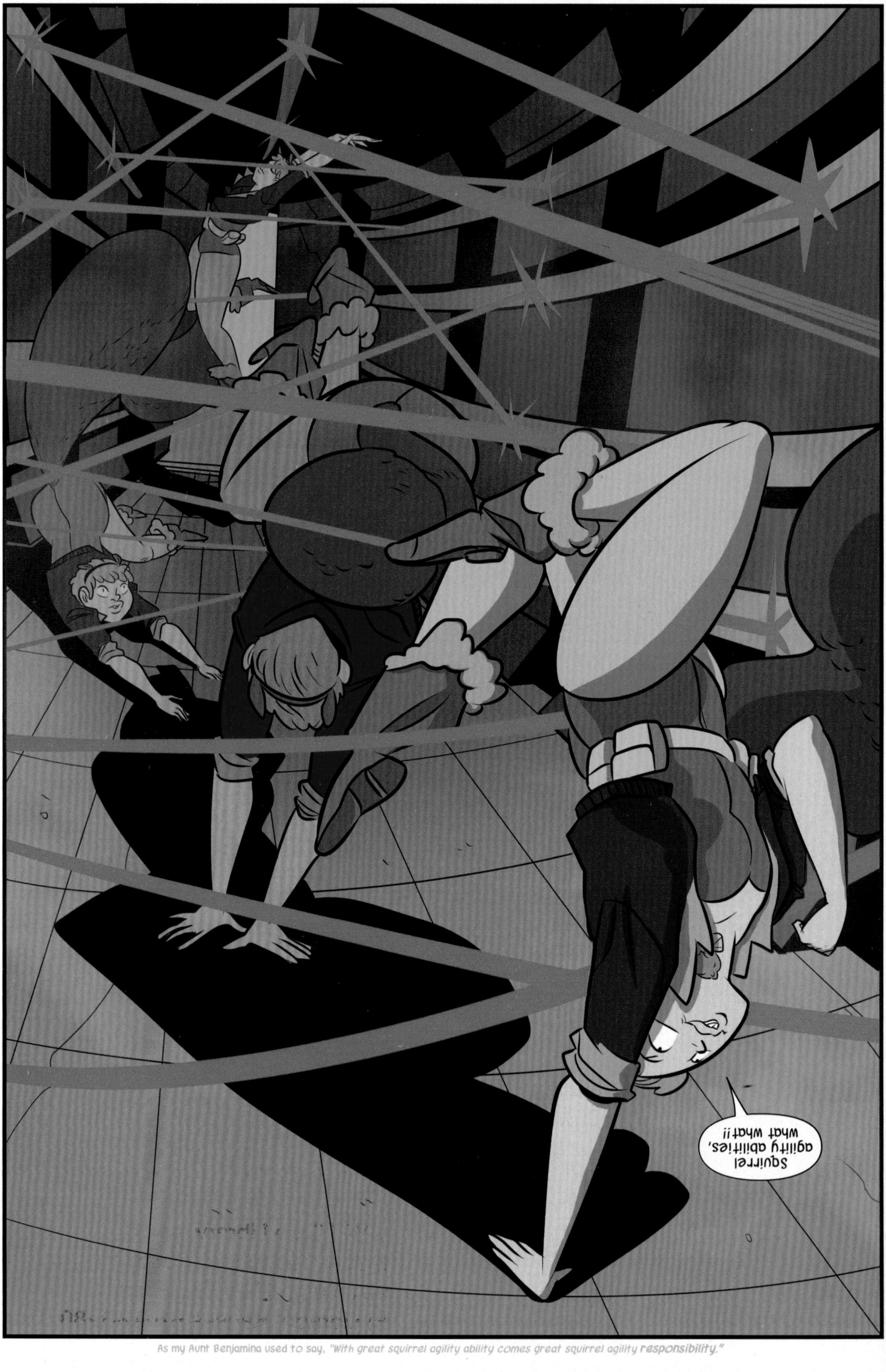
squirrel agility abilities, what what!!

As my Aunt Benjamina used to say, *"With great squirrel agility ability comes great squirrel agility **responsibility.**"*

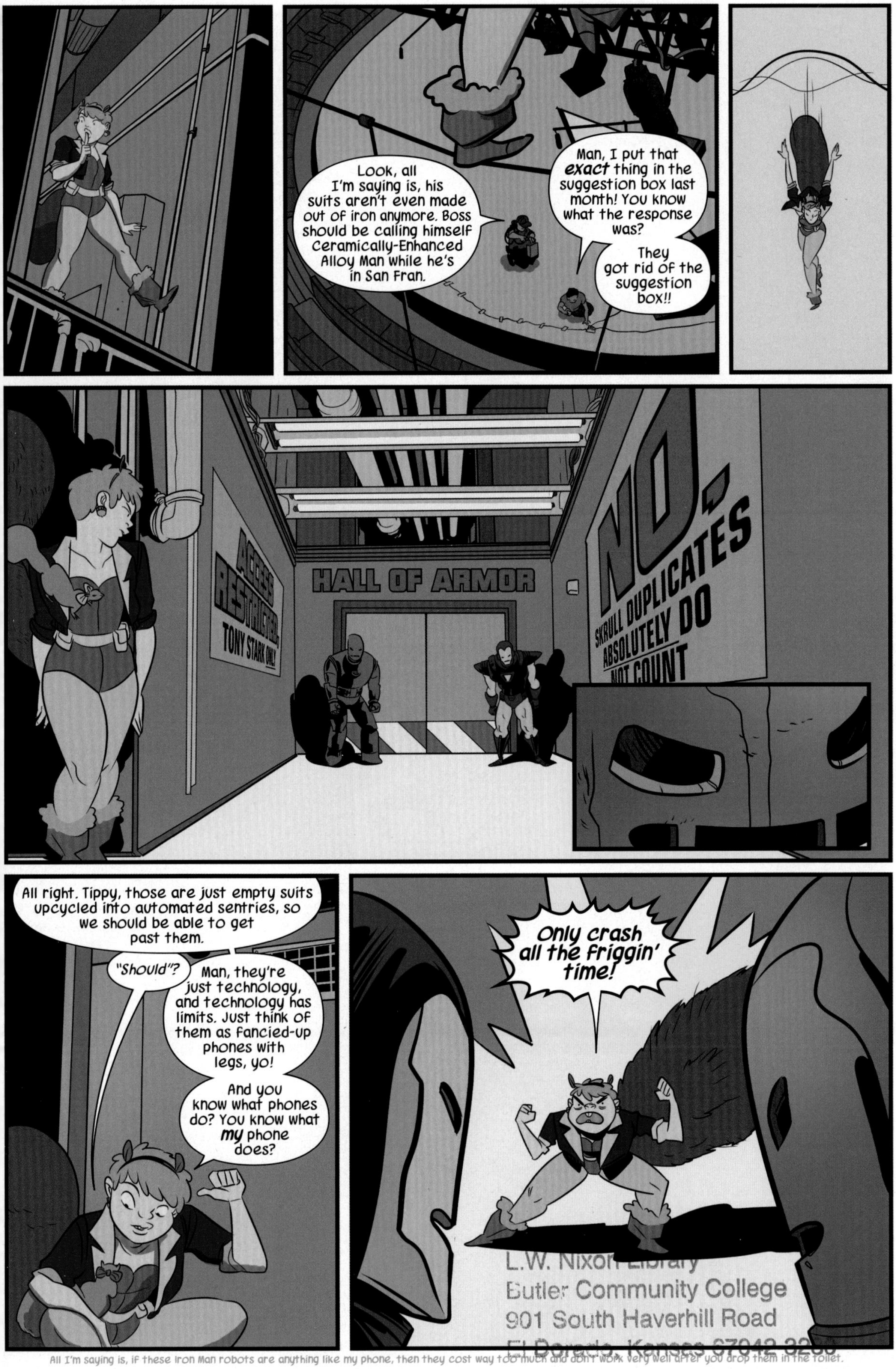
Look, all I'm saying is, his suits aren't even made out of iron anymore. Boss should be calling himself Ceramically-Enhanced Alloy Man while he's in San Fran.
Man, I put that *exact* thing in the suggestion box last month! You know what the response was?
They got rid of the suggestion box!!
ACCESS RESTRICTED
TONY STARK ONLY
HALL OF ARMOR
NO, SKRULL DUPLICATES ABSOLUTELY DO NOT COUNT
All right. Tippy, those are just empty suits upcycled into automated sentries, so we should be able to get past them.
"Should"?
Man, they're just technology, and technology has limits. Just think of them as fancied-up phones with legs, yo!
And you know what phones do? You know what *my* phone does?
Only crash all the friggin' time!

All I'm saying is, if these Iron Man robots are anything like my phone, then they cost way too much and don't work very well after you drop them in the toilet.

Whoa!

All right, robots! This is me, Squirrel Girl, speaking loudly and clearly so your speech recognition can understand!

I'm throwing this grenade at you! It will explode in one second unless you destroy it!

Okay, here comes my grenade!

PHWEE

KAKOOM

See? *See? This* is why we need to invest in the computer sciences. Now all we need to do is open the door and we're...

PHWEEE

...huh?

Security from eight different zones? All for me?

Me, a regular girl who, um--

--who got really, really lost from the tour group while trying to find the bathroom??

That "PHWEEEEEEeeee" is the sound of the repulsors charging up. The robots aren't saying the "PHWEEEEEEeeee" noises themselves, although that would've been *kinda adorable.*

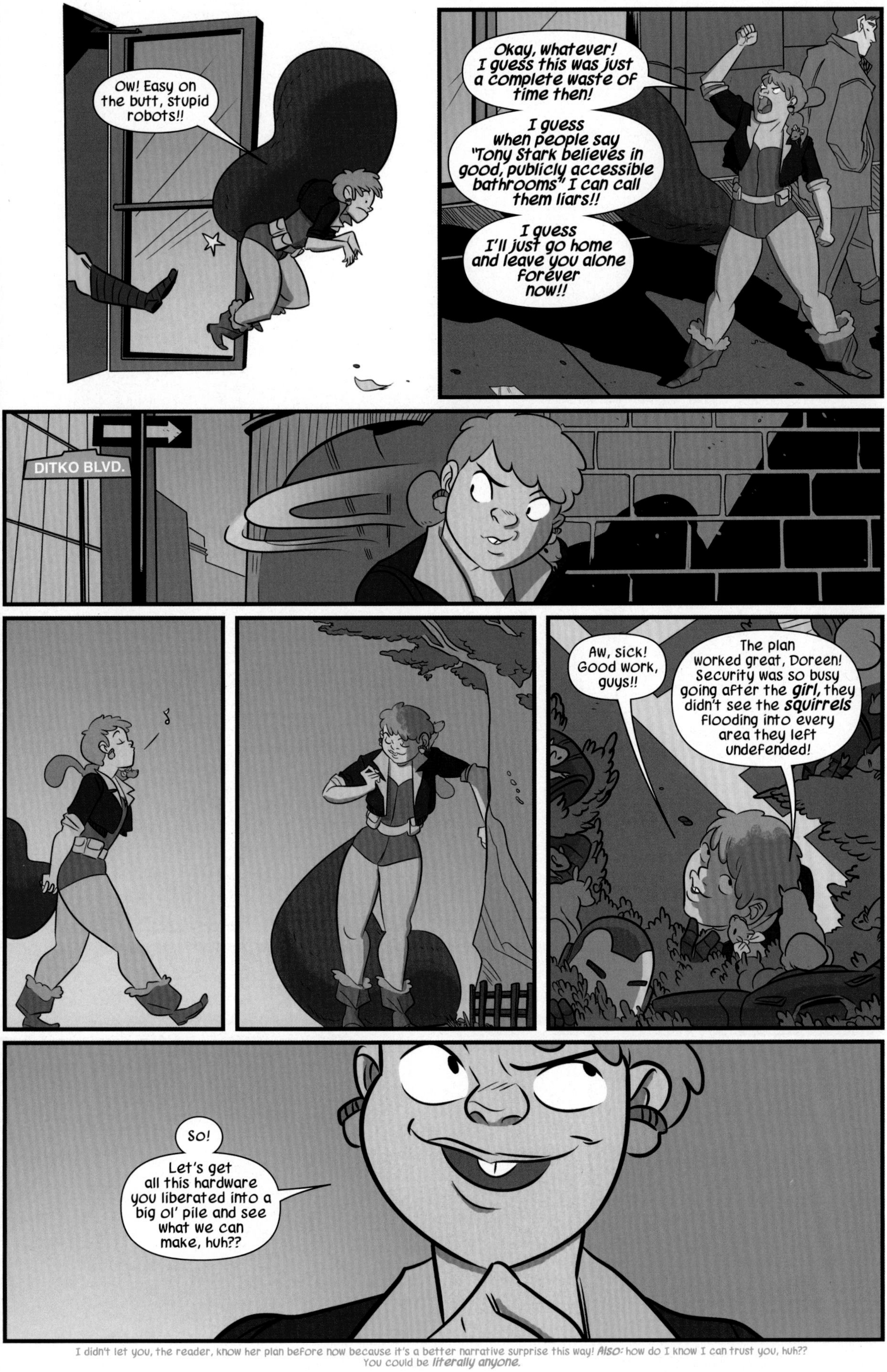

Ow! Easy on the butt, stupid robots!!
Okay, whatever! I guess this was just a complete waste of time then!
I guess when people say "Tony Stark believes in good, publicly accessible bathrooms" I can call them liars!!
I guess I'll just go home and leave you alone forever now!!
DITKO BLVD.
Aw, sick! Good work, guys!!
The plan worked great, Doreen! Security was so busy going after the *girl,* they didn't see the *squirrels* flooding into every area they left undefended!
So!
Let's get all this hardware you liberated into a big ol' pile and see what we can make, huh??

I didn't let you, the reader, know her plan before now because it's a better narrative surprise this way! *Also:* how do I know I can trust you, huh??
You could be *literally anyone.*

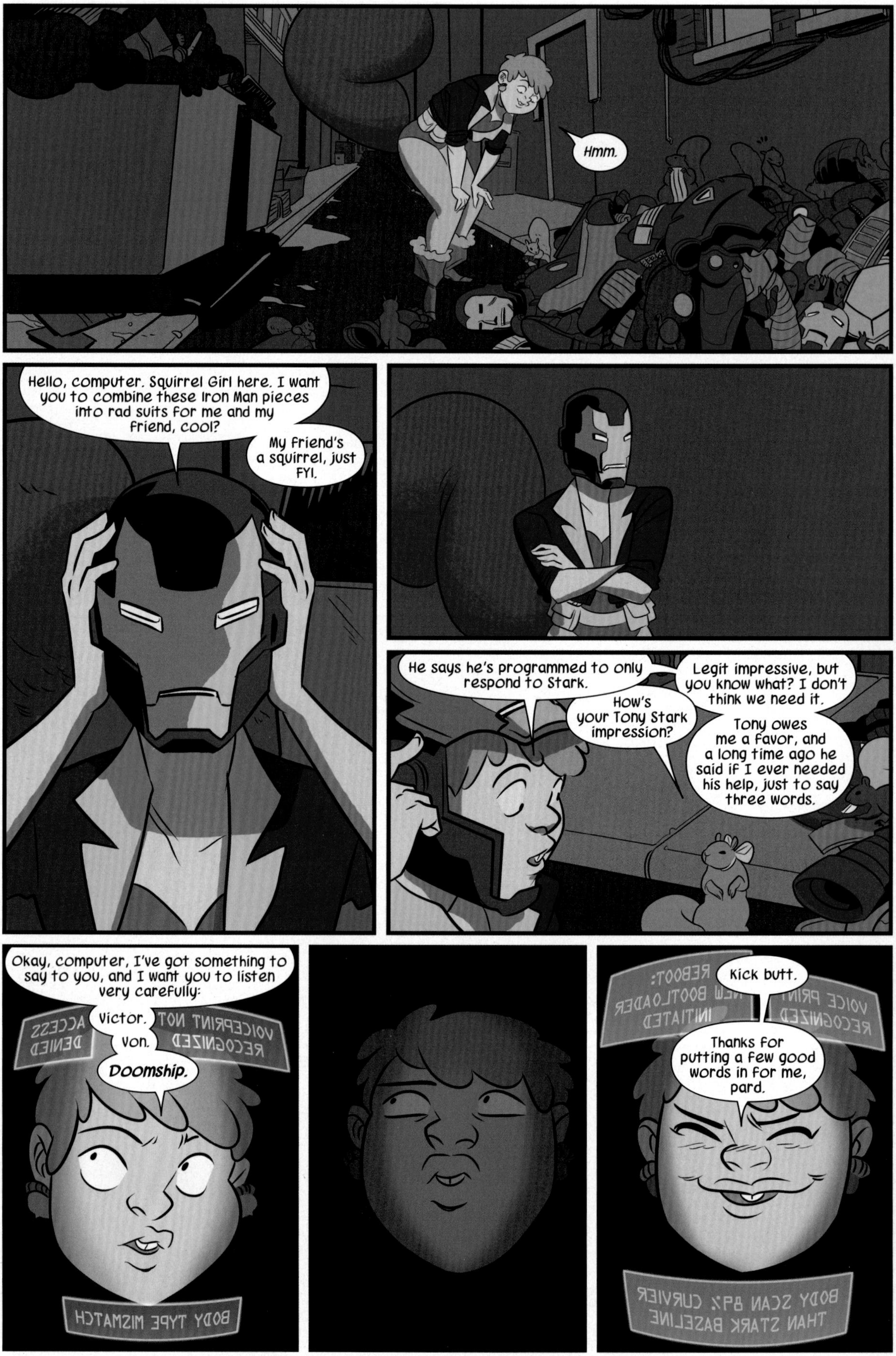
Hmm.
Hello, computer. Squirrel Girl here. I want you to combine these Iron Man pieces into rad suits for me and my friend, cool?
My friend's a squirrel, just FYI.
He says he's programmed to only respond to Stark.
How's your Tony Stark impression?
Legit impressive, but you know what? I don't think we need it.
Tony owes me a favor, and a long time ago he said if I ever needed his help, just to say three words.
Okay, computer, I've got something to say to you, and I want you to listen very carefully:
ACCESS DENIED
VOICEPRINT NOT RECOGNIZED
Victor.
Von.
Doomship.
BODY TYPE MISMATCH
REBOOT: NEW BOOTLOADER INITIATED
VOICE PRINT RECOGNIZED
Kick butt.
Thanks for putting a few good words in for me, pard.
BODY SCAN 89% CURVIER THAN STARK BASELINE

BODY TYPE: Rad / TAIL TYPE: Unexpected / CLAW TYPE: Geez, Tony, you really need to get these nails under control.

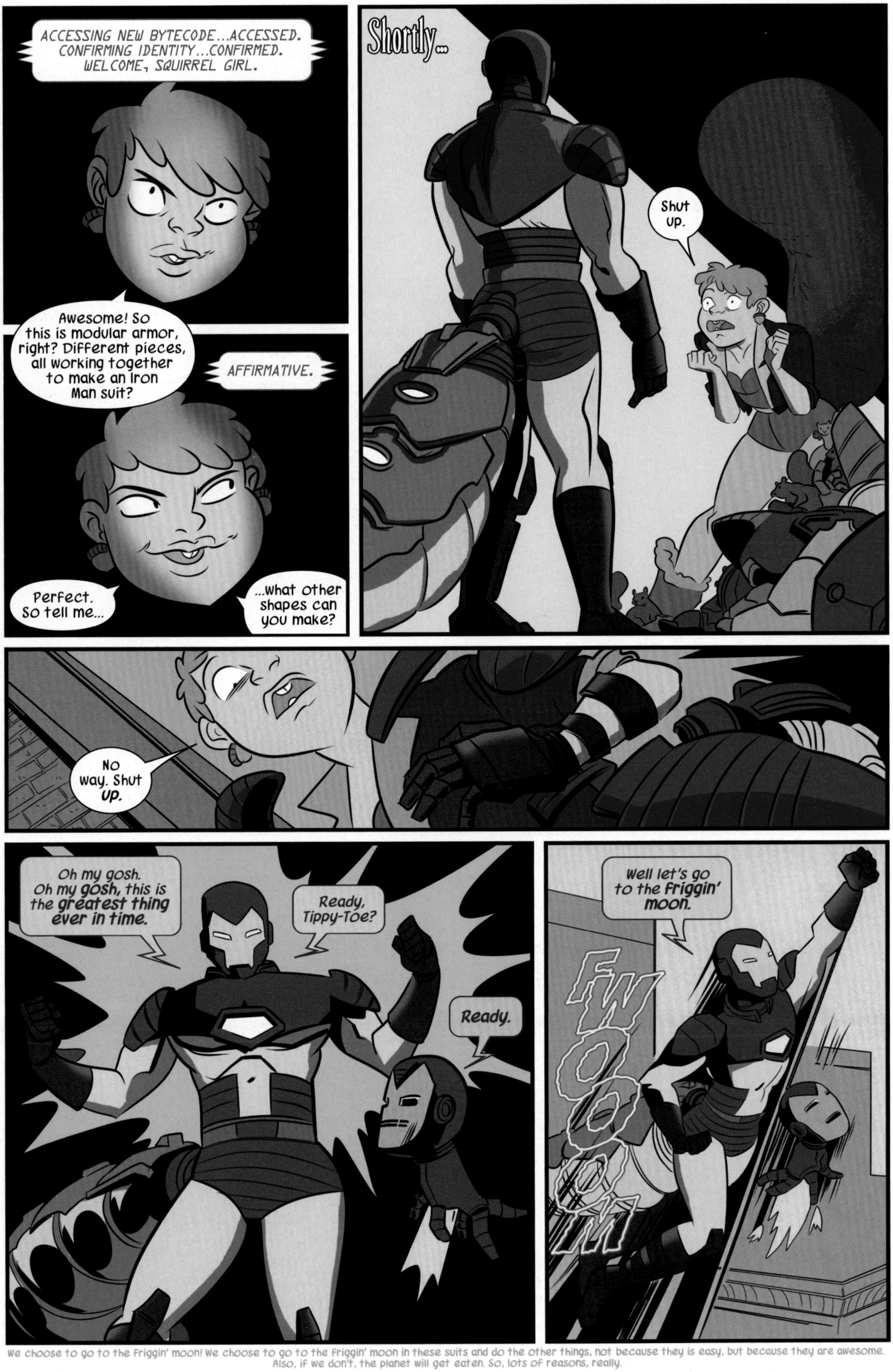
ACCESSING NEW BYTECODE...ACCESSED. CONFIRMING IDENTITY...CONFIRMED. WELCOME, SQUIRREL GIRL.
Awesome! So this is modular armor, right? Different pieces, all working together to make an Iron Man suit?
AFFIRMATIVE.
Perfect. So tell me...
...what other shapes can you make?
Shortly...
Shut up.
No way. Shut up.
Oh my gosh. Oh my gosh, this is the greatest thing ever in time.
Ready, Tippy-Toe?
Ready.
Well let's go to the friggin' moon.
FWOOOOM

We choose to go to the friggin' moon! We choose to go to the friggin' moon in these suits and do the other things, not because they is easy, but because they are awesome. Also, if we don't, the planet will get eaten. So, lots of reasons, really.

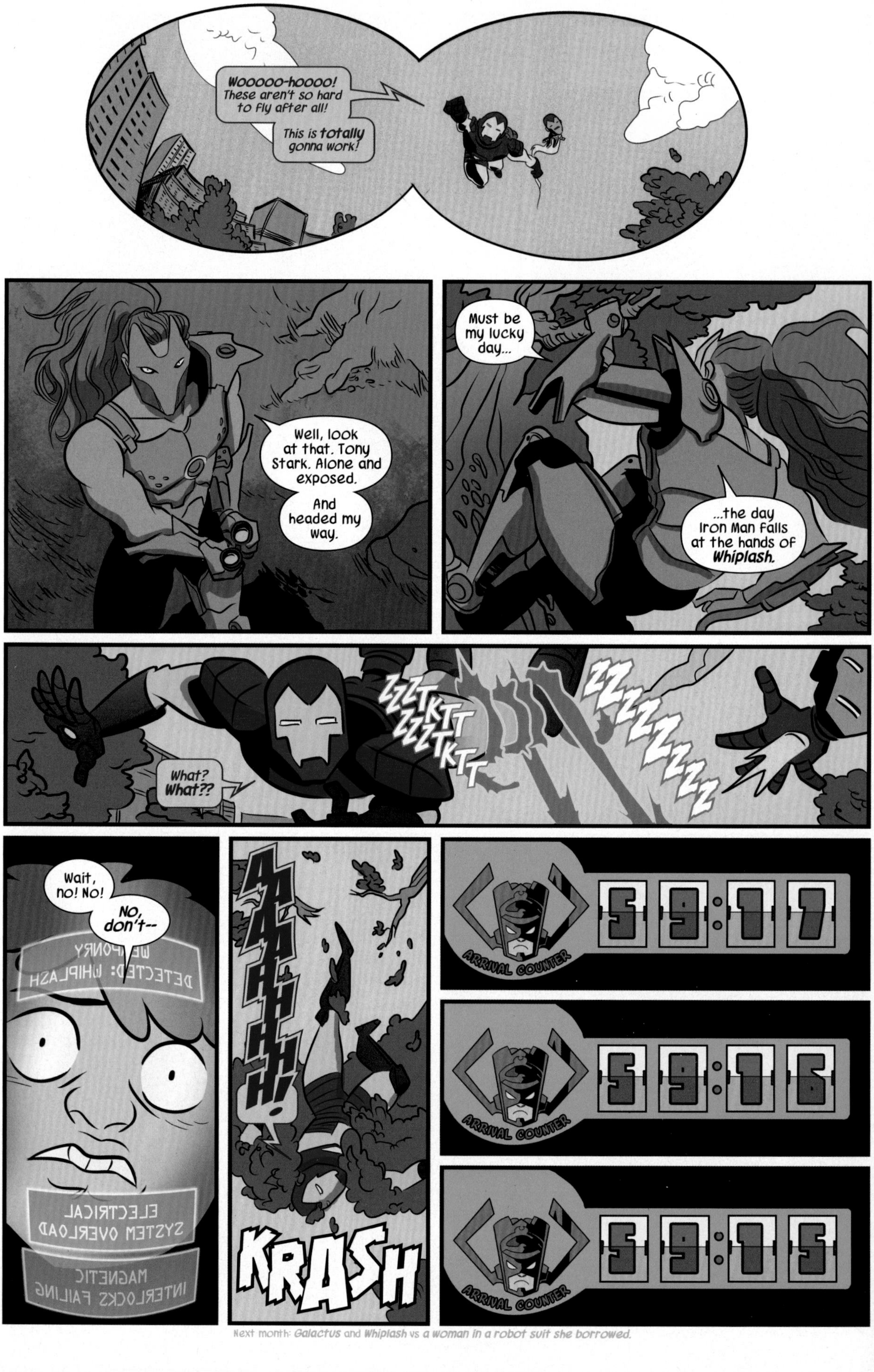

Wooooo-hoooo! These aren't so hard to fly after all!
This is totally gonna work!
Well, look at that. Tony Stark. Alone and exposed.
And headed my way.
Must be my lucky day...
...the day Iron Man falls at the hands of Whiplash.
ZZZTKTT ZZZTKTT
What? What??
ZZZZZZZZZ
Wait, no! No!
No, don't--
WEAPONRY DETECTED: WHIPLASH
ELECTRICAL SYSTEM OVERLOAD
MAGNETIC INTERLOCKS FAILING
AAAAHHHHH!
KRASH
ARRIVAL COUNTER
59:17
ARRIVAL COUNTER
59:16
ARRIVAL COUNTER
59:15

Next month: *Galactus* and *Whiplash* vs *a woman in a robot suit she borrowed.*

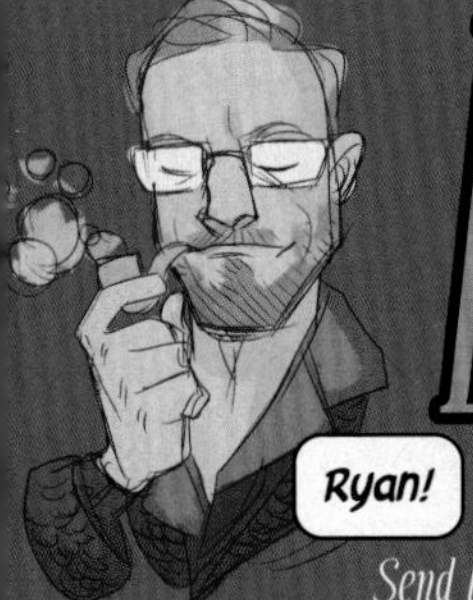
Ryan!

Letters From Nuts

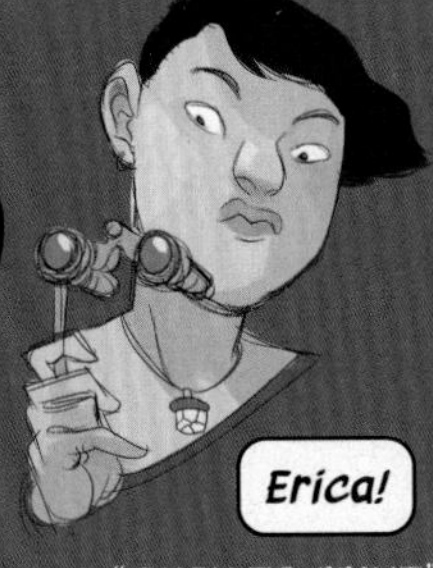
Erica!

Send letters to mheroes@marvel.com or 135 W 50th St. 7th Floor, New York, NY 10020 (Please mark "OKAY TO PRINT")

Last month we said all the letters were fake because you hadn't sent us any yet, but now we have TONS and all the letters are real! We love to hear from you: send your email to MHEROES@MARVEL.COM, and don't forget to mark "OKAY TO PRINT" in there somewhere. And be sure to follow our production blog at unbeatablesquirrelgirl.tumblr.com! We post fan art, sneak peeks, sketches, recordings of Squirrel Girl's theme song we made in our kitchens - all sorts of fun stuff!

YOUR LETTERS:

Q: In issue #1's letters you wrote, "Can a book like this find an audience?" We live in a post-Superior Foes of Spider-Man world; more and more we readers like having the "comic" in our comics. You've found an audience in this guy, that's for sure! Was it Ryan/Erica or the editors who wrote the subscript footnotes? Because that was NUT a bad idea. I hope the footnotes are a continued part of the comic mag!

- Trent H.

A: Yeah, that was me (Ryan) doing that! I like the idea of secrets that you get to discover when you read a comic, and I really hope there are people who only noticed those secret words halfway through (or perhaps, just now, as they're reading this, and now they're going back to see what they missed?). They will continue forever because I love writing them forever!

Q: Squirrels. Cannot. Give. You. RABIES!!! Look it up!! Doreen would have known this and corrected her new roommate (even if she didn't know about the squirrel observatories).

-Benjamin G.
True Squirrel Fan

A: ATTENTION EVERYONE: I looked into this and BENJAMIN IS CORRECT. Squirrels don't even normally GET rabies, because to get it they'd have to hang around with animals that typically carry it, and most of those animals try to eat all the squirrels they see. Squirrel bites are apparently one of the few animal bites that don't trigger a hospital vaccination protocol! GOOD TO KNOW.

PS: if you get bitten by a squirrel, maaaaybe still check with a doctor just in case? You know, before you take the medical advice you found in the letters page of a comic book.

ERICA: I have personal experience with this, actually. As a young teenager, I think you call them tweens now, during the time when most Marvel characters gain their superhuman abilities, I was bitten by a squirrel. I was tested, but did not get rabies. We did not test for radiation. It might have been a radioactive squirrel. If you ask, I'll show you my scar.

Q: Thank you, Erica, for drawing Squirrel Girl not like a sex symbol (I feel awkward when I discovered about she and Logan...). And thank you, Ryan, for showing us that Squirrel Girl is a geek too. It's good to read comics about a girl who is a fan of comics too, and a little tomboy (I'm a tomboy girl too).

Will we see romance between Speedball and Squirrel Girl? I know we are gonna see a lot of Marvel stars in this comic. But I hope to see those love birds together again.

- ScarlettShana

A: Aw, thanks! I wouldn't worry about that Wolverine thing though: all we knew for SURE is that she and Wolverine at one point agreed to never see each other again. BUT NOW I CAN TELL YOU WHY: several years ago, Doreen was about to get into a cab when Wolverine ran up and hopped inside, stealing it from her. Squirrel Girl was (understandably) SUPER-CHEESED and shouted that he was a jerk and his jerkiness must have its OWN healing factor and that she never wanted to see him again. As the cab drove off Wolverine rolled down the window and shouted "You too, bub!". And that's why things were awkward when they met again! THE END.

As for romance with Speedball, everyone has a little romance in their lives at some point, right? But I have a feeling Doreen might have feelings for someone new now...

ERICA: You're welcome, but honestly I just drew her the way I saw her and I don't see her as a sexy character. She's not exactly Emma Frost, you know?

Q: Does Doreen have a flying squirrel costume that opens up and lets her glide?

- Simon S.

A: SPOILER ALERT (IF YOU'RE READING THIS COMIC FROM BACK TO FRONT, THAT IS): She gets an Iron Squirrel outfit this issue, so - kinda! But a base-jumping suit would be PRETTY AMAZING for her to get down the road.

ERICA: Well, I know that S.H.I.E.L.D. has had base-jumping suits for decades and Dum Dum Dugan did invite Doreen to join S.H.I.E.L.D. at one point, so she might have access to some later...

Q: First off, I have to say how absolutely MARVELous (ha!) the first issue of Unbeatable Squirrel Girl was! Wow! Artwork and writing combined, it's pretty much the most perfect comic book of all time and space. Secondly, I have to say how super AWESOME it is to have another female-fronted book, but also one where the character is hilarious and clumsy and endearing and basically a lot more like me than any of the other beautiful, graceful super-women out there. (I love them too, though!) I love everything you've done and I absolutely canNUT wait for the next issue! (One day I'll stop with the puns. Today is NUT that day.)

- Holly R.

A: Thank you! One thing both Erica and I discovered while making this book is how often every day (without thinking!) we would say something is "nuts" or "nutty" or how we'd like "acorn" ("a corn") for dinner. The puns come almost TOO easily!

ERICA: My main thing is I like to draw heartier super ladies, if their powers are mostly physical, because I feel like I shouldn't be able to take down a super hero by sitting on her.

Q: Is it true Squirrel Girl would've been in Avengers 2, but Ultron was too chicken to fight her?

- Andy D.

A: That movie isn't even out yet! How do you know she's NOT in it?? ...But on the off chance that for some reason she isn't, yeah, probably that's the reason! I'm guessing the after-credits scene is just Ultron peeking around corners to make sure Squirrel Girl isn't there, then wiping his forehead and saying "PHEW! CLOSE CALL."

ERICA: I don't know about that, but they need to add her to the movies soon because who's going to take down Thanos???

That's all we have room for, but look for a double-sized letters page next issue! See y'all next month! Stay nutty!

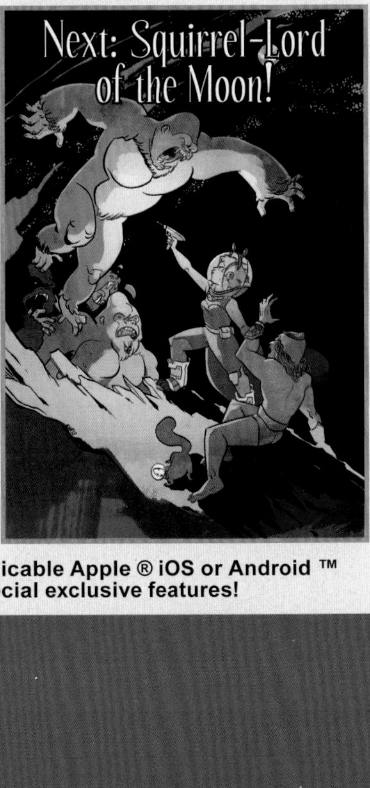
Next: Squirrel-Lord of the Moon!

When you see this: AR, open up the MARVEL AR APP (available on applicable Apple ® iOS or Android ™ devices) and use your camera-enabled device to unlock extra-special exclusive features!

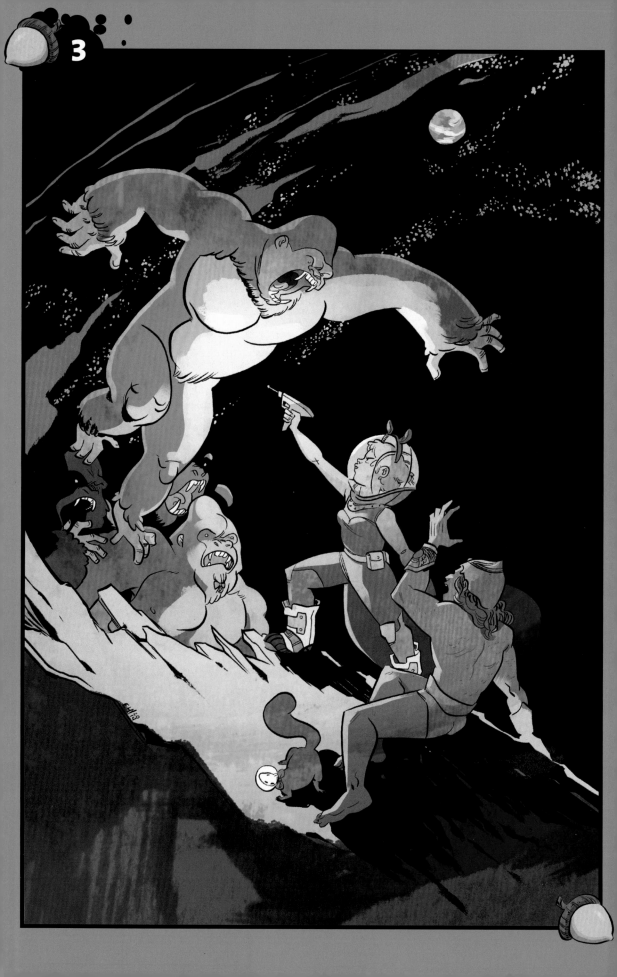

3

Doreen Green isn't just a first-year computer science student: she secretly also has all the powers of both squirrel and girl! She uses her amazing abilities to fight crime **and** be as awesome as possible. You know her as...*The Unbeatable Squirrel Girl!* Let's catch up with what she's been up to until now, with...

Squirrel Girl in a nutshell

 Squirrel Girl! @unbeatablesg
Did you guys see how I took care of Kraven the other day?

 xKravenTheHunterx @unshavenkraven
NOBODY LISTEN TO @unbeatablesg, SHE DIDN'T TAKE CARE OF ME, I MERELY DECIDED TO STOP FIGHTING HER

 Squirrel Girl! @unbeatablesg
@unshavenkraven hey dude did you kill any gigantos underwater like I suggested?

 xKravenTheHunterx @unshavenkraven
@unbeatablesg listen

 xKravenTheHunterx @unshavenkraven
@unbeatablesg these things take time

 Squirrel Girl! @unbeatablesg
Apparently I'm the only one that can see that GALACTUS IS COMING TO EARTH!!

 Tippy-Toe @yoitstippytoe
CHIT CHUKKA CHITTY

 Squirrel Girl! @unbeatablesg
Apparently me and @yoitstippytoe are the only ones that can see GALACTUS IS COMING TO EARTH!!

 Squirrel Girl! @unbeatablesg
Oh well

 Squirrel Girl! @unbeatablesg
guess we'll just have to stop him ourselves then

 Squirrel Girl! @unbeatablesg
ON THE FRIGGIN' MOON

 Tony Stark @starkmantony ✓
Whoever "borrowed" Iron Man armor parts from my NYC offices, please return them. Looking at you, @unbeatablesg.

 Squirrel Girl! @unbeatablesg
@starkmantony Tony it's REALLY IMPORTANT. Like COSMIC important.

Squirrel Girl! @unbeatablesg
@starkmantony I don't know why I'm being coy. It's for Galactus.

 Squirrel Girl! @unbeatablesg
@starkmantony I'm gonna beat up @xGALACTUSx, Tony!! ON THE MOON

 Tony Stark @starkmantony ✓
@unbeatablesg You break it, you bought it.

Whiplash @realwhiplash22
I JUST WHIPPED @STARKMANTONY OUT OF THE SKY WITH MY ENERGY WHIPS YES YES #OWNED

Tony Stark @starkmantony ✓
Wasn't me. I'm in San Francisco, @realwhiplash22.

Whiplash @realwhiplash22
@starkmantony SORRY I CANNOT HEAR YOU OVER HOW BADLY YOU GOT #OWNED

search!

#OWNED

#everythingisnormalinspace

Welcome to

#USG

Number Three

Hope you like falafel jokes

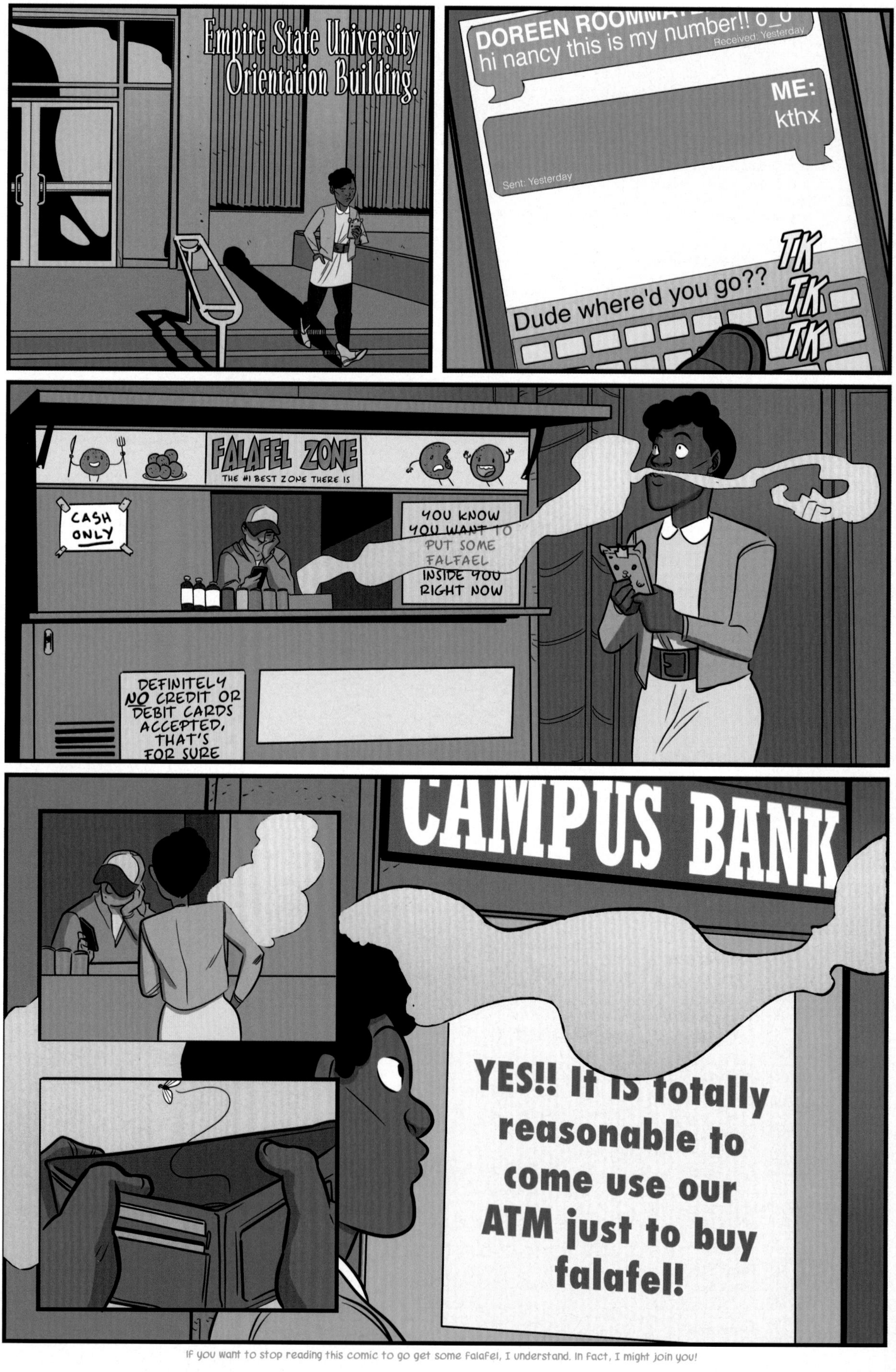
Empire State University Orientation Building.
DOREEN ROOMMATE
hi nancy this is my number!! o_o
Received: Yesterday
ME:
kthx
Sent: Yesterday
Dude where'd you go??
TK
TK
TK
FALAFEL ZONE
THE #1 BEST ZONE THERE IS
CASH ONLY
YOU KNOW YOU WANT TO PUT SOME FALFAEL INSIDE YOU RIGHT NOW
DEFINITELY NO CREDIT OR DEBIT CARDS ACCEPTED, THAT'S FOR SURE
CAMPUS BANK
YES!! It IS totally reasonable to come use our ATM just to buy falafel!

If you want to stop reading this comic to go get some falafel, I understand. In fact, I might join you!

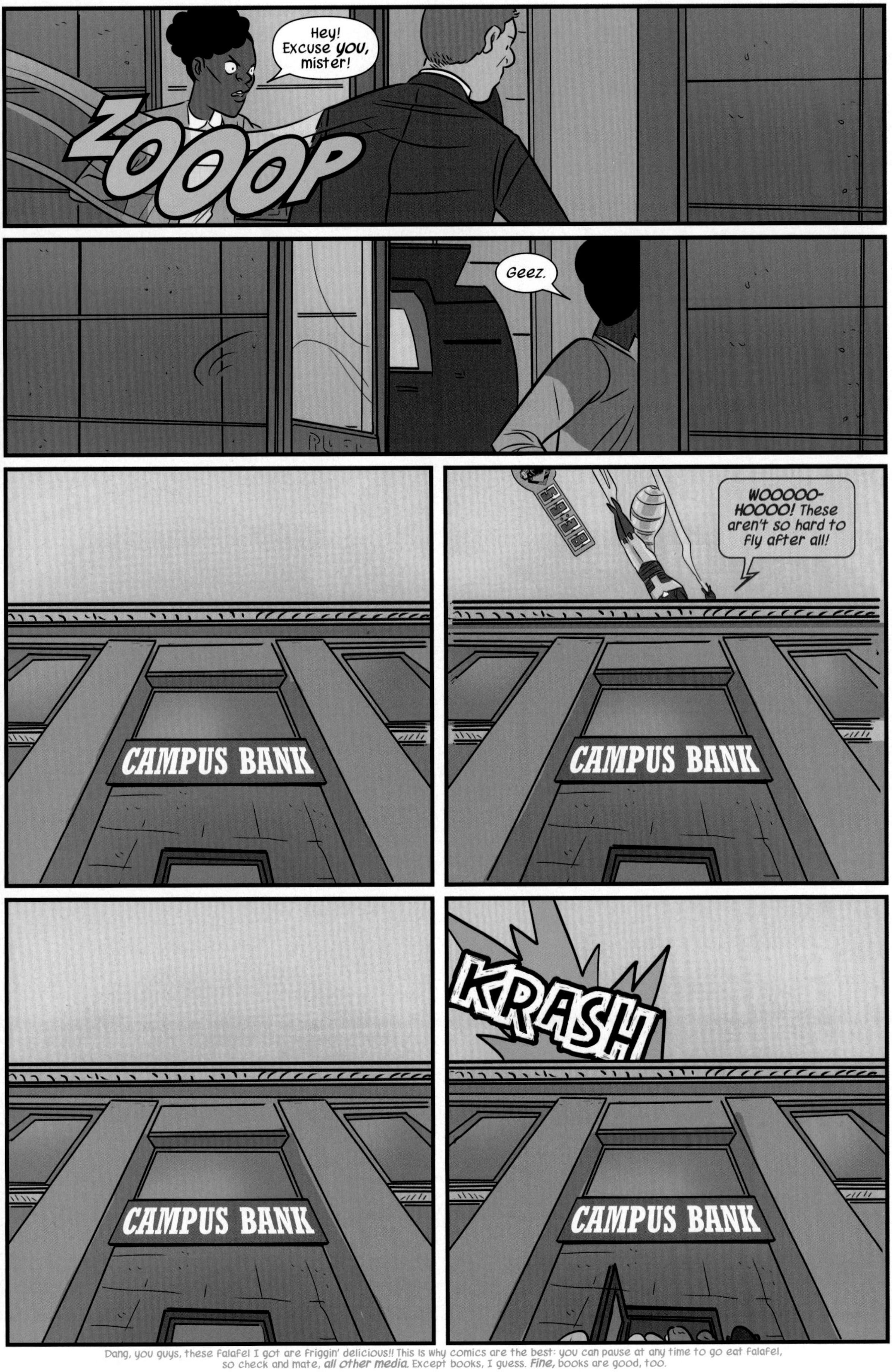
Hey! Excuse *you*, mister!
ZOOOP
Geez.
CAMPUS BANK
WOOOOO-HOOOO! These aren't so hard to fly after all!
CAMPUS BANK
CAMPUS BANK
KRASH
CAMPUS BANK

Dang, you guys, these falafel I got are friggin' delicious!! This is why comics are the best: you can pause at any time to go eat falafel, so check and mate, ***all other media***. Except books, I guess. ***Fine***, books are good, too.

the unbeatable Squirrel Girl

Words by Ryan North
Art by Erica Henderson
Trading Card Art by Kyle Starks
Color Art by Rico Renzi
Lettering by VC's Clayton Cowles

Cover by Erica Henderson
Variant Covers by Jill Thompson,
Gurihiru

Starring:

Squirrel Girl	Whiplash	Nancy Whitehead	Galactus	Galactus Counter
SECRET IDENTITY: Doreen Green **FUN FACT:** Likes Iron Man, and borrowed his armor!	**SECRET IDENTITY:** Anton Vanko **FUN FACT:** Hates Iron Man, and reverse-engineered his armor!	**SECRET IDENTITY:** Nancy Whitehead **FUN FACT:** That guy who barged through the door she opened also cut in line for the teller! Sheesh, dude!	**SECRET IDENTITY:** G. Alactus **FUN FACT:** I may have just made that secret identity up! **FUN SUPPOSITION:** But maybe I didn't??	**SECRET IDENTITY:** G. Alactus Counter **FUN FACT:** instead of being a character, Galactus Counter is simply a narrative conceit, and does not actually exist!!

Okay, real talk: If you look it up online, you'll find Galactus's *actual* name is "Galan." I'm not joking, it's Galan. Galan A. Lactus.

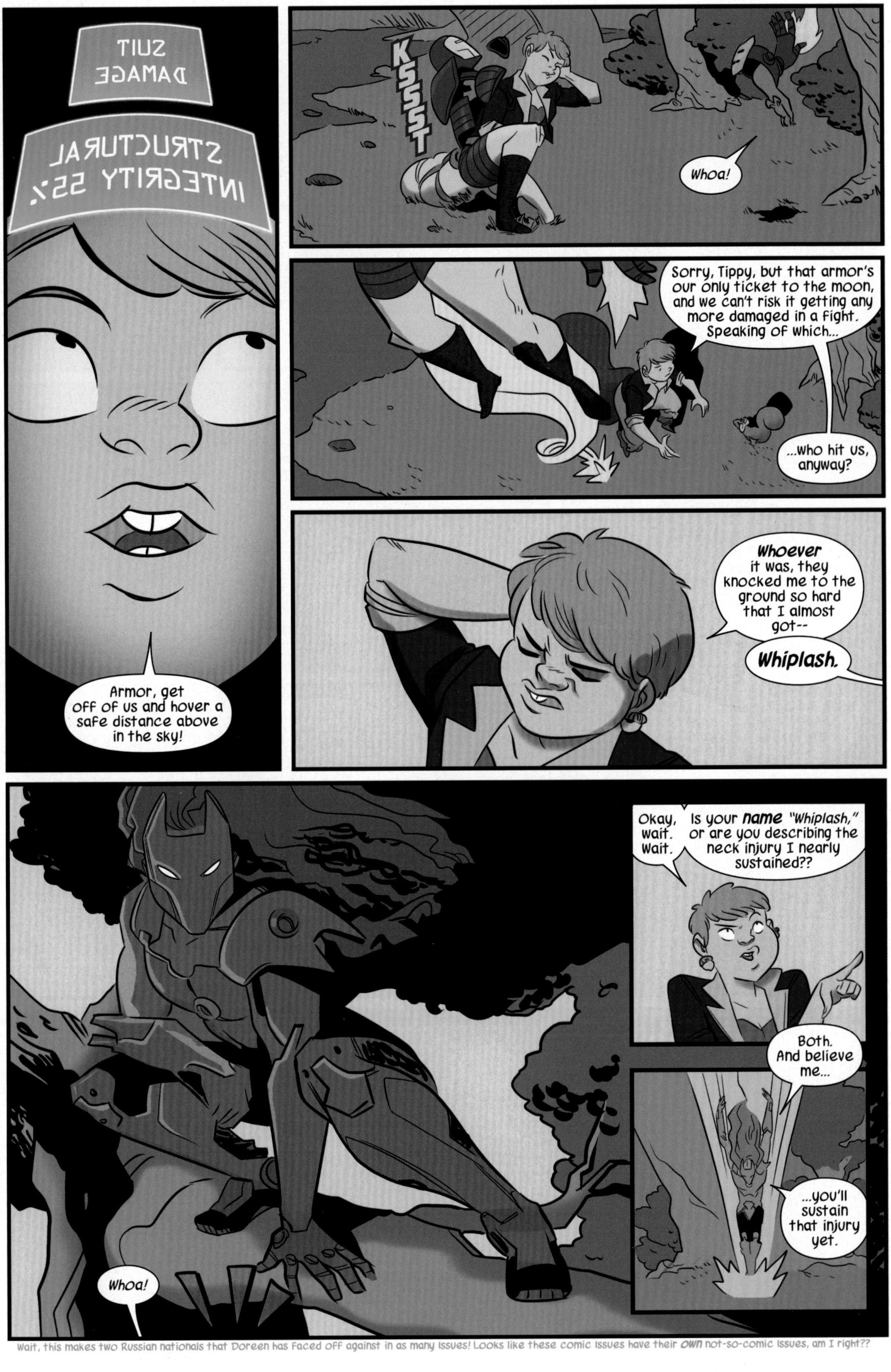
SUIT DAMAGE
STRUCTURAL INTEGRITY 55%
Armor, get off of us and hover a safe distance above in the sky!
KSSST
Whoa!
Sorry, Tippy, but that armor's our only ticket to the moon, and we can't risk it getting any more damaged in a fight. Speaking of which...
...who hit us, anyway?
Whoever it was, they knocked me to the ground so hard that I almost got--
Whiplash.
Whoa!
Okay, wait. Wait.
Is your name "Whiplash," or are you describing the neck injury I nearly sustained??
Both. And believe me...
...you'll sustain that injury yet.

Wait, this makes two Russian nationals that Doreen has faced off against in as many issues! Looks like these comic issues have their *own* not-so-comic issues, am I right??

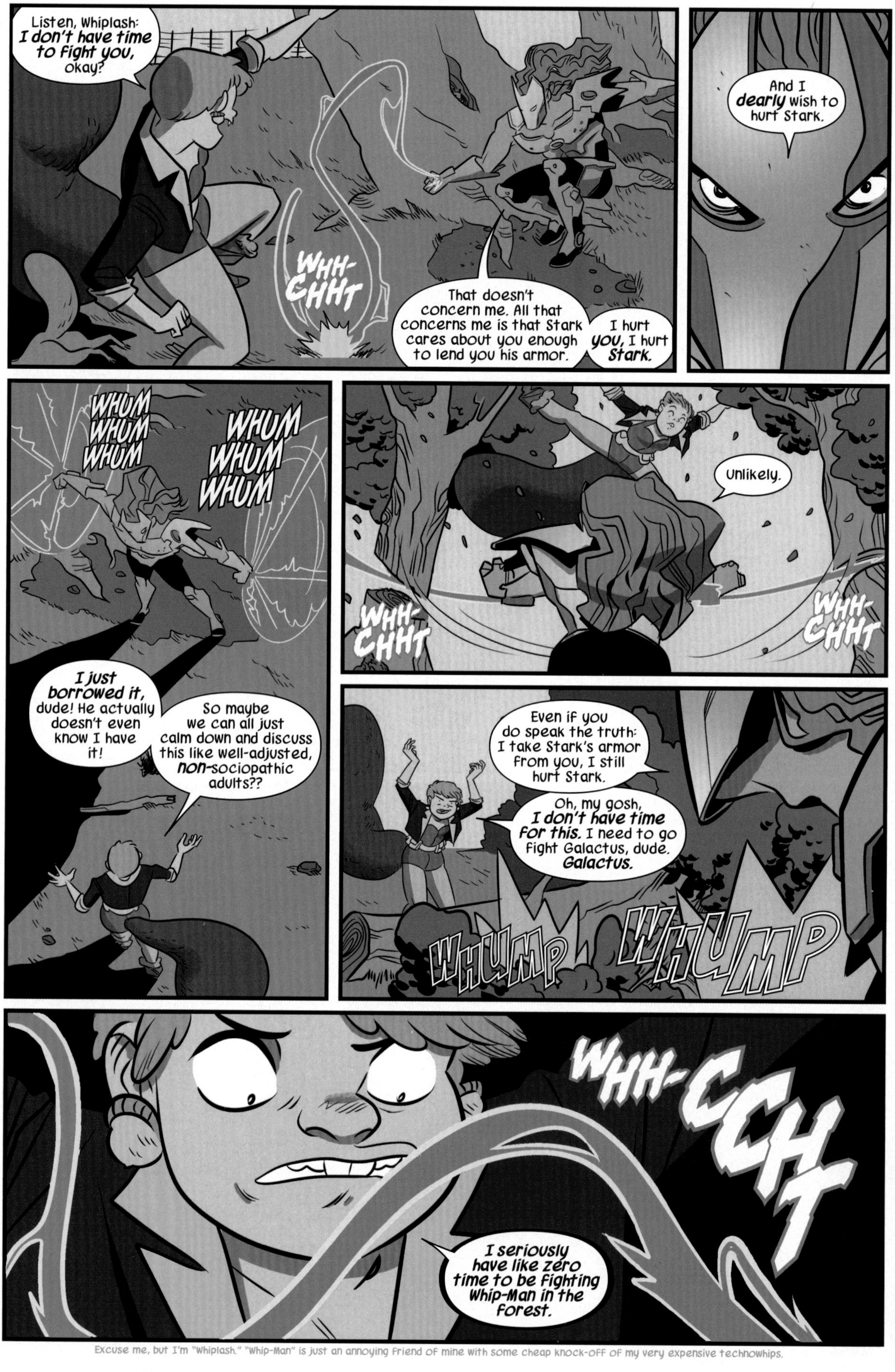

Listen, Whiplash: I don't have time to fight you, okay?
WHH-CHHT
That doesn't concern me. All that concerns me is that Stark cares about you enough to lend you his armor.
I hurt you, I hurt Stark.
And I dearly wish to hurt Stark.
WHUM WHUM WHUM
WHUM WHUM WHUM
I just borrowed it, dude! He actually doesn't even know I have it!
So maybe we can all just calm down and discuss this like well-adjusted, non-sociopathic adults??
Unlikely.
WHH-CHHT
WHH-CHHT
Even if you do speak the truth: I take Stark's armor from you, I still hurt Stark.
Oh, my gosh, I don't have time for this. I need to go fight Galactus, dude. Galactus.
WHUMP
WHUMP
WHH-CCHT
I seriously have like zero time to be fighting Whip-Man in the forest.

Excuse me, but I'm "Whiplash." "Whip-Man" is just an annoying friend of mine with some cheap knock-off of my very expensive technowhips.

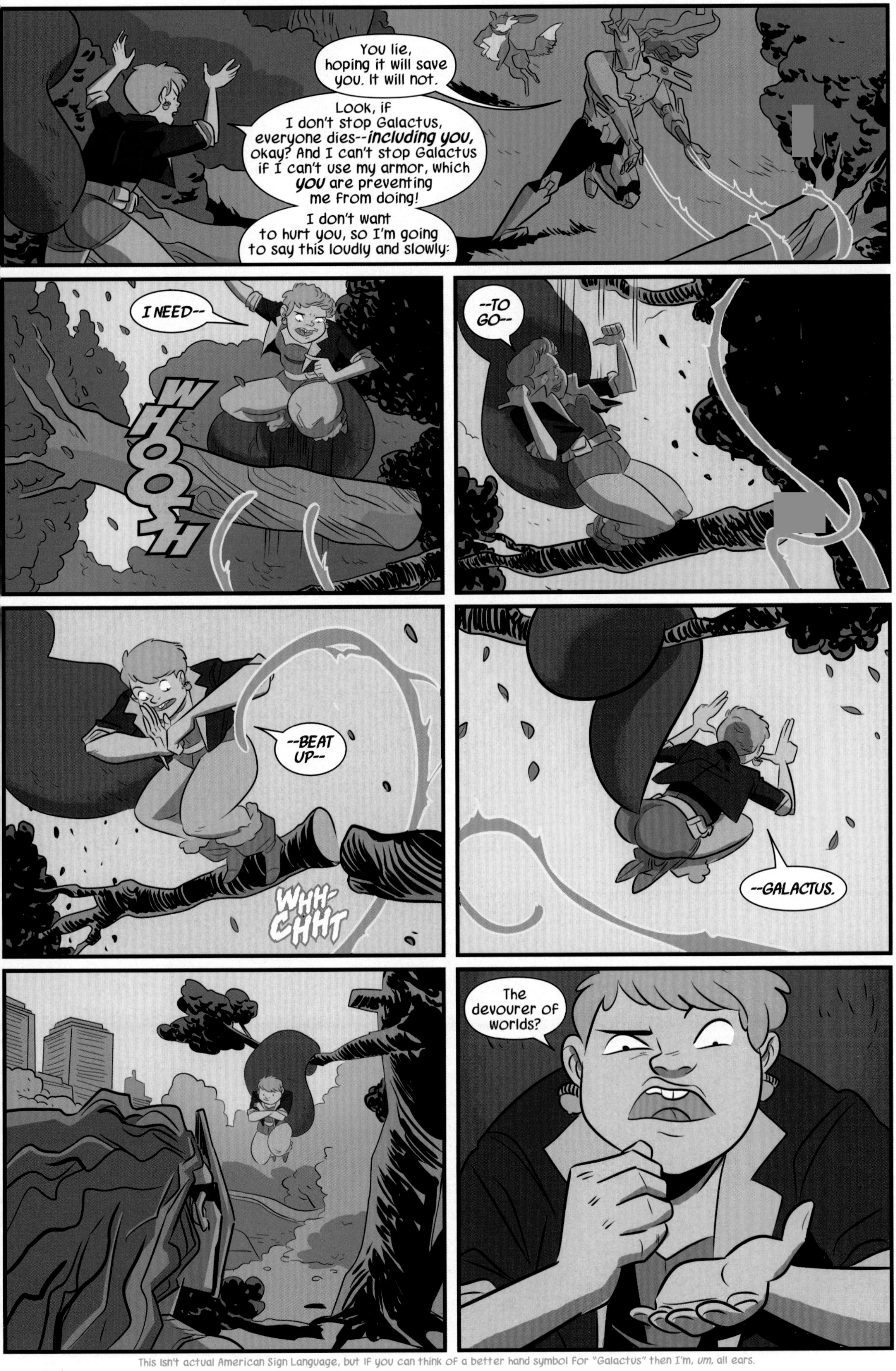
You lie, hoping it will save you. It will not.
Look, if I don't stop Galactus, everyone dies--including you, okay? And I can't stop Galactus if I can't use my armor, which you are preventing me from doing!
I don't want to hurt you, so I'm going to say this loudly and slowly:
I NEED--
WHOOOSH
--TO GO--
--BEAT UP--
WHH-CHHT
--GALACTUS.
The devourer of worlds?

This isn't actual American Sign Language, but if you can think of a better hand symbol for "Galactus" then I'm, *um,* all ears.

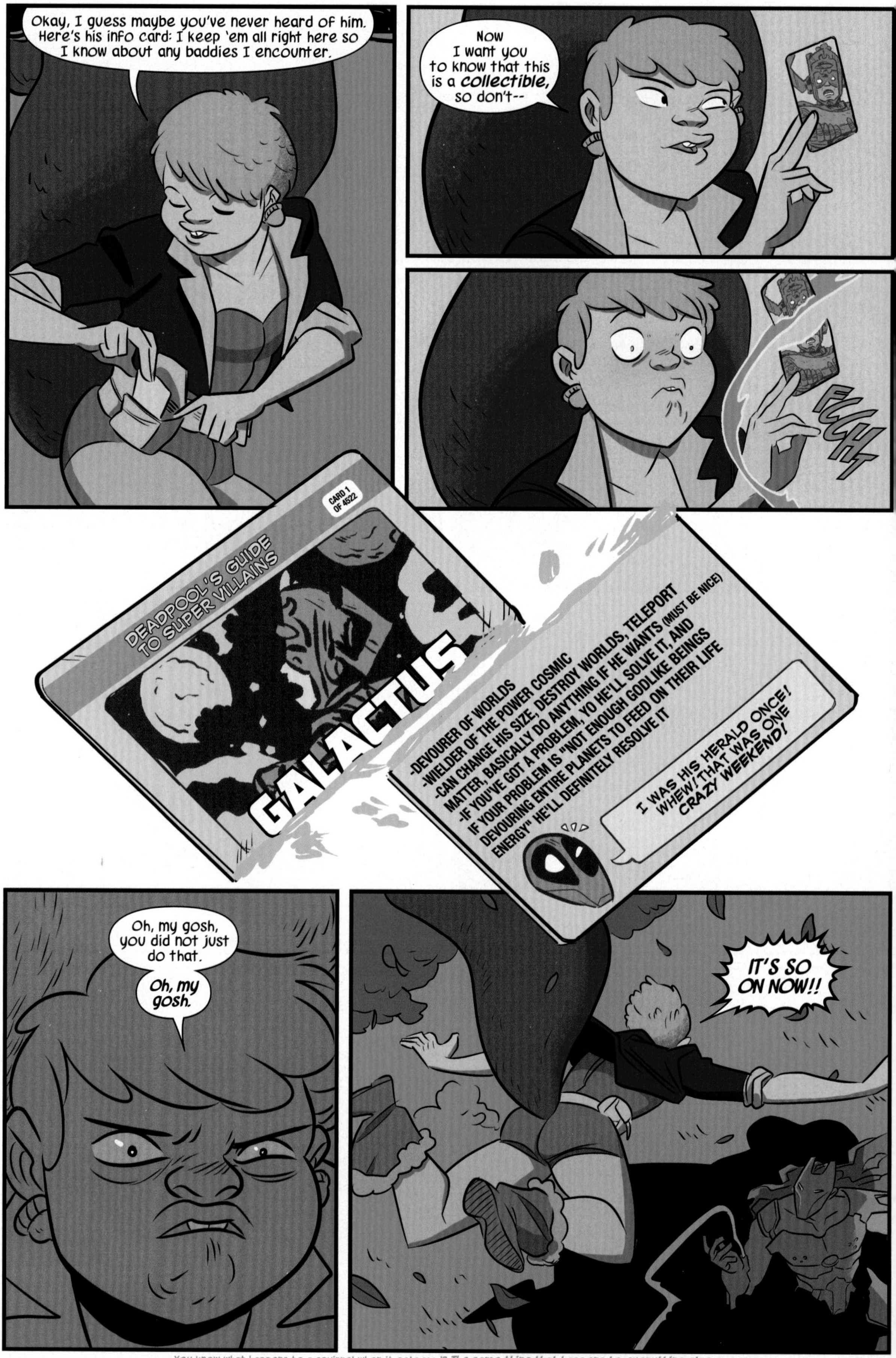
Okay, I guess maybe you've never heard of him. Here's his info card: I keep 'em all right here so I know about any baddies I encounter.
Now I want you to know that this is a collectible, so don't--
FCCHT
DEADPOOL'S GUIDE TO SUPER VILLAINS
CARD 1 OF 4522
GALACTUS
-DEVOURER OF WORLDS
-WIELDER OF THE POWER COSMIC
-CAN CHANGE HIS SIZE, DESTROY WORLDS, TELEPORT MATTER, BASICALLY DO ANYTHING IF HE WANTS (MUST BE NICE)
-IF YOU'VE GOT A PROBLEM, YO HE'LL SOLVE IT, AND IF YOUR PROBLEM IS "NOT ENOUGH GODLIKE BEINGS DEVOURING ENTIRE PLANETS TO FEED ON THEIR LIFE ENERGY" HE'LL DEFINITELY RESOLVE IT
I WAS HIS HERALD ONCE! WHEW! THAT WAS ONE CRAZY WEEKEND!
Oh, my gosh, you did not just do that.
Oh, my gosh.
IT'S SO ON NOW!!

You know what happens to a squirrel when it gets mad? *The same thing that happens to everything else.* Which is to say, increased heart rate, elevated adrenaline and norepinephrine production, a lessened capacity for self-monitoring, etc., etc.

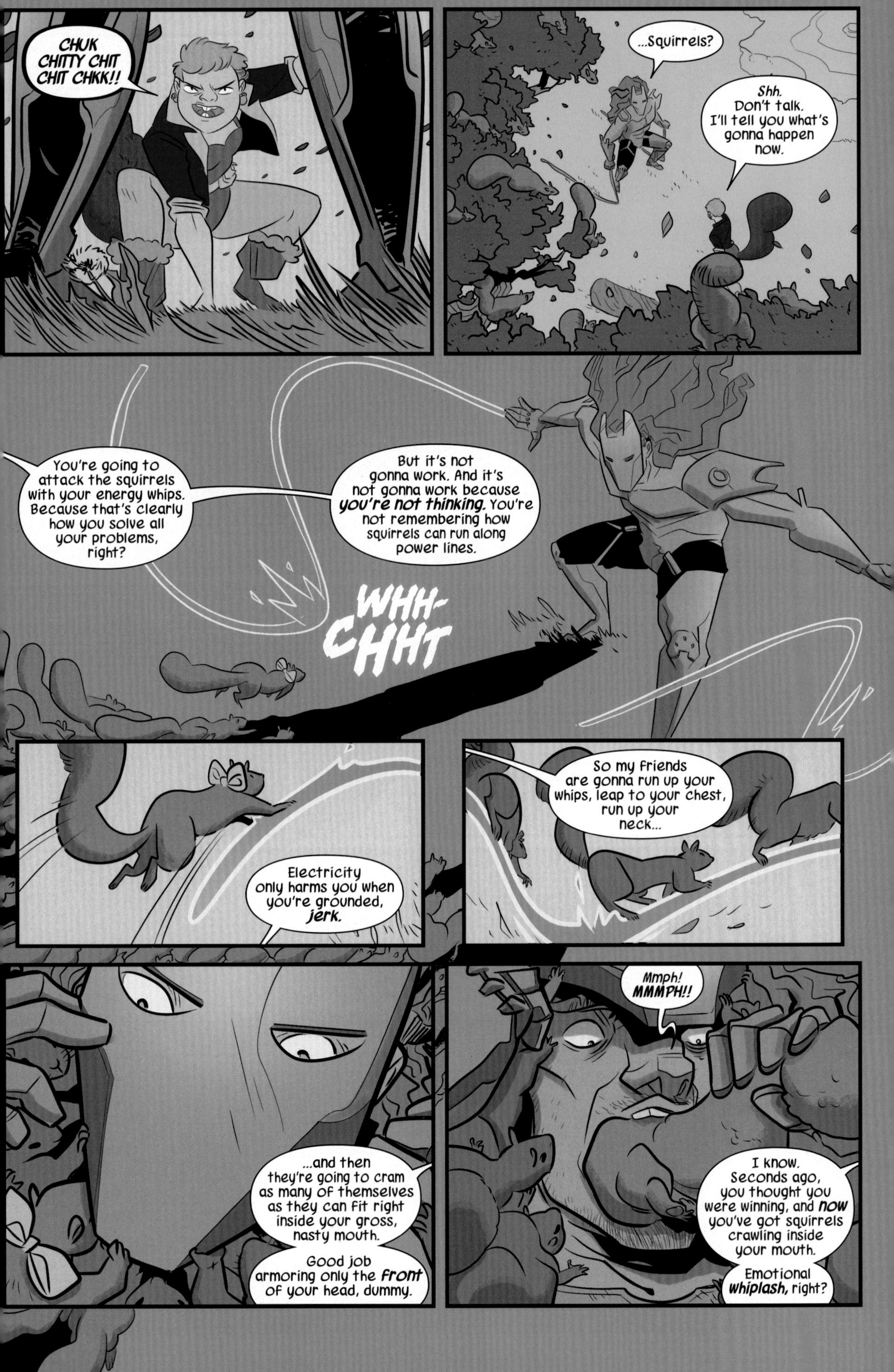

CHUK CHITTY CHIT CHIT CHKK!!
...Squirrels?
Shh. Don't talk. I'll tell you what's gonna happen now.
You're going to attack the squirrels with your energy whips. Because that's clearly how you solve all your problems, right?
But it's not gonna work. And it's not gonna work because *you're not thinking.* You're not remembering how squirrels can run along power lines.
WHH-CHHT
Electricity only harms you when you're grounded, *jerk.*
So my friends are gonna run up your whips, leap to your chest, run up your neck...
...and then they're going to cram as many of themselves as they can fit right inside your gross, nasty mouth.
Good job armoring only the *front* of your head, dummy.
Mmph! *MMMPH!!*
I know. Seconds ago, you thought you were winning, and *now* you've got squirrels crawling inside your mouth.
Emotional *whiplash,* right?

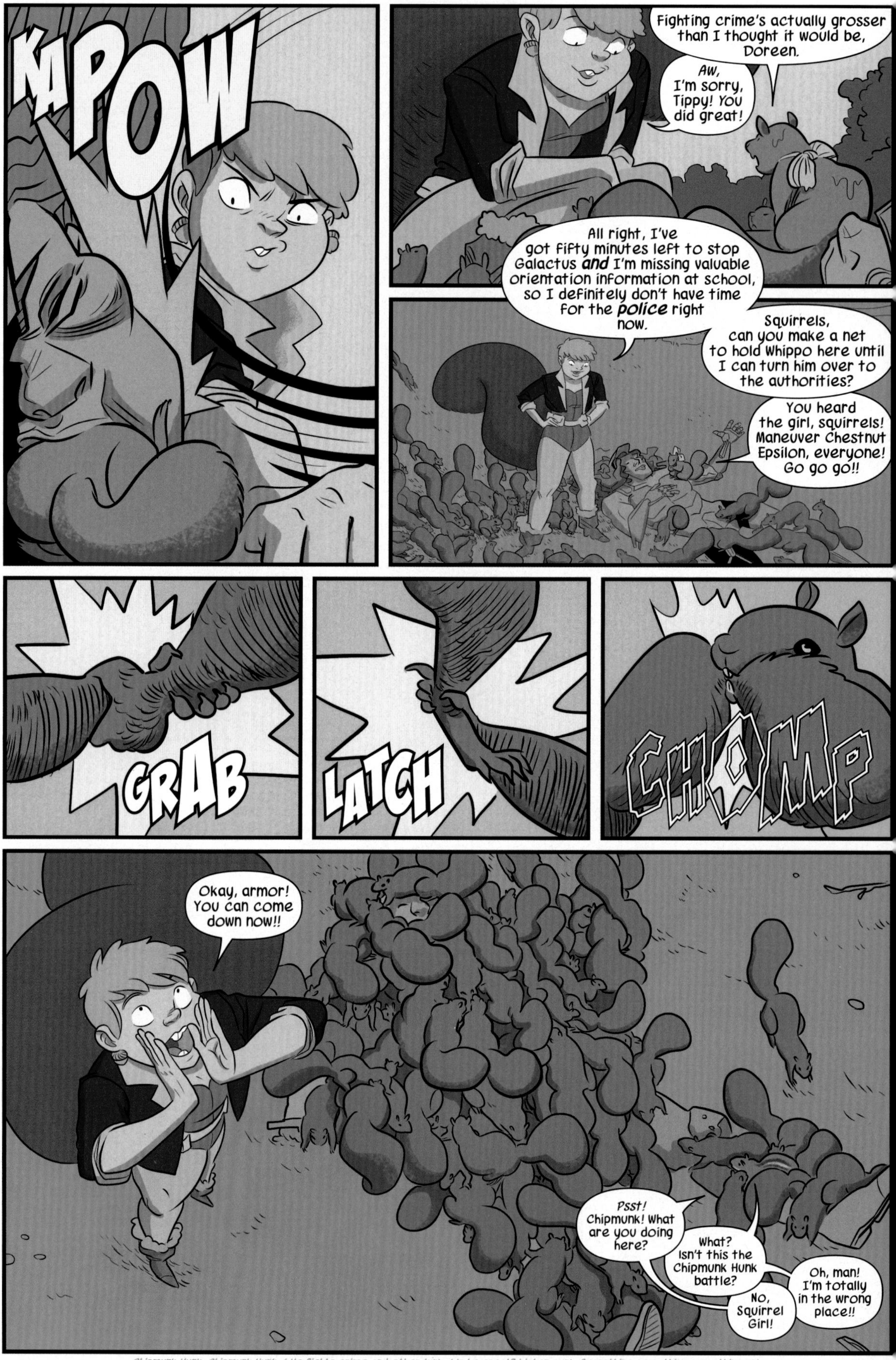

KAPOW
Fighting crime's actually grosser than I thought it would be, Doreen.
Aw, I'm sorry, Tippy! You did great!
All right, I've got fifty minutes left to stop Galactus **and** I'm missing valuable orientation information at school, so I definitely don't have time for the **police** right now.
Squirrels, can you make a net to hold Whippo here until I can turn him over to the authorities?
You heard the girl, squirrels! Maneuver Chestnut Epsilon, everyone! Go go go!!
GRAB
LATCH
CHOMP
Okay, armor! You can come down now!!
Psst! Chipmunk! What are you doing here?
What? Isn't this the Chipmunk Hunk battle?
No, Squirrel Girl!
Oh, man! I'm totally in the wrong place!!

Chipmunk Hunk, Chipmunk Hunk / He fights crime and other junk / Is he great? Listen punk: Something something something unk

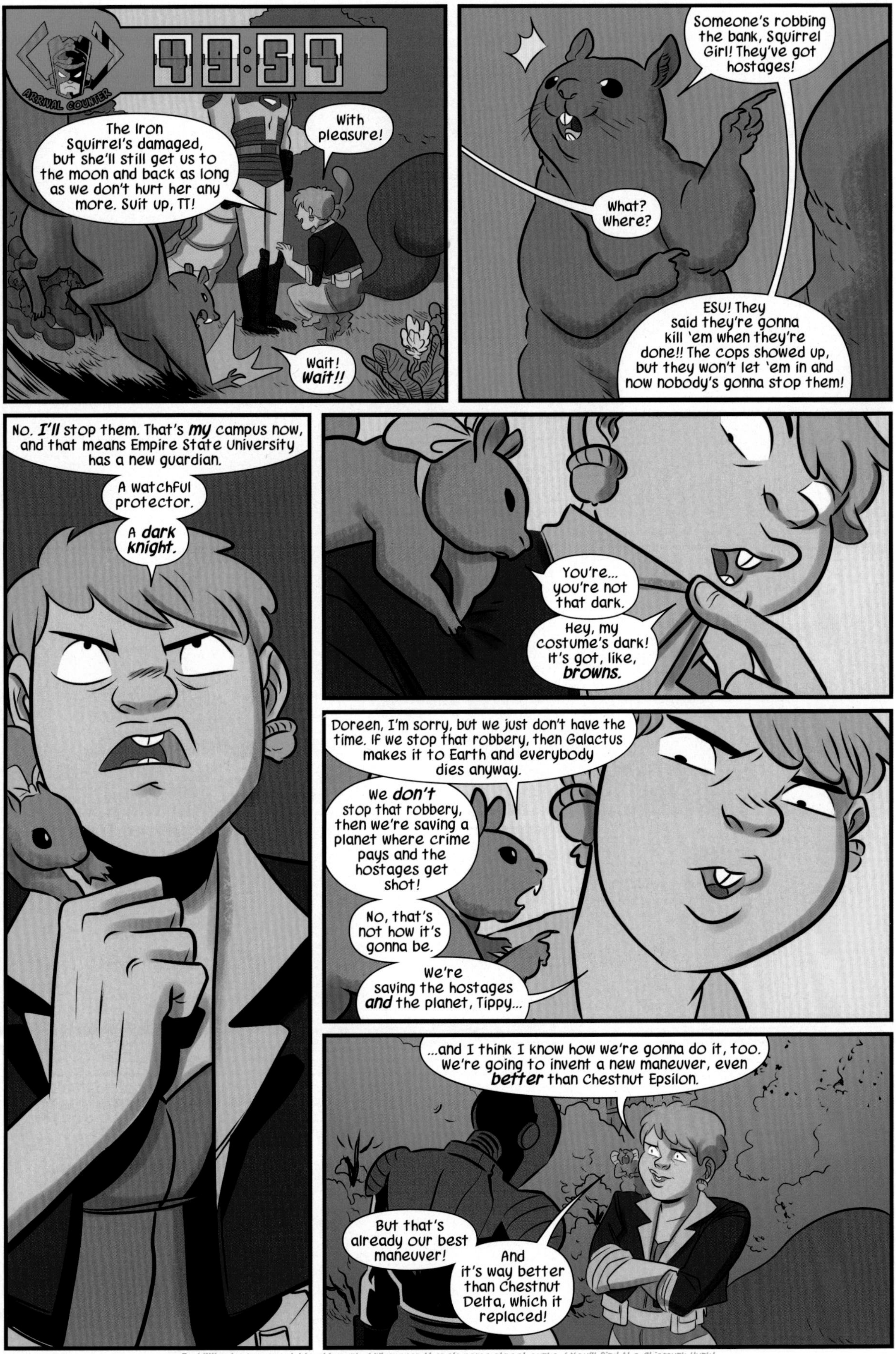
ARRIVAL COUNTER
49:54
The Iron Squirrel's damaged, but she'll still get us to the moon and back as long as we don't hurt her any more. Suit up, TT!
With pleasure!
Wait! *Wait!!*
Someone's robbing the bank, Squirrel Girl! They've got hostages!
What? Where?
ESU! They said they're gonna kill 'em when they're done!! The cops showed up, but they won't let 'em in and now nobody's gonna stop them!
No. *I'll* stop them. That's *my* campus now, and that means Empire State University has a new guardian.
A watchful protector.
A *dark knight.*
You're... you're not that dark.
Hey, my costume's dark! It's got, like, *browns.*
Doreen, I'm sorry, but we just don't have the time. If we stop that robbery, then Galactus makes it to Earth and everybody dies anyway.
We *don't* stop that robbery, then we're saving a planet where crime pays and the hostages get shot!
No, that's not how it's gonna be.
We're saving the hostages *and* the planet, Tippy...
...and I think I know how we're gonna do it, too. We're going to invent a new maneuver, even *better* than Chestnut Epsilon.
But that's already our best maneuver!
And it's way better than Chestnut Delta, which it replaced!

To hiiiiim, he is a great big chipmunk / Wherever there's some street punks / You'll Find the Chipmunk Hunk!

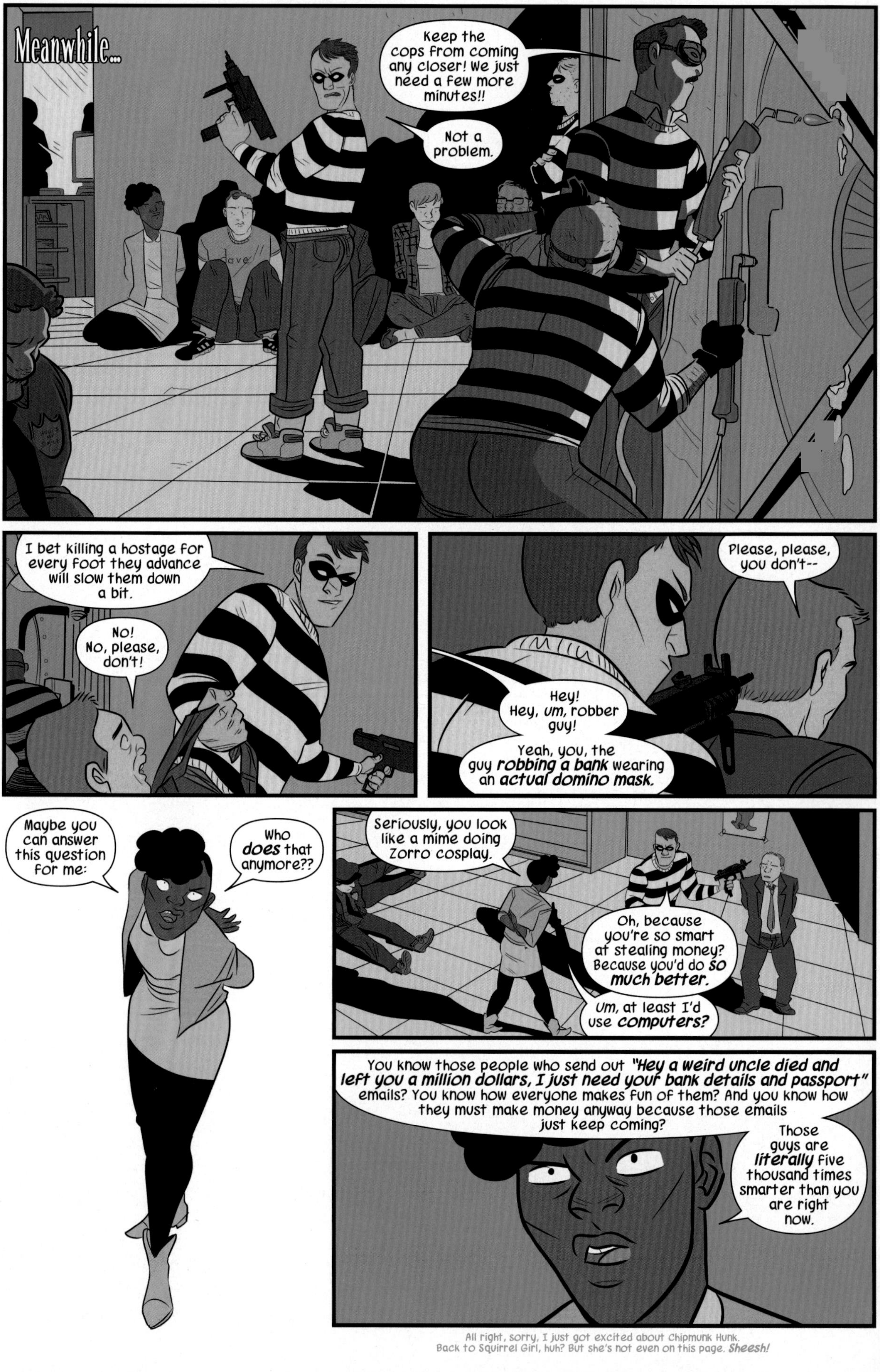
Meanwhile...
Keep the cops from coming any closer! We just need a few more minutes!!
Not a problem.
I bet killing a hostage for every foot they advance will slow them down a bit.
No! No, please, don't!
Please, please, you don't--
Hey! Hey, um, robber guy!
Yeah, you, the guy *robbing a bank* wearing an *actual domino mask.*
Maybe you can answer this question for me:
Who *does* that anymore??
Seriously, you look like a mime doing Zorro cosplay.
Oh, because you're so smart at stealing money? Because you'd do *so much better.*
Um, at least I'd use *computers?*
You know those people who send out *"Hey a weird uncle died and left you a million dollars, I just need your bank details and passport"* emails? You know how everyone makes fun of them? And you know how they must make money anyway because those emails just keep coming?
Those guys are *literally* five thousand times smarter than you are right now.

All right, sorry, I just got excited about Chipmunk Hunk.
Back to Squirrel Girl, huh? But she's not even on this page. *Sheesh!*

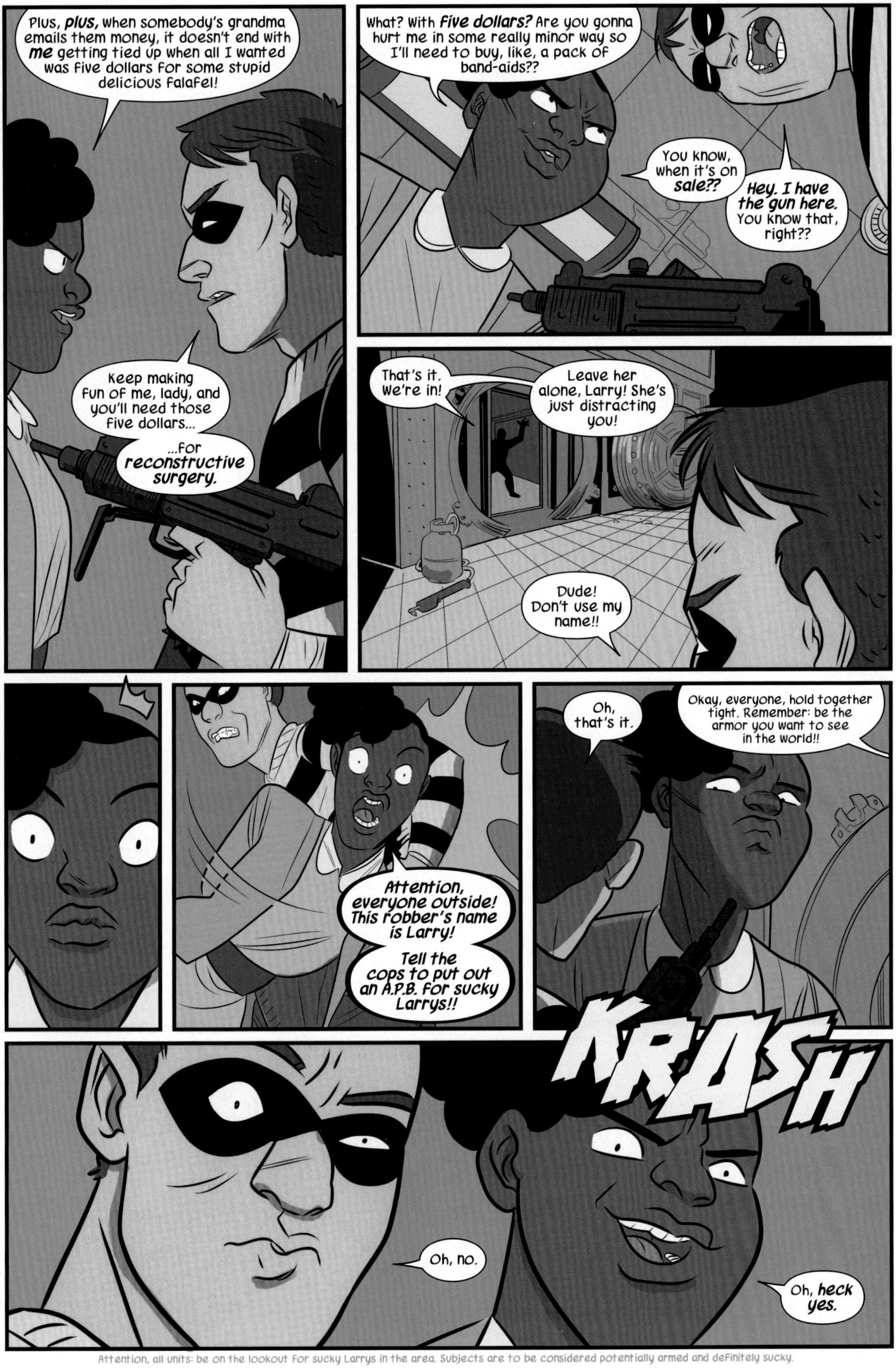

Plus, *plus,* when somebody's grandma emails them money, it doesn't end with *me* getting tied up when all I wanted was five dollars for some stupid delicious falafel!
Keep making fun of me, lady, and you'll need those five dollars...
...for *reconstructive surgery.*
What? With *five dollars?* Are you gonna hurt me in some really minor way so I'll need to buy, like, a pack of band-aids??
You know, when it's on *sale??*
Hey. I have the gun here. You know that, right??
That's it. We're in!
Leave her alone, Larry! She's just distracting you!
Dude! Don't use my name!!
Attention, everyone outside! This robber's name is Larry!
Tell the cops to put out an A.P.B. for sucky Larrys!!
Oh, that's it.
Okay, everyone, hold together tight. Remember: be the armor you want to see in the world!!
KRASH
Oh, no.
Oh, *heck yes.*

Attention, all units: be on the lookout for sucky Larrys in the area. Subjects are to be considered potentially armed and definitely sucky.

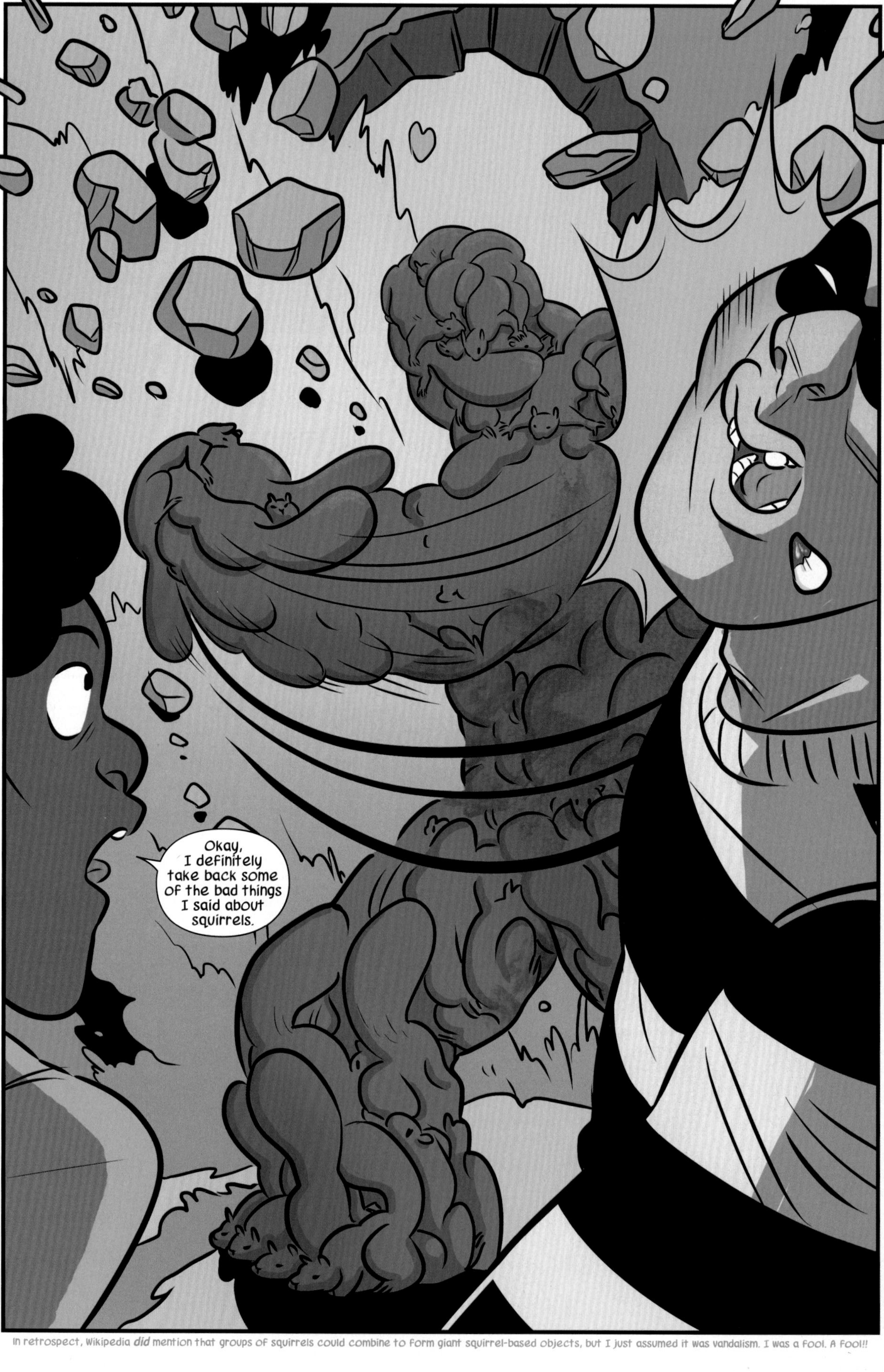
Okay, I definitely take back some of the bad things I said about squirrels.

In retrospect, Wikipedia *did* mention that groups of squirrels could combine to form giant squirrel-based objects, but I just assumed it was vandalism. I was a fool. A fool!!

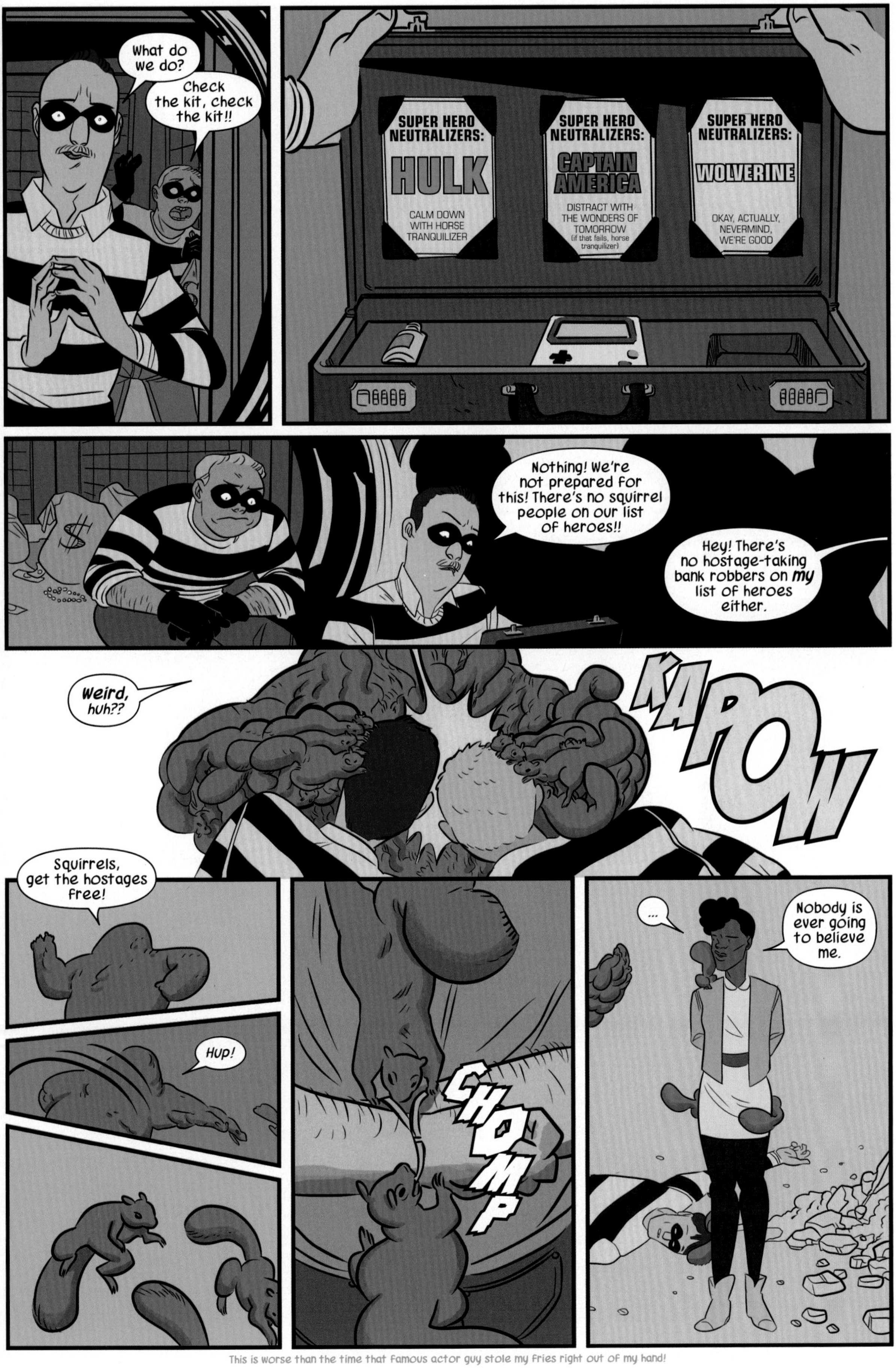
What do we do?
Check the kit, check the kit!!
SUPER HERO NEUTRALIZERS: HULK
CALM DOWN WITH HORSE TRANQUILIZER
SUPER HERO NEUTRALIZERS: CAPTAIN AMERICA
DISTRACT WITH THE WONDERS OF TOMORROW
(if that fails, horse tranquilizer)
SUPER HERO NEUTRALIZERS: WOLVERINE
OKAY, ACTUALLY, NEVERMIND, WE'RE GOOD
Nothing! We're not prepared for this! There's no squirrel people on our list of heroes!!
Hey! There's no hostage-taking bank robbers on my list of heroes either.
Weird, huh??
KAPOW
Squirrels, get the hostages free!
Hup!
CHOMP
...
Nobody is ever going to believe me.

This is worse than the time that famous actor guy stole my fries right out of my hand!

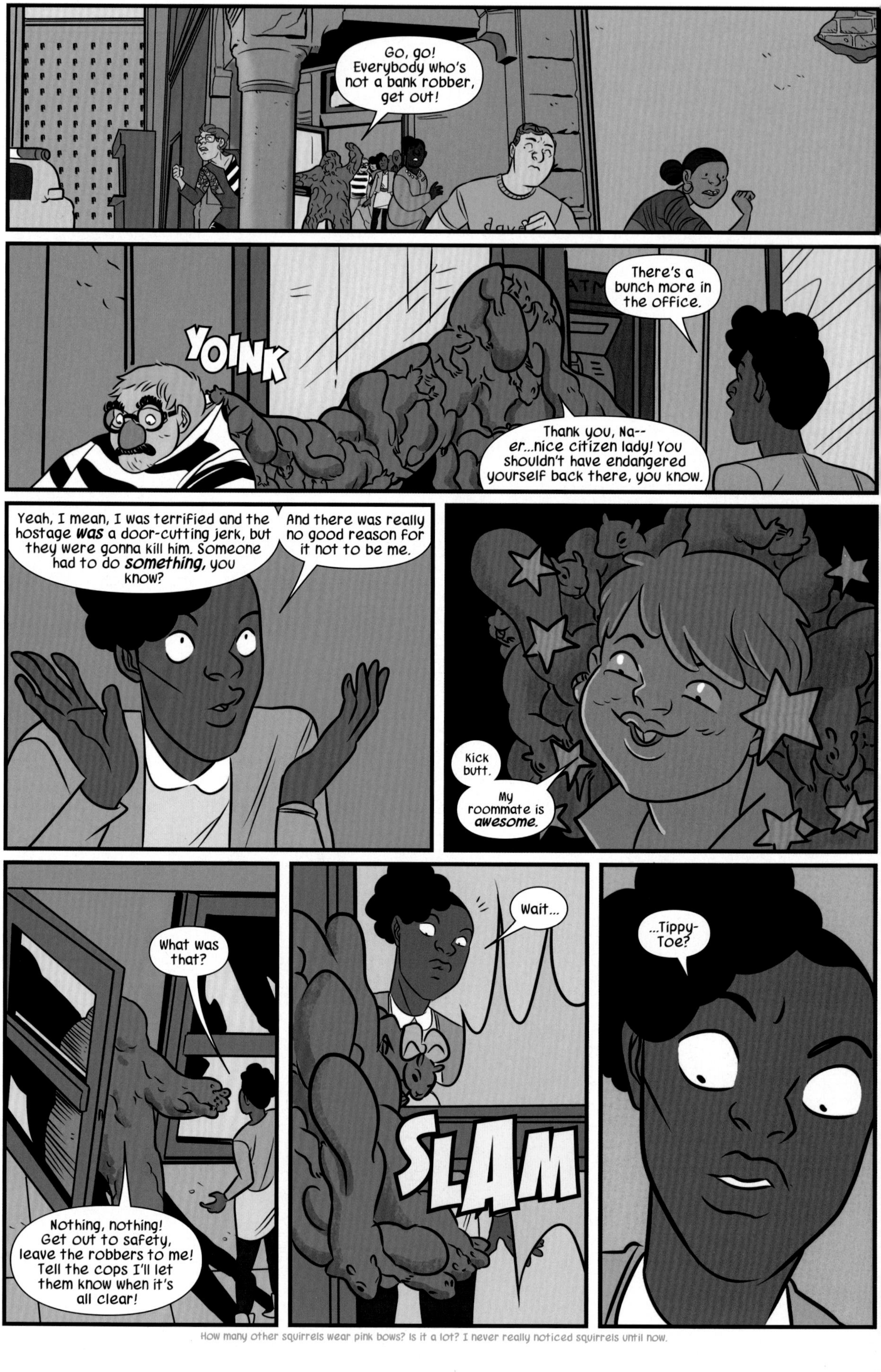
Go, go! Everybody who's not a bank robber, get out!
YOINK
There's a bunch more in the office.
Thank you, Na-- er...nice citizen lady! You shouldn't have endangered yourself back there, you know.
Yeah, I mean, I was terrified and the hostage **was** a door-cutting jerk, but they were gonna kill him. Someone had to do **something,** you know?
And there was really no good reason for it not to be me.
Kick butt.
My roommate is **awesome.**
What was that?
Nothing, nothing! Get out to safety, leave the robbers to me! Tell the cops I'll let them know when it's all clear!
Wait...
SLAM
...Tippy-Toe?

How many other squirrels wear pink bows? Is it a lot? I never really noticed squirrels until now.

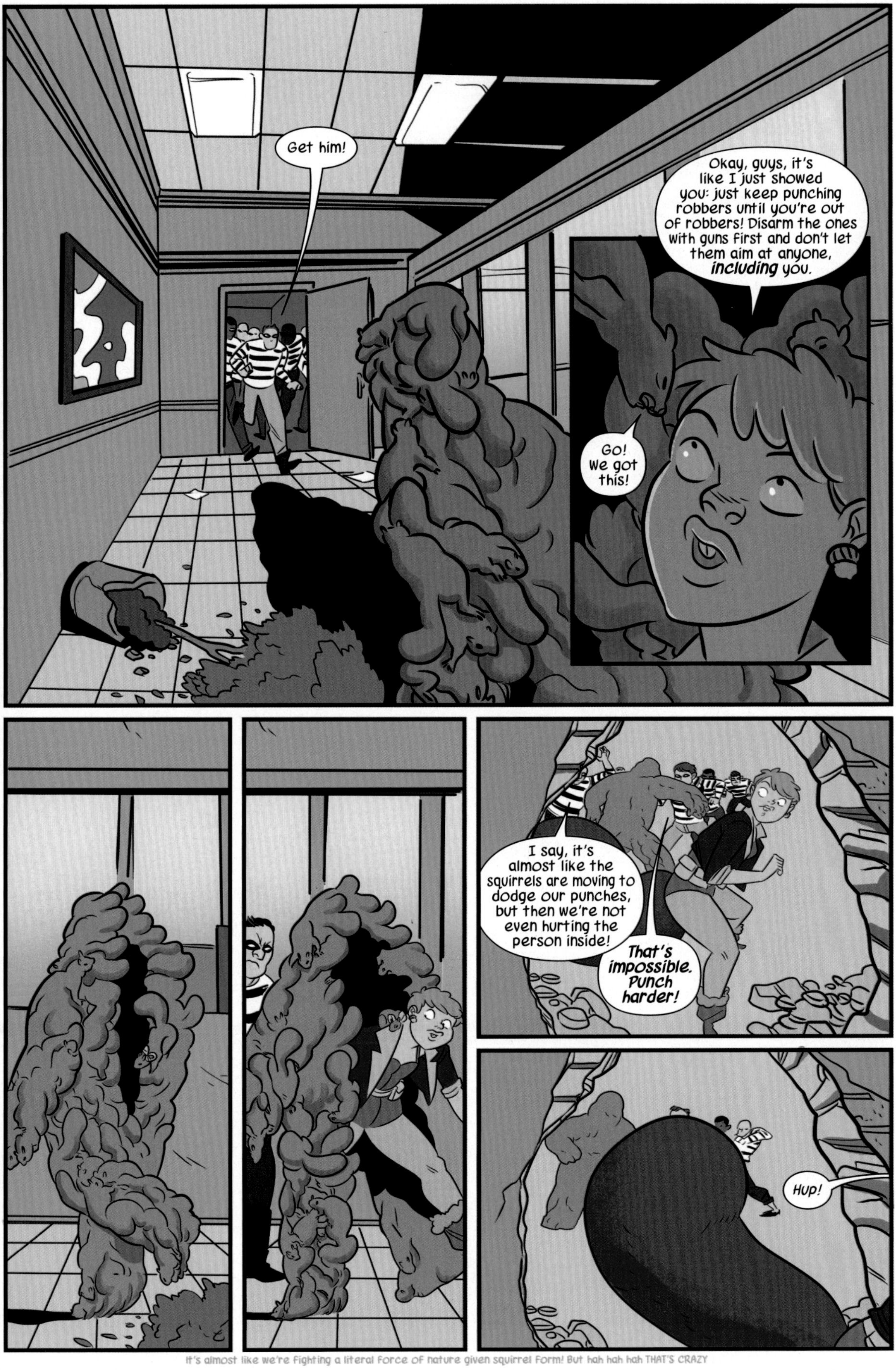

Get him!
Okay, guys, it's like I just showed you: just keep punching robbers until you're out of robbers! Disarm the ones with guns first and don't let them aim at anyone, *including* you.
Go! We got this!
I say, it's almost like the squirrels are moving to dodge our punches, but then we're not even hurting the person inside!
That's impossible. Punch harder!
Hup!

It's almost like we're fighting a literal force of nature given squirrel form! But hah hah hah THAT'S CRAZY

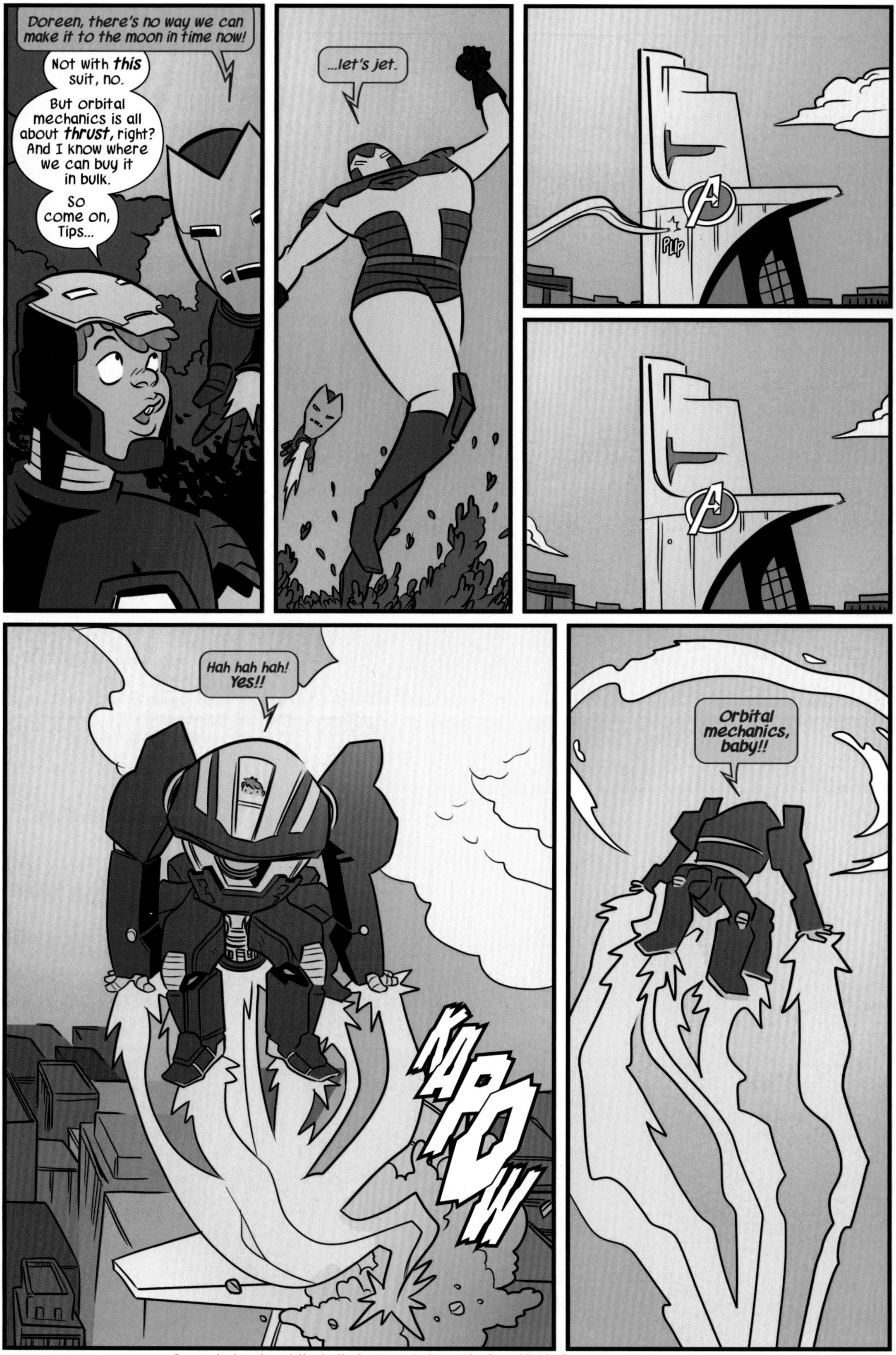
Doreen, there's no way we can make it to the moon in time now!
Not with this suit, no.
But orbital mechanics is all about thrust, right? And I know where we can buy it in bulk.
So come on, Tips...
...let's jet.
PLIP
Hah hah hah! Yes!!
KAPOW
Orbital mechanics, baby!!

I was going to put a solution to the inverse Kepler's equation for orbital bodies here but ran out of room, so you'll just have to take my word for it that the physics in my talking squirrel comic are 100% ultralegit

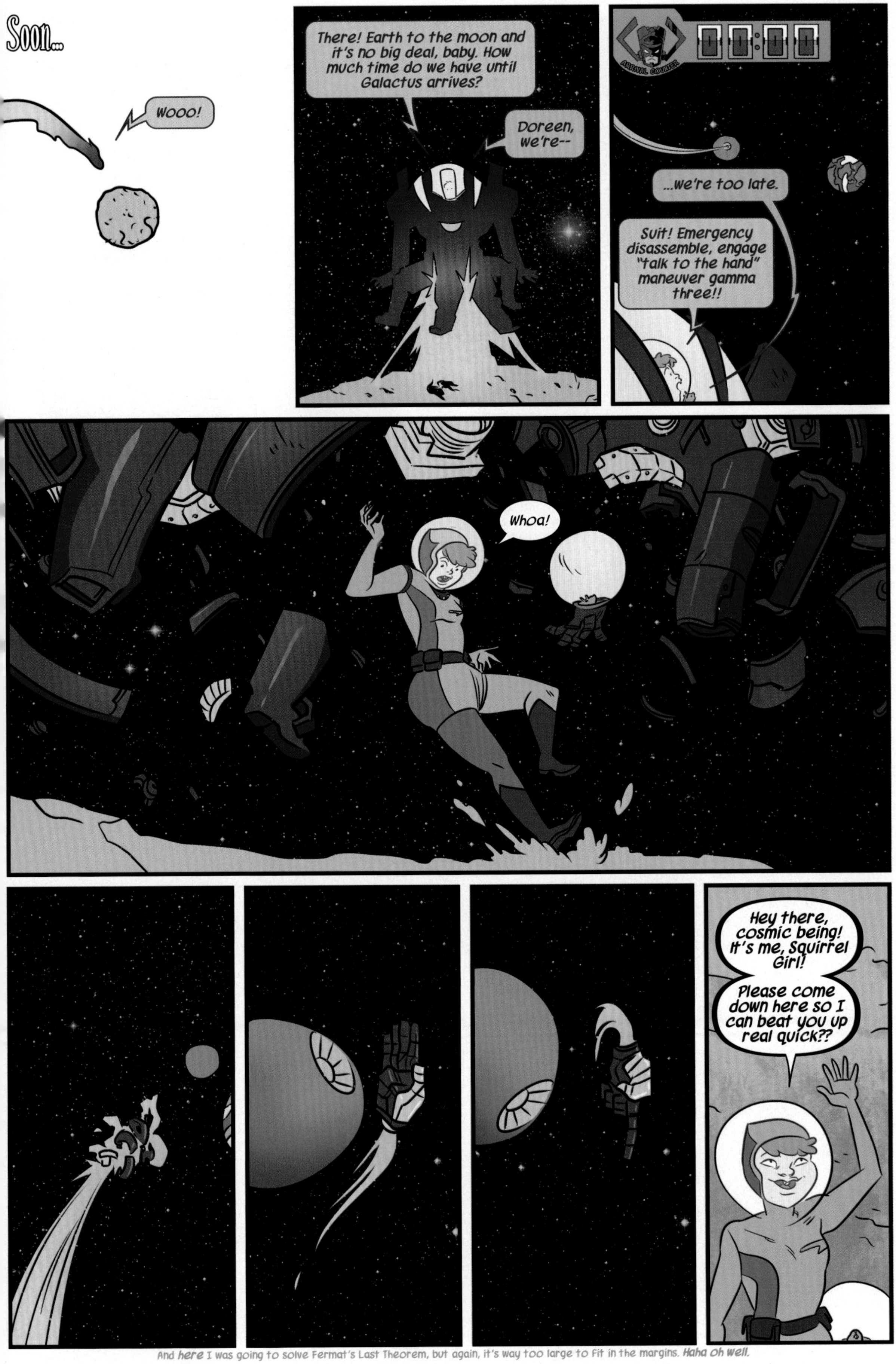
Soon...
WOOO!
There! Earth to the moon and it's no big deal, baby. How much time do we have until Galactus arrives?
Doreen, we're--
00:00
...we're too late.
Suit! Emergency disassemble, engage "talk to the hand" maneuver gamma three!!
Whoa!
Hey there, cosmic being! It's me, Squirrel Girl!
Please come down here so I can beat you up real quick??

And *here* I was going to solve Fermat's Last Theorem, but again, it's way too large to fit in the margins. *Haha oh well.*

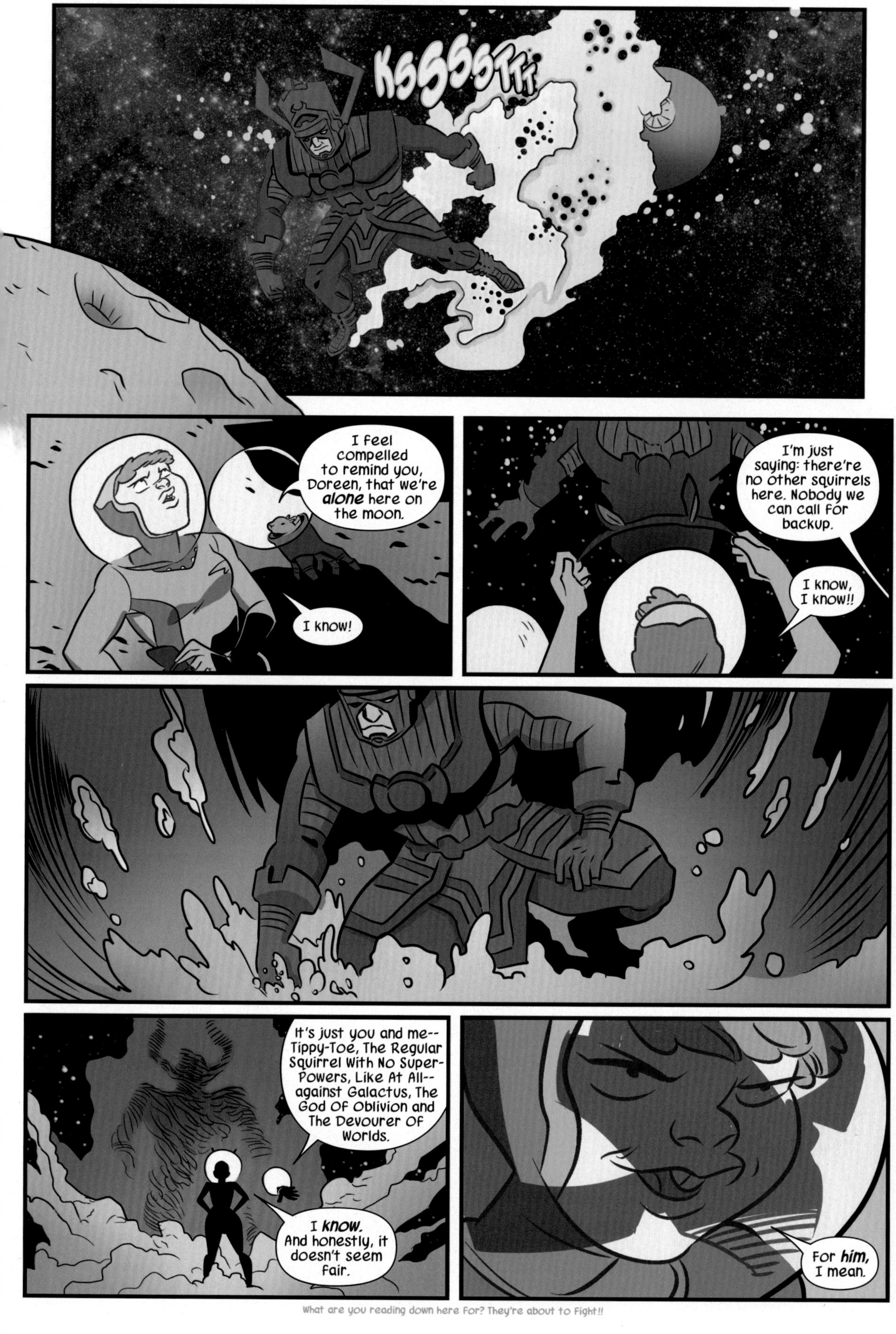
KSSSSTTT
I feel compelled to remind you, Doreen, that we're *alone* here on the moon.
I know!
I'm just saying: there're no other squirrels here. Nobody we can call for backup.
I know, I know!!
It's just you and me-- Tippy-Toe, The Regular Squirrel With No Super-Powers, Like At All-- against Galactus, The God Of Oblivion and The Devourer Of Worlds.
I *know.* And honestly, it doesn't seem fair.
For *him,* I mean.

What are you reading down here for? They're about to fight!!

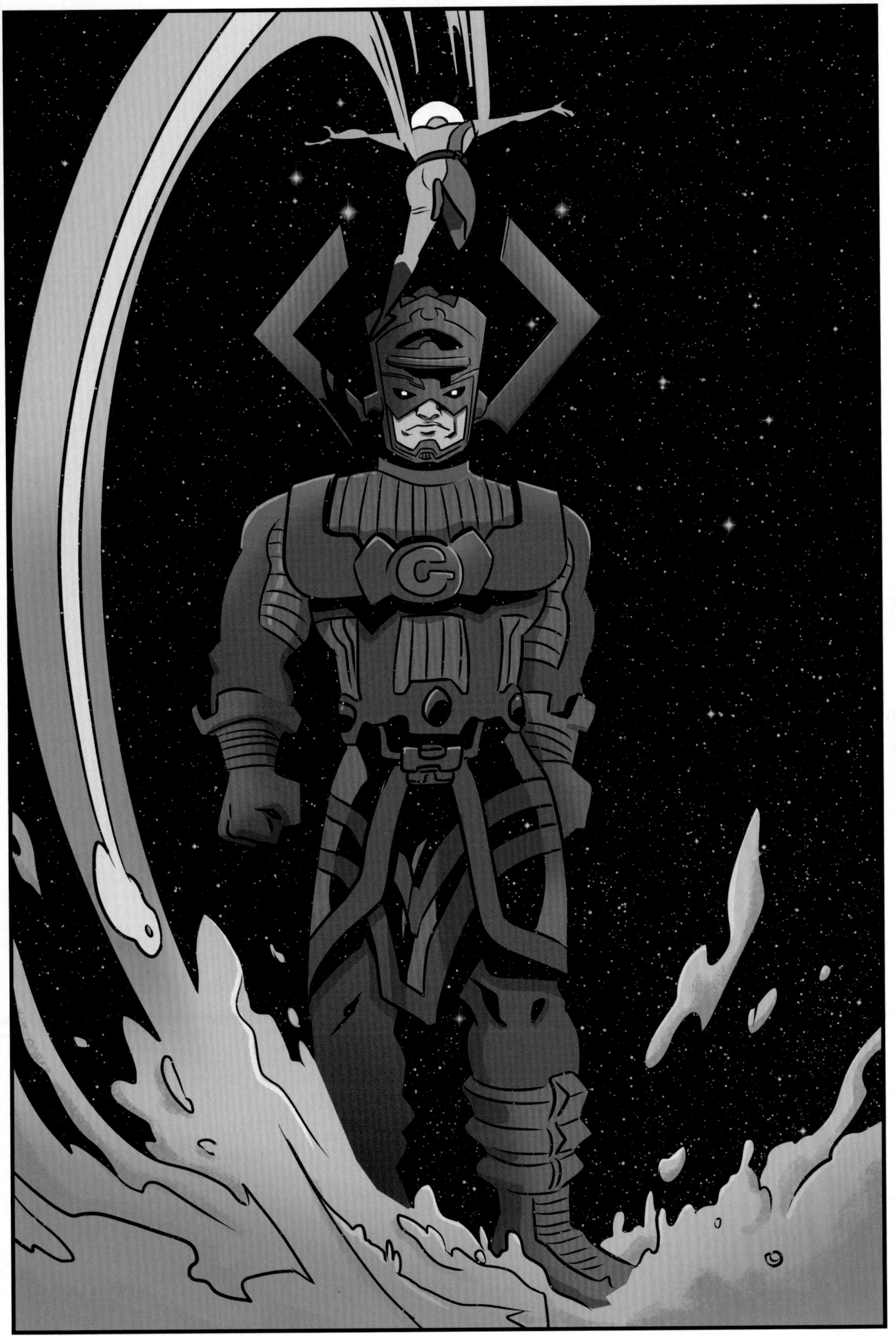

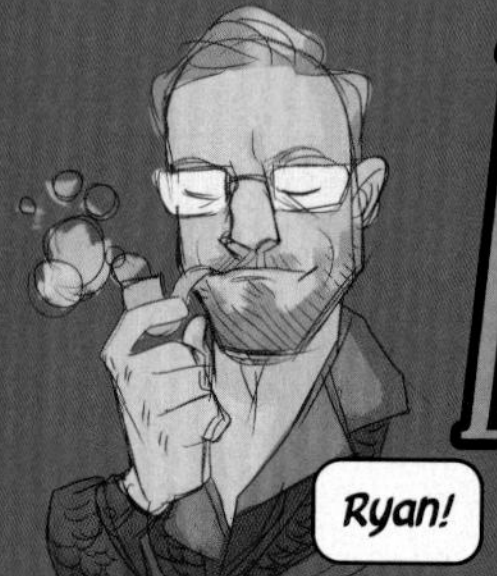
Ryan!

Letters From Nuts

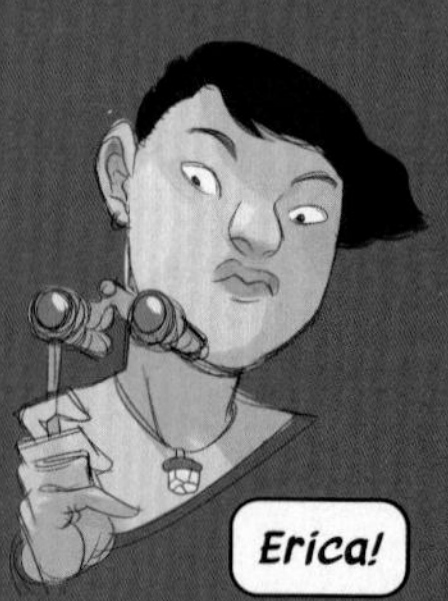
Erica!

Send letters to mheroes@marvel.com or 135 W 50th St, 7th Floor, New York, NY 10020 (Please mark "OKAY TO PRINT")

Welcome to the special triple-sized you-guys-are-awesome-and-are-really-vocal-about-your-feelings-for-this-book letters page!!!

Q: Do squirrels and kitties usually get along? Are you concerned that Tippy-Toe and Mew will come to blows?

Michelle K.

RYAN: They don't usually, I think! But Tippy-Toe and Mew aren't your usual squirrel and kitten. Besides, Nancy would never have said it was okay for Tippy-Toe to stay with them unless she was already PRETTY SURE Mew was on board.

Dear Ryan, Erica, Rico, & VC's Clayton (or just Clayton, idk),

You guys, your Squirrel Girl comic is the coolest! Ryan, I've followed your writing online for a number of years, and have been SUPER PUMPED to see you busting out of the internet and on to printed paper held together by staples!

Can we expect to see some Asgardian tomfoolery within these pages? I demand a Doreen vs. Thor/ Tippy-Toe vs. **[CENSORED]** throwdown/team-up! I mean, come on, Norse mythology has **[MEGA CENSORED]** (whose name, I learned today, means **[YES, THIS TOO IS CENSORED]** which is pretty cool)! How are you NOT going to use that?!

Keep up the amazing work, everybody!

Adam Barnett
Portland, OR

RYAN: Thanks, Adam! We are actually planning to see that person you mentioned showing up down the line, so I just went ahead and censored your letter here as to not spoil the surprise. I'm sorry! But when it happens you can say "See? CALLED IT" and point to this page for proof. Attention future generations: ADAM WAS TOTALLY RIGHT.

ERICA: Hah! That character might have been the topic of my first frantic middle-of-the-night email to Ryan about Squirrel Girl matters. My first foray into self-publishing was a little bestiary and [REDACTED] is totally in there. I love that dude.

Dear Nutty Buddies,

Thanks so much for producing a title that I can confidently share with my niece, Paislee!

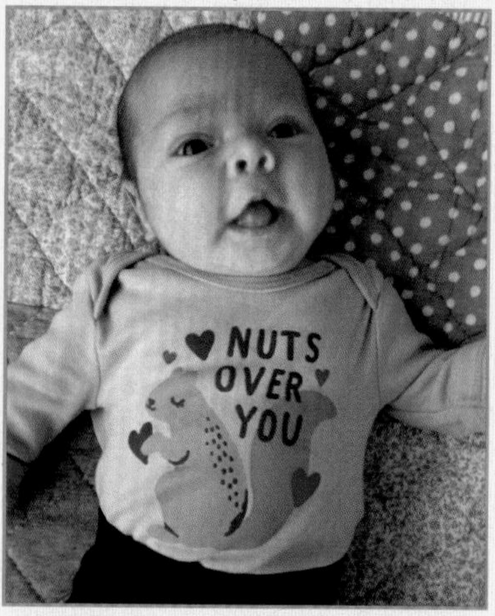
NUTS
OVER
YOU

We're both nuts for Squirrel Girl and it's refreshing to know there's a strong, positive, female role-model out there in the Marvel Universe for her to admire on a monthly basis as she grows from being just a tiny little acorn herself.

Here's a question for you: Did you know that in Norse mythology there was **[CENSORED FOR THE EXACT SAME REASONS AS THE LAST LETTER]**? Really! **[THIS OTHER BIT IS CENSORED TOO. EVERYONE, YOU ARE TOO GOOD AT GUESSING OUR STORY IDEAS]** - and then **[AGAIN, CENSORED, SORRY, I GUESS??]**.

Nuts over you,
Paislee H. & Darryl E.

RYAN: Paislee is adorable! #1 Paislee fan over here. Also: I'm glad we're putting out a book you can share with her once she's old enough to realize that if she looks at a certain idiosyncratic series of squiggles in the right order she can hear a voice in her head telling her a story! Once that happens we will be ALL OVER that.

Hi Team Squirrel Girl!

My friend and I just finished the first issue and we both loved it! But we are concerned about Squirrel Girl! Will she have time to go to her classes with all of the crime-fighting that she'll be doing? What are her classes? Thanks!

Beck and Bida

RYAN: I haven't seen her full course selection, but I know there's Introduction to Database Systems, Introduction to Compilers, Linear Algebra, Punching Dudes 101, etc. But yeah, it's tough to balance your social life and your studies. That's why I recommend crime-fighting students cultivate arch-enemies whose powers can dovetail nicely into your education. For example, a super villain who along with trying to take over the world also constructs linear equations in n-dimensional Euclidean vector spaces would be ideal, because that way you can LEARN as you TURN him away from his life of crime.

Q: Now that Squirrel Girl is in college, will she join any clubs or sports teams?

Zachariah W.

RYAN: Zachariah, you clearly wrote this letter before issue #2, where we saw her attempts to join some clubs! So since your question has already been answered, I'm gonna pretend you asked a different question. LIKE SO:

Q: Squirrel Girl has the proportional speed and strength of a squirrel, so what would happen if she got shrunk? Would she lose her powers?

Zachariah W.

RYAN: Excellent question, Zachariah!! This question has not been asked before and I'm glad you definitely came up with it on your own just now. The answer is that while her speed and strength are proportional TO her normal size, they don't change WITH her size. If Ant-Man shrunk her, she'd still be super tough. Similarly, if she ate a bunch and got heavier, that wouldn't make her any stronger. It's too bad, because that would be the EASIEST and MOST FUN way to enhance your super powers ever!

Q: What breed of squirrel is Tippy-Toe? There are 256 species of squirrel worldwide so it's pretty hard to narrow it down.

Sarah Yu
Hong Kong
Squirrel Enthusiast

RYAN: Sarah, I'm glad that as a Squirrel Enthusiast there is finally a comic for you! I don't know what species of squirrel Tippy-Toe is, because while I too am a Squirrel Enthusiast, I am a rank amateur. Are there any Professional Squirrel Enthusiasts who can determine Tippy-Toe's exact squirrel type out there?? (No, "rad type" does not count as an answer.)

ERICA: WELL. I think as someone who gets paid to think about and draw squirrels, I can count myself as a Professional Squirrel Enthusiast, Ryan. Tippy-Toe joined the team after the untimely death of Monkey Joe (RIP) while Doreen was a member of the Great Lakes Avengers, who are based out of Milwaukee. Wisconsin has five varieties of tree squirrel: grey, fox, red, northern flying and southern flying. Tippy is clearly a grey squirrel. Fun fact: Grey is a variety and does not necessarily reflect the actual color of individual animals.

Dear Ryan, Erica, and Rico,

THE UNBEATABLE SQUIRREL GIRL #1 has to be one of the best comic books I've ever read. It was funny, cool, quirky, wacky, and a lot of other good things. Thank you for giving us such an awesome comic book with great art and writing. It's nice to have another super-heroine who doesn't go around fighting crime in her underwear. Some people think the art is "too cartoonish" but 'TIS NOT TRUE! THE ART IS PERFECT!

The Mighty M

P.S. Where can I read Nancy's Cat Thor fan fiction? And where can I get that Purl Jam poster?!

RYAN: Thanks! I actually really like how Squirrel Girl dresses in layers, because you gotta figure sometimes it'd get too hot or too cold and you'd want to be able to adjust. It's just sensible!! As for Nancy's fan fiction epic Cat Thor: Cat God of Cat Thunder, I'd love to have that show up at some point, but for now it lives only in our dreams of a better, impossibly perfect world.

ERICA: Ahhhhhh! Thank you so much! I think clothing choices are pretty important in getting across who someone is. Some people do want to run around in their underwear and that's great for them (looking at you, Emma and Namor), but that's not everyone's bag. I don't want to get too deep into it but our clothing choices say a lot about what we want to get across to people, even if you're not actively thinking about what you're putting on at the time. I mean, you still had to go out and buy it, or, if you're a super hero, probably MAKE IT. I want the clothes to feel like something those characters would choose for themselves.

Hey guys!

Keep up the good work with Squirrel Girl. It's refreshing to see a female super hero that has the body type a lot of us girls have. How did you guys come up with the character design?

Can't wait to read more!

Alexa

ERICA: For the body, I didn't think about it much. I tend to draw super heroines with more physical powers thicker because I honestly have a hard time believing that a 90-pound woman can take down a 200-pound steroidal dude who has equal fighting ability. So yeah. Her body type in the book is the same as the first finished drawing of her I

ever did because that's just how I see Squirrel Girl. Besides, have you seen people who do crossfit? Their thighs are HUUUUUGE.

Hey gang,
I rarely if ever write in to comics but I had to drop a line regarding SQUIRREL GIRL #1 to let you guys know I think it's great stuff. I've been a fan of SG since the GREAT LAKES AVENGERS specials back in the day and it's nice to see the character step out into her own series. My hope was that this would be a return to fun comics without the gloom and grit teeth so prevalent in most titles on the stands and I am happy to report you guys hit it out of the park with a funny, entertaining read. Kudos!
Galactus in the second issue? Nice. I guess Franklin Richards is going to need a new herald after SG gets through with him, huh? I think a college dorm lacks the space for a trophy room to keep the giant purple moon boots, so a headquarters might soon be an item on Doreen's To-Do List. . .
Thanks again for a great comic!
Take care,
Stacy Dooks

This book is so much fun. I had no earthly intention of buying it, I liked the character, and I really enjoyed the Dan Slott GREAT LAKES AVENGERS miniseries from a decade ago, but Squirrel Girl as a lead? My budget is paper thin, and I didn't even consider it. But then the reviews came pouring in, all overwhelmingly positive. And I thought about how disillusioned I've become as a comics fan. Neverending event series, tie-in series to the events, ret-cons, deaths that last six months to spike sales, major changes to flagship characters that everyone knows won't last, another fun She-Hulk series getting cancelled, FANTASTIC FOUR getting shelved, I'm sick to death of it. I thought "this might be what I need." Something purely fun, unapologetically upbeat.
So I bought it, and I laughed out loud at nearly every page. It was so funny. This is exactly what I needed right now. A comic to remind me why I love comics. And now Squirrel Girl is going to fight Galactus. This is going to be incredible. You could do an issue where she does nothing but converse with Tippy-Toe while onlookers look on in bewilderment, and I would love it. Between this and ANT-MAN #1, this has been the most enjoyable week I've had reading comics in at least a decade, I'm completely serious. I truly hope the fanboys and fangirls sample this book, because if they do, it will last.
Jason Smith
Buena Park, Ca

RYAN: Jason this is the nicest! You sure know how to make a guy feel good about his squirrel lady comic: thank you. Our secret is we're just making the sort of book we'd like to read, and we've been really lucky that other people want to read it too. Hooray for comics!
ERICA: I think it's been said before, but I think we were all worried/curious about the reception of this book. It's definitely different from what people associate with mainstream comics so I'm glad that you like it and that we can fill that gap for you.

Dear Ryan North, Eric Henderson, and the Squirrel Girl gang,
I always loved Squirrel Girl and was sad to see how it wasn't appearing as a solo issue in recent years. As a result, when I heard that Squirrel Girl was getting its own series I was jumping up and down like a squirrel would seeing an acorn!!! The art also brings out the best of the college story of Squirrel Girl. It is awesome seeing how Squirrel Girl isn't depicted as a dark, gritty super hero, but a cheerful, just super hero and the art brings out the best of that. I really am honored to be reading this issue and I wish this story continues on forever!!! The jokes make me laugh a lot and her cheerful attitude makes me blissful too!
Thanks,
Andre Lee

P.S. I totally love squirrels in real life too!

RYAN: Thanks Andre! Funny thing about squirrels in real life: I never noticed them before, and now I see them EVERYWHERE. So I'll be walking my dog Chompsky to the park and see squirrels in the trees and think "Oh right I'm late

on the issue #5 script, I should get on that." So now there's these reminders for me to get back to work distributed WORLDWIDE, on every continent except Antarctica.
Therefore I'm moving to Antarctica, see y'all later!!

Dear Ryan & Erica,
When in 1933 a bunch of newspaper comic strips were put together in a periodical, thus creating the first comic book, if its creators could only know that it would one day lead to THE UNBEATABLE SQUIRREL GIRL, they would have reveled with paroxysms of joy, knowing with happy certainty that they had played such a crucial role to the betterment of Western Civilization.
I could go on, but I fear I might start to tilt toward a touch of hyperbole.
Gene Popa

RYAN: One of my favorite things to think about is how your entire life has technically been leading up to THIS one moment, right now. So if I've just made a good sandwich, my entire life has been leading up to that one delicious sandwich. Then a few seconds later my life has been leading up to me eating it, then cleaning up the dishes, etc. Anyway, Gene: my ENTIRE LIFE has been leading up to me answering your letter just now. Thank you for sending it in!

To the nut that answers these letters,
I have been waiting years (make that 2) for Squirrel Girl to have her own comic book series and when I finally got my hands on issue #1, I went absolutely nuts! And if THE AMAZING SPIDER-MAN can have a 700 issue run, then surely, THE UNBEATABLE SQUIRREL GIRL can have at least 800...I mean, 001 on the cover does mean there's room for up to 999 issues, right? Which brings me to a totally unrelatable question...I know Squirrel Girl speaks English as well as Squirrel and is going to school to learn to speak 1s and 0s, but does she speak any other languages such as Japanese, Chinese, Spanish, or Chipmunk?
Philip Hanan

RYAN: Hah hah, I did not notice until JUST NOW that our book does have two leading zeros on the cover. It's not issue 1, it's issue 001. So that's 999 comics in total that Marvel expects from us, and at one a month, that's...83 ¼ years?! LET THIS BE A LESSON TO US ALL: always read the contracts BEFORE you sign them, lest you find out in a letters page you have SIGNED THE REST OF YOUR LIFE AWAY.
Still. No regrets!!
ERICA: Did you know that chipmunks are also part of the family Sciuridae? They are! They probably speak the same language. PROBABLY.

Q: Will Squirrel Girl ever team up with any female characters to kick some major butt?
Maryam F.

RYAN: Yep! AND HOW.
ERICA: ALL THE BUTTS.

Dear Erica and Ryan and Rico,
I just finished the first issue of THE UNBEATABLE SQUIRREL GIRL and I am vexed. I was wondering: How can I be more like Squirrel Girl? I am neither a girl nor a squirrel and have a severe nut allergy. The doctors say I shouldn't even be alive! What should I do?
Your Scholar,
James Kislingbury

RYAN: Okay first off, if you're going to doctors who say "you shouldn't even be alive," you should get a new doctor. Get one who says "you SHOULD be alive and I'm glad you are, holla" instead. And while you might not be able to be Squirrel Girl, you could still be Chipmunk Hunk!
ERICA: Well, the important thing with squirrels isn't so much nuts as much as they're opportunistic omnivores that can't digest cellulose. So try to find foods that have a lot of protein, carbs and fat.

To the inspired minds behind THE UNBEATABLE SQUIRREL GIRL,

I'm gonna be honest here - Squirrel Girl wasn't a hard sell for me. I like comics, I like squirrels. I'm a girl and I like reading about girls. In the title alone Squirrel Girl has almost everything I like in life (still needs: Oreos, posters, high speed car chases, etc).
So I figured I was going to like SQUIRREL GIRL #1 because HOW CAN YOU NOT and then I read it (as I made my own move to college, funnily enough) and was STILL wowed! I AM IN LOVE! It is so much fun, from start to finish! The dialogue is hilarious, the facial expressions are to die for, and the colors are so vibrant and delightful ajskdlfjkasdfj IT IS SO. GOOD.
I can't wait to see more of Doreen's adventures - crime-fighting! Attending classes! Punching and studying, aw yeah! It's all great. Fingers crossed for a long and happy series for Doreen and co.!
Marley

RYAN: Thanks, Marley! You're RIGHT that we haven't had high-speed car chases yet, but it's been tricky because how often do you see squirrels inside a car? INFREQUENTLY AT BEST. I guess... we could change that?

Guys and Gals,
You're all nuts. Irrevocably and gloriously so. ANT-MAN? SQUIRREL GIRL? Astonishing and unbeatable first issues!
More importantly, my sick four-year-old was so engaged as we read (an edited, age-appropriate version of) these comics out loud to her (along with issues of ROCKET RACCOON and MS. MARVEL, whom she loves); it lends such a positive experience to her being in a hospital. In times past (the early 80s), I actually looked forward to plowing through back issues of EARTH'S MIGHTIEST while recuperating from surgery or high fever. Isn't that nuts?

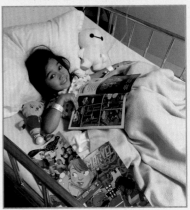

That's probably because every True Believer knows that Marvel Comics are the best medicine. Nuts, but true.
Papa Joe
Cville, VA

P.S. I do hope Kamala Khan and Doreen Green make it to the MCU!

RYAN: Joe, this is adorable and I wish I got comics when I was sick. I hope your daughter is feeling better and never makes the causal connection between illness and GETTING TO READ ALL THE COMICS EVER, because if I had as a kid I'm sure I'd be faking tummy aches every week.

Dear Erica, Ryan, and Rico,
I've just finished reading issue #1 of your new series and I have to say I absolutely loved it. The humor is spot on, the art is ADORABLE, and she has the best theme song ever.
Also, I've been wondering where I can get myself a pack of those Deadpool super villain trading cards? I could really use them in my top secret crime-fighting endeavors. (Maybe I shouldn't be mentioning this in a, possibly, published letter.)
Sarah Y.
Hong Kong

RYAN: Sarah Y. from Hong Kong, your secret of fighting crime is safe with me! I won't tell anyone that Sarah Y. in Hong Kong fights crime. Also, I would love to see those Deadpool cards in real life

too, but I'm a little worried because then they'd need me to write descriptions for EVERY SINGLE MARVEL VILLAIN EVER IN TIME, which I dunno, might take a while. A long weekend, easy.

First off, thank you so much for giving Squirrel Girl her own comic, it's a breath of fresh air and something I have been waiting for...forever. Because squirrels. Second, yay! The bestest and most awesomest marvel heroine gets some recognition for saving us all from the real threats! Yay again!

Um...this was just a thank you letter really, but if I had to ask questions. Ok. Love the addition of acorn earrings, but have the eye stripes gone for good? They were cute...

Also, any chance we get to meet the parents? Doreen's mum and dad must be the proudest parents, or the most laid back, ever.

I have another thank you, to Ryan and Erica, thank you for giving us an upbeat and completely positive lighthearted book, in an industry where everyone is dark, edgy and gritty. (And depressing... Is it me? Or has every hero got problems? Except Squirrel Girl who has squirrels!)

Love you all!
Tim P.
Plymouth, England.

ERICA: Can you imagine having to take that makeup on and off every time though? Squirrel Girl's back in NYC and there's NO TIME TO STOP FOR ANYTHING.

Dear Squirrel Girl Team,

Hello there, you fabulous people in comic book world! When I heard that they were going to be bringing Squirrel Girl back to the Marvel Universe, I was all filled with glee and dancing a jig. I let that simmer on the back burner, until I heard that Ryan North would be writing it. I can't actually put into print how excited this made me. I guess to go with my previous metaphor, you could say I boiled over. (This is the part where you all are laughing and telling me how clever I am; at least, it is in my head.) I've seen what you can do with six panels of dinosaurs, and I am among those who helped with that Kickstarter of yours for the *Hamlet Choose Your Own Adventure.* Who better to take the helm of this new series?

From the second I pulled the first issue off of the shelf at my comic store, I knew I would not be disappointed. The art is amazing! Doreen didn't look quite how I pictured the new Squirrel Girl to look, but that's okay because she looks even better. I love that pretty much everything is round and colorful. Makes the book so much more approachable to someone like me who is new to the world of comic book buying/collecting. I wish I had a convention coming up so I could cosplay her already. And the story! I want to ask so many questions about where you are heading, but I think I'm just going to wait until the comics come out. Thank you all for your work that you're doing. I look forward to seeing what adventures lay ahead for Doreen and Tippy-Toe. And on that note, I'm off to see if Rosetta Stone offers a course on the Northeastern variant of Squirrelese.

Your Unbeatable Fan,
Stefanie M.

RYAN: Thank you, Stefanie! And I am secretly really excited for convention season this year, because I really want to see the Squirrel Girl cosplay. Everyone dress up as her forever, thanks in advance!!

UNBEATABLE SQUIRREL GIRL was the absolute highlight of my day, week, and possible even year (though it's a little early to tell). I'm so excited to see Doreen not only put bad guys in their place but also tackle the exciting world of Computer Science - how incredibly rad. It's the kind of book that gives me hope for super-hero comics. In the mean time, I have two questions for you:

1) Will any of Doreen's past friends (the GLA, Devil, or the Cage-Jones family) be making appearances?

2) If Doreen could have lunch with any other Marvel super hero who would it be?

Congratulations and I'm sure you'll continue to knock it out of the park.

Arielle B.

RYAN: I know Erica loves Flatman (AND WHO DOESN'T?) so I'd love to have him appear at some point! Of course, who's to say that he hasn't ALREADY appeared, only he was standing at just the right angle as to be invisible? WHO INDEED. Well in fact it's the artists and writers who can say, and we're here saying he hasn't done that in Squirrel Girl.

YET.

ERICA: If Doreen could have lunch with any other hero it would be Dazzler because, oh my god, she has, like, ALL of her albums.

Dear Squirrel Girl Creative Team (can I call you the Squirrel Squad?)

I'm absolutely nuts about Doreen! Thank you for bringing back one of my favorite Marvel characters from obscurity into a book I can shove in all my friends' faces. The first issue was all I hoped it would be and more.

I am foaming at the mouth for the next one already! (I should probably go get that checked out.) I am curious, how did you choose between Tippy-Toe and Monkey Joe to appear in the series?

Amy Chase

Ok I've been obsessed with Squirrel Girl and waiting for this moment for a while now... great job on the first issue! I really wanted her to kick some major butt in the first issue but next one looks pretty crazy so I already can't wait.

I MUST know what her MJ necklace stands for. If it's Marc Jacobs I will die but I think there's another meaning... Also, I need her purse, any idea where I can get one?!

Last, Squirrel Girl needs to go into psychiatry or psychology. She has a way with talking to this guy that shows a gift.

Love,
Squirrel Girl super fan for life

RYAN: It stands for "Monkey Joe," her first squirrel companion! He was the squirrel she hung out with before Tippy-Toe. It could also stand for "My Jewelry," in case she only wears jewelry that describes itself. They only way to confirm that for sure though is if she ever wears earrings that just say "earring," which I think... might be amazing??

ERICA: I totally own a brown version of that purse. I think it's sold out. I'm sorry. I'm just going to be honest here, I pretty much own all of Doreen's clothes.

I want to say "chitter chit chit chitter" THANK YOU for bring Squirrel Girl back. The fact that she wears the MJ in homage to Monkey Joe makes me want to tear up.

I can't wait for the next issue! My squirrel friend Ladro is throwing nuts at me asking how he can join the squirrel army?

Sincerely,
Beth 'the Squirrel' Jankowski

ERICA: I'm glad I'm not the only one who tears up over Monkey Joe. (RIP)

Hi Squirrel Girl Team!

So I'm writing this on a Tuesday night because I run a shop and I totally stayed late tonight just to read your book.

I just want to say going in I wasn't convinced. I wasn't a fan of the art, but by the second page (that we hadn't seen in the preview yet) I was totally won over. I love it! I can't wait to sell this to everyone that comes in tomorrow and days after that until I run out then I can sell the 2nd and 3rd and 4th printings too, and the hardcovers and trade paperbacks. This book rocks and it will be great for anyone that loves fun and maybe we can win over some of the people that hate fun too.

One little thing, any chance the color on the bottom page tidbits can be altered a teensy bit? They were really hard to read. Or I just need new glasses.

Thanks for the fun comic!

Jenn Swackhamer
Comic City Pontiac, MI

Hello!

First off, I have to say how absolutely MARVELlous (ha!) the first issue of UNBEATABLE SQUIRREL GIRL was! Wow! Artwork and writing combined, it's pretty much the most perfect comic book of all time and space.

Secondly, I have to say how super AWESOME it is to have another female-fronted book, but also one where the character is hilarious and clumsy and endearing and basically a lot more like me than any of the other beautiful, graceful super-women out there. (I love them too though!) I love everything you've done and I absolutely canNUT wait for the next issue! (One day I'll stop with the puns. Today is NUT that day.)

Holly Ringsell

Well, we've used up all the extra room we have this month! But keep writing! We want to hear from every dang one of you! And don't forget to check out our behind-the-scenes tumblr: unbeatablesquirrelgirl.tumblr.com! See y'all next month! Stay nutty!

Next: Squirrel Girl vs. Planet-Eating Man!

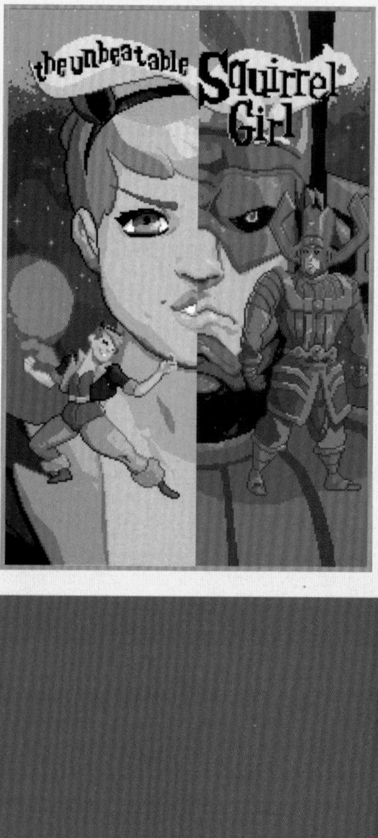
the unbeatable Squirrel Girl

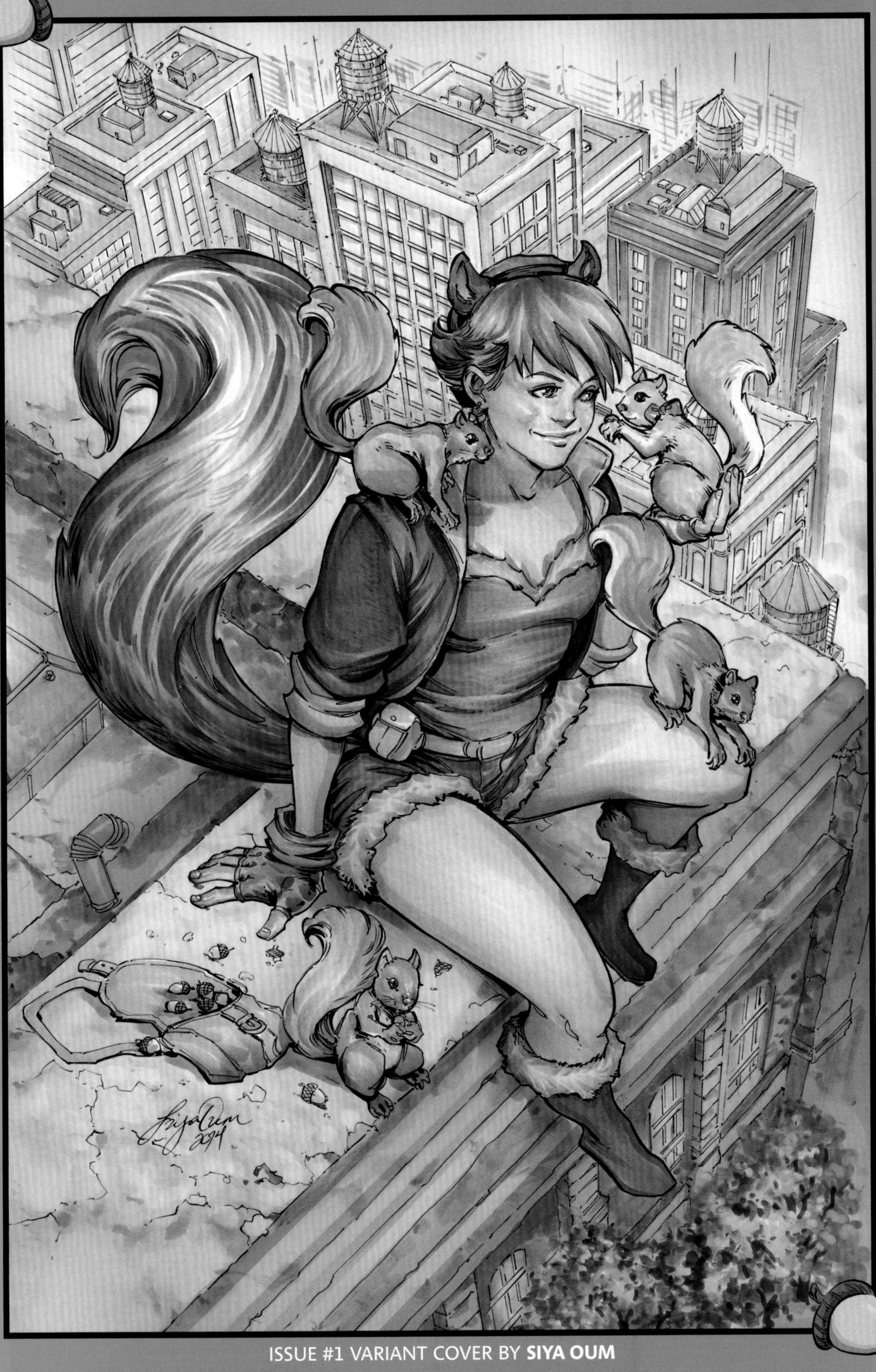

ISSUE #1 VARIANT COVER BY **SIYA OUM**

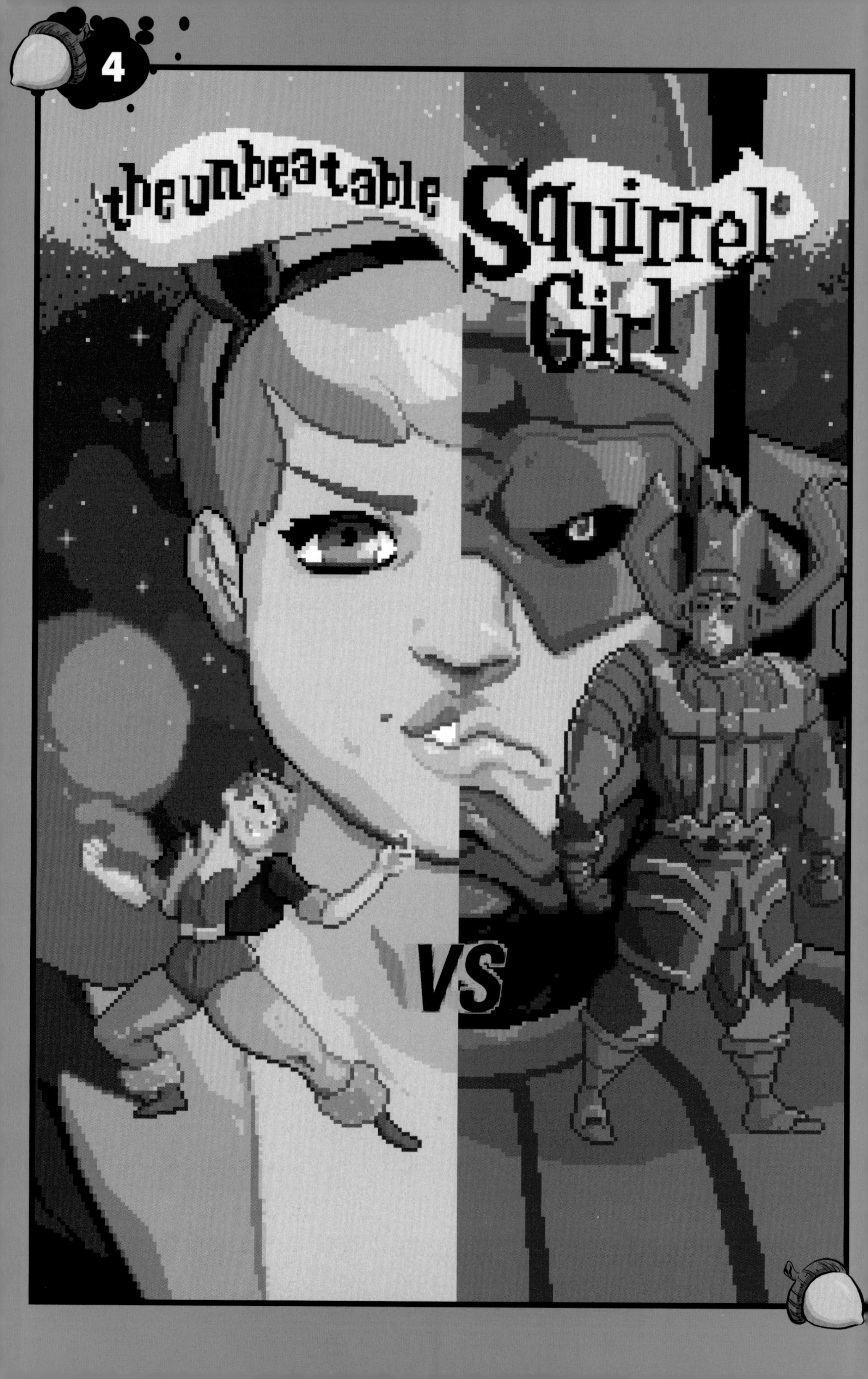
4
the unbeatable Squirrel Girl
VS

Doreen Green isn't just a first-year computer science student: she secretly also has all the powers of both squirrel and girl! She uses her amazing abilities to fight crime **and** be as awesome as possible. You know her as...**The Unbeatable Squirrel Girl!** Let's catch up with what she's been up to until now, with...

Squirrel Girl *in a nutshell*

search! 🔍

#bankrobbery

#banksnobbery

#mew

#squirrelsuitcrochetpattern

#snackcakes

#squirrelman

G. ALACTUS
GALACTUS @xGALACTUSx
HEY GUESS WHAT I'M COMING TO EARTH TO DEVOUR THE ENTIRE PLANET

G. ALACTUS
GALACTUS @xGALACTUSx
AND NOBODY KNOWS BECAUSE I PUT MY SHIP IN A STEALTH FIELD

G. ALACTUS
GALACTUS @xGALACTUSx
"BUT WAIT," YOU SAY, "AHA! NOW WE KNOW YOU'RE COMING BECAUSE YOU JUST POSTED IT ON SOCIAL MEDIA!!"

G. ALACTUS
GALACTUS @xGALACTUSx
ONLY YOU AREN'T SAYING THAT BECAUSE NOBODY KNOWS I'M COMING BECAUSE NOBODY FOLLOWS ME ON THIS STUPID SITE

G. ALACTUS
GALACTUS @xGALACTUSx
...

G. ALACTUS
GALACTUS @xGALACTUSx
#ff @xGALACTUSx

Tony Stark @starkmantony ✓
@unbeatablesg Just heard more of my Iron Man parts have been "borrowed," and now there's a big hole in my building too. Any ideas?

Squirrel Girl! @unbeatablesg
@starkmantony Oh wow dude these suits have wifi in them??? I can go online on my way to the MOON?? Tony ur the best <3

Tony Stark @starkmantony ✓
@unbeatablesg That "wifi" works even in Mars orbit, uses proprietary Stark technology, and costs several thousand dollars a kilobyte.

Squirrel Girl! @unbeatablesg
@starkmantony um I already downloaded some songs for the trip to the moon. Sorry!!!

Tony Stark @starkmantony ✓
@unbeatablesg Don't reply to say you're sorry! That ALSO costs money!

Squirrel Girl! @unbeatablesg
@starkmantony sorry sorry!

Tony Stark @starkmantony ✓
@unbeatablesg Don't reply! Stop replying!

Squirrel Girl! @unbeatablesg
@starkmantony whoooooooooooooooooooooooooooooops

Nancy W. @sewwiththeflow
Story time, friends. Your hero, me, thought she'd eat some delicious (cash-only) falafel. So I went to the bank.

Nancy W. @sewwiththeflow
And you know how banks are always the worst even when you're NOT being taken hostage? WELL GUESS WHAT?

Nancy W. @sewwiththeflow
Yep. But then we got saved by @unbeatablesg who appeared in SQUIRREL SUIT ARMOR MODE. Not even joking.

Nancy W. @sewwiththeflow
This really happened. I was saved by a squirrel suit Squirrel Girl. I know you don't believe me.

Nancy W. @sewwiththeflow
tl;dr: doesn't matter, ate falafel

Whiplash @realwhiplash22
I am trapped in #CentralPark and need #squirrelrepellant, PLEASE RT!!!!! #please #rt #please #rt #please #rt

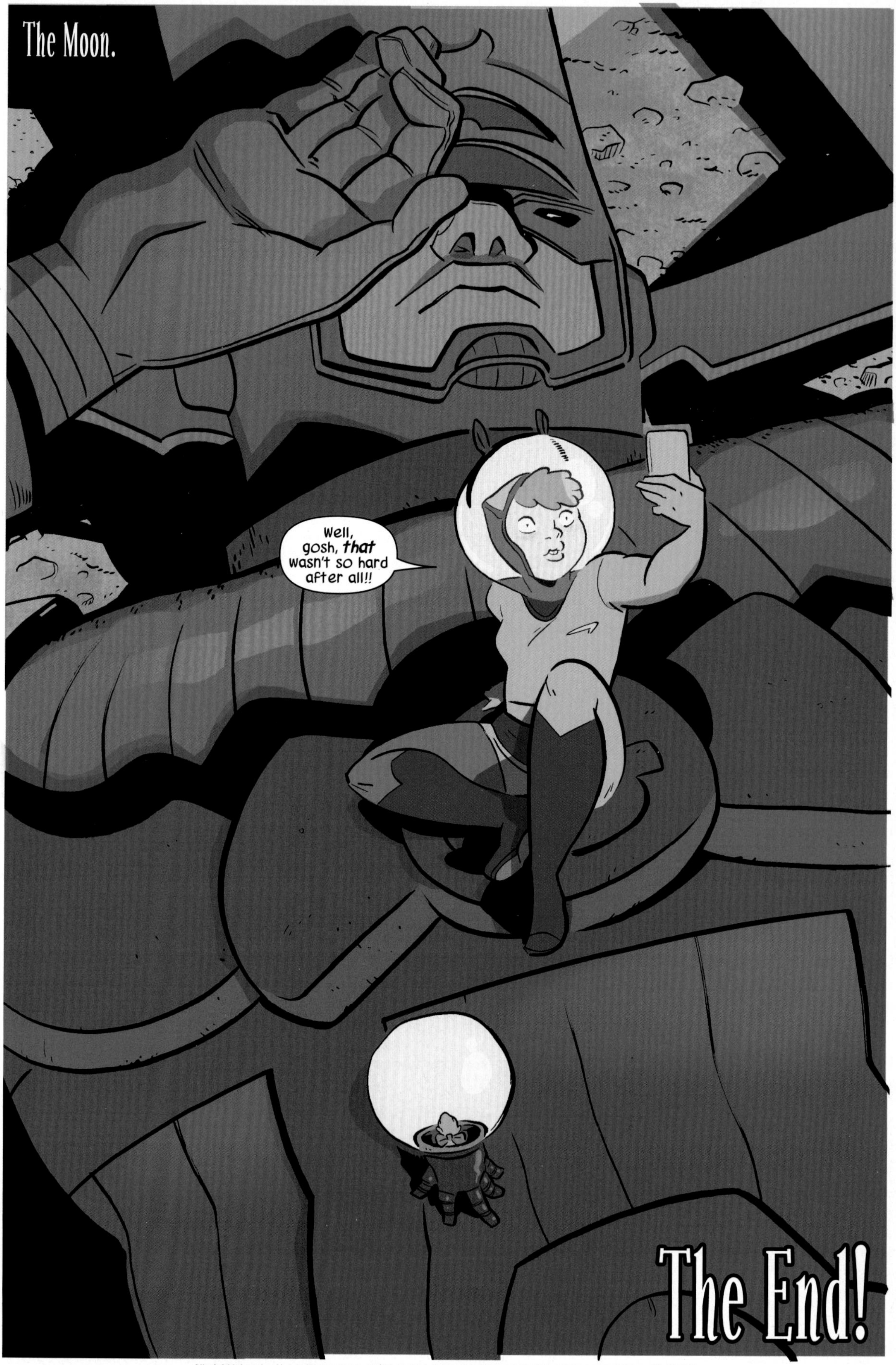
The Moon.
Well, gosh, *that* wasn't so hard after all!!
The End!

All right! Now to the letters page, and then the rest of this book is just blank pages! Haha, *Oh well!!*

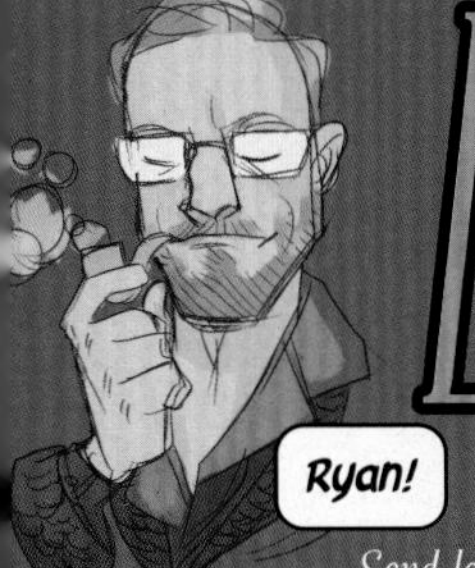
Ryan!

Letters From Nuts

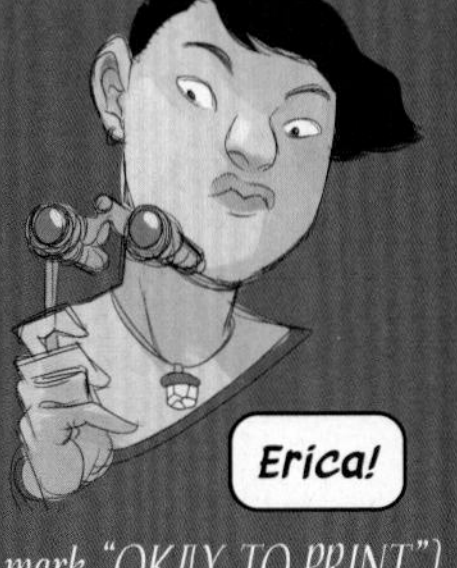
Erica!

Send letters to mheroes@marvel.com or 135 W 50th St, 7th Floor, New York, NY 10020 (Please mark "OKAY TO PRINT")

Dear Squirrel Girl comics,

I really liked Tippy-Toe's squirrel armor. I can't believe that Squirrel Girl's fighting Galactus. I mean, that's a big thing, you know! I find that the cover is very funny because Squirrel Girl is using Iron Man as a surfboard. I mean, a surfboard? That's cray-cray!

Signed,
Elsa McQuaid

RYAN: Thanks! To invent Tippy-Toe's armor I held out my hand in an approximately squirrel shape and confirmed, yes, that would fit inside a glove. And if you're reading this, then you just read the page that showed the aftermath of Squirrel Girl beating Galactus off panel, which we can all agree was really very satisfying! Writing: it's easy!!

ERICA: I remember getting an e-mail saying we needed the second cover and that it should be Squirrel Girl surfing on an Iron Man suit and my first thought was "That's stupid." I'll admit when I'm wrong-- just don't tell Ryan I told you that. Any part of that.

Dear "Letters from Nuts" crew,

As a comic collector of over 20 years, I want to thank you for creating such a great comic. Over the past several years, my love of comics has crossed over with another love - squirrels! I have been a squirrel fanatic since my college days when I worked on an independent study project to identify squirrel parasites. In the last few years, I have been taking a sketchbook to the comic conventions that I attend and I have been asking various artists to draw a Squirrel mashed-up with any character of their choosing! I have attached several of the sketches for your enjoyment (including some of my own):

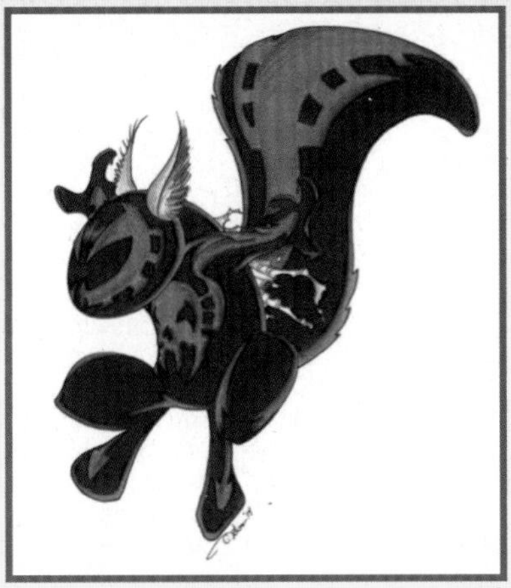

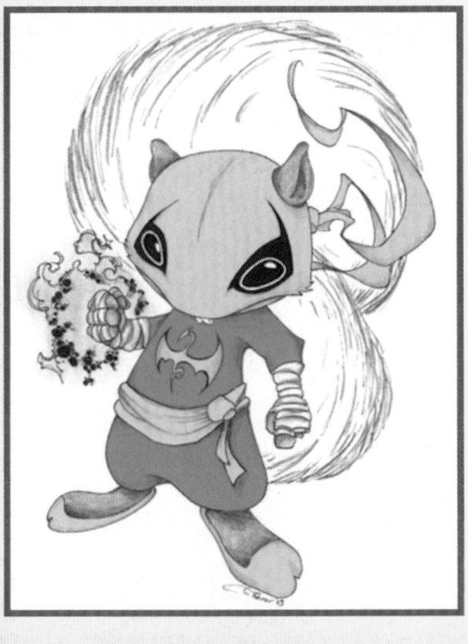

Question: Based on Marvel's summer plans, is there any way we could get a small landmass on Battleworld assigned to a whole universe where all of the Marvel characters are squirrels (and maybe Squirrel Girl could rule them all)? In my opinion, that would be the most important part of the Secret Wars crossover!

Your loyal fan,
Corey Fuhrer

RYAN: Those pictures are amazing. If only we had made this comic more than one page long, we could've shown you Squirrel Galactus! But alas, we decided to publish this book with only one page of comics, some letters, and then a whole bunch of blank pages.

I have pitched your idea to Marvel and they informed me that it's "way too late" to rewrite their Battleworld plans to include Squirrel Island, although they "wish they had thought of that sooner" and "feel regret about not doing Squirrel Island more keenly than [they] have ever felt any emotion before, including love." So – that's something!

ERICA: Although we SHOULD do Squirrel Island but like Spider Island. (Because let's follow up on ALL of Dan Slott's ideas.) Everyone on Manhattan gets bitten by radioactive squirrels but nobody turns into a Squirrel Girl equivalent because that's not how she got her powers. Pretty sure this is a one-page story. Is NOT BRAND ECHH still a thing?

Is Chipmunk Hunk perhaps a monk? Look, I'm just trying to think of rhymes for the theme song.

Stephen,
Kansas City

RYAN: All I know for sure is: he's been shrunk, he can dunk, spelunk, his car's got a trunk, and if you bring him to a cabin he'll steal the top bunk.

ERICA: RYAN. Leave the rhyming to the professionals. Like Adam WarRock. Have you HEARD his Squirrel Girl rap? (www.adamwarrock.com) Step down, buddy.

My four-year-old twin daughters enjoy squirrels quite a bit. They are always asking if we can leave some peanut butter and crackers outside to feed our neighborhood squirrel crew. They also love comic books, as they've been exposed to them pretty much since they were born. So, it was a no-brainer to hip them to THE UNBEATABLE SQUIRREL GIRL series.

There aren't very many comics that the girls will allow me to read them from start to finish. They generally prefer to tear through 'em on their lonesome, looking at the artwork and making up their own dialogue. SQUIRREL GIRL is one of the exceptions though.

One constant with each issue I've noticed is that they keep asking me where Gamora is. So if you end up having the Guardians of the Galaxy make an appearance, that would seal the deal with their appreciation of Squirrel Girl.

Darrick Patrick
Dayton, Ohio

P.S. I'm including a photograph of Nola and Logann showing off their Unbeatable collection so far:

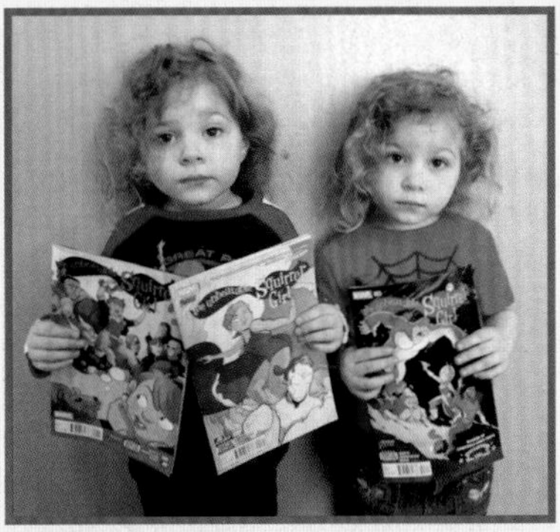

RYAN: Awesome, a complete set! You can tell Nola and Logann that I, the writer of these comics, say that Gamora is secretly there, just hidden. She and Doreen were going to get lunch together before Doreen got wrapped up in this Galactus thing, so while Doreen's there fighting Whiplash and bank robbers and Galactus, Gamora's standing there, just out of frame, gesturing

to her watch, impatiently waiting.

ERICA: Yes! My favorite compliment this book gets is being able to share it with your kids, so I love that! Side note: peanuts aren't great for squirrels and apparently can get some sort of weird invisible toxic mold (citation needed)??? If you want to leave a snack out, nuts in shells are great. It's something they love and the shell provides good gnawing exercise.

Well Hi there!

This is why I really like Squirrel Girl: she's really funny-looking. On a new-comics wall, I can look across all Marvel's titles; lots of angry-looking, grim but very buff-looking hero-suited figures, and there's Squirrel Girl, happy and goofy-looking. I have to support that. And apparently she's the most powerful super-powered person in the whole Marvel Universe? Y'know, I get a lot of comics, but now I'm down to just two Marvel comics, this one, and Captain Marvel. Guess I just like strong, pleasant women in my life. Carol and Doreen are like that, nice people. One's goofy-looking: y'know? -- in the Marvel Universe, that just makes her exceptional.

It certainly helps that SQUIRREL GIRL's written well. And works well with a slightly 'cartoony' edge to the artwork. The words and pictures really support one-another. You could do me a favor, though, by using a darker ink to your teeny tiny bottom-page typings. Old eyes, y'know? Thanks for a good, fun comic.

Best wishes,
Matt Levin
Hatfield, MA

ERICA: I'm glad you're into it! I really stressed out when I was first asked to draw this character. One of the only pieces of mine that Wil (our editor) mentioned when we were starting out was a much more realistic-looking movie poster I drew, and I went back and forth on how the style should look. In the end I took a gamble on a looser and more animated look and I'm super happy that it's worked out.

Loved, loved, loved UNBEATABLE SQUIRREL GIRL #2. Art and story - killing it! Thank you for this book.

Any chance we'll see the Great Lakes Avengers at some point? I mean, that's where I first met Doreen, and now she's way more popular than the GLA so it'd be nice to use her popularity to bolster them up. Also, when you inevitably get to your big, triple-sized anniversary spectacular, could you reprint her first appearance? It's not an easy "tail" to come by. Thanks!

Charles Albert,
Richmond VA

RYAN: I'd like to! I really like Flatman because he has all the powers of being a man AND all the powers of being flat. I can't tell you how many times I've looked at tiny cracks under doors and wanted to see what was on the other side and said "If only I was a flat, but alas, I am a man." Okay, I can: it's several. I have done that several times.

ERICA: I keep picturing the GLA reunion like a high school reunion and Doreen is the one kid that left their small town to do something big and is home for the first time in 10 years and just has no idea if it's going to be super awkward or not. Also, everyone is worried Deadpool is going to show up. THAT GUY, AMIRIGHT?

I just wanted to thank you guys for starting to write/print this comic at such an opportune time. Just two weeks ago I was mentioning that Squirrel Girl existed to a friend and he didn't really believe me, so I looked her up to show him and simultaneously found out that these were being printed! Now, hopefully, I'll get to show him a physical copy with my name in it! It also gives me a great read to look forward to every week with my best-friend-roommates. So...Thank you for such a humorously written and expertly drawn comic!

On an unrelated note though, any chance of us ever seeing any physical copies of Deadpool's Guide to Super Villains and Super Villain Accessories in the future?

Andre W.

RYAN: I'd love to see the Deadpool cards as a set! I don't know if anyone higher up at Marvel Headquarters reads the letters page of our squirrel comic BUT IF THEY DO: Yo, that's two months in a row people have asked for these cards! Please make them immediately. PS: this counts as market research, and I have never been wrong before.

ERICA: Henderson and North, MAKING IT HAPPEN. (The comic/continuation of Squirrel Girl, not the cards. We don't really have control over merchandising- yet.)

To whom it may concern,

I got the first two issues of UNBEATABLE SQUIRREL GIRL recently, and I can't wait to for next month's issue. Thank you for making Tippy-Toe so cute, and for Nancy. I knit and crochet, too (and now I know next year's Halloween costume). I couldn't resist making a little Tippy-Toe for myself. Thank you for creating something so cute and fun.

Keep up the amazing work!
Katie H.

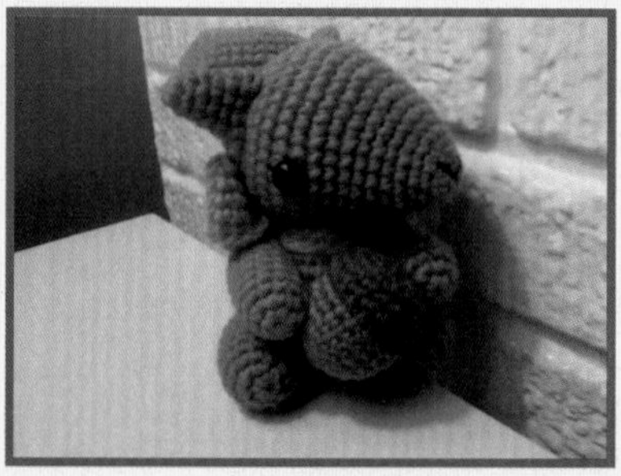

RYAN: Katie, GUESS WHAT: I love that Tippy-Toe so much! Nancy's knitting is inspired by my mom, who made me a sweater with a dinosaur on it, and the sweater has a hood with a tassel, AND THE DINOSAUR ON THE SWEATER IS WEARING THE SAME SWEATER WITH THE SAME HOOD AND TASSEL. It's the best ever.

ERICA: AHHHHH. WHAAAAAT. I do some sewing, but knitting and crocheting are amazing mystery arts to me. I'm so in awe! That Tippy is just so cute! Fun Fact: When I first saw Nancy in the script she was so much like a friend of mine that I grew up with that I had to reread her intro a few times. When issue 1 came out, other friends asked if it was her. So I love that people are getting into Nancy because she rocks!

Hey guys,

Thanks for making such an epic comic, first of all! Secondly, I really like Mew and also knitting. How can I join Mew Club?

Jane
Cat, Squirrel, and Yarn Enthusiast

RYAN: To join Mew Club you have to write down "Mew is a great cat" on a piece of paper and sign your name, and then you are a member of Mew Club. Mew is based on two cats we know in real life (one I know, and one Erica knows) and when you perform this ritual, we will be alerted, and will inform the Actual Mews of this Actual News.

Wanted to say that, as one of two comics I'm reading, this one is my personal favorite. Just wanted to ask, have you ever come across negative reception for the comic? How did you deal with it?

Felix

RYAN: Thanks for reading our comic! Also, you should read more comics!

There's always going to be people who don't like what you're doing, and it's like, that's fine? There are books I don't like but I don't hate them or want them destroyed or anything. I just don't read them! So if I see someone reacting negatively to anything I do, I don't take it personally, I just think "Oh that's too bad, this person's tastes are not my own. I guess their opinions are different from my clearly objectively correct ones, oh well."

ERICA: I'm with Ryan. There are going to be some people that you just don't agree with on taste and even if they're jerks about it there's not much you can do there, so there's no point in dealing with that. The only time I address it is when I get "won't read because Squirrel Girl isn't hot anymore" because UGH. Anyway, it's pretty easy to get those dudes to back off with a quick "why are you so concerned about a minor being hot?" Also, I'm so curious about this one other comic you're reading. Tweet us about it when you see this answer!

Next: Readers Beware!

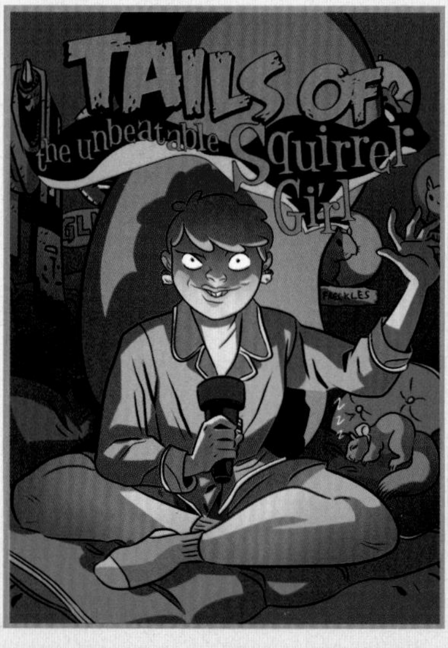
TAILS OF
the unbeatable Squirrel Girl

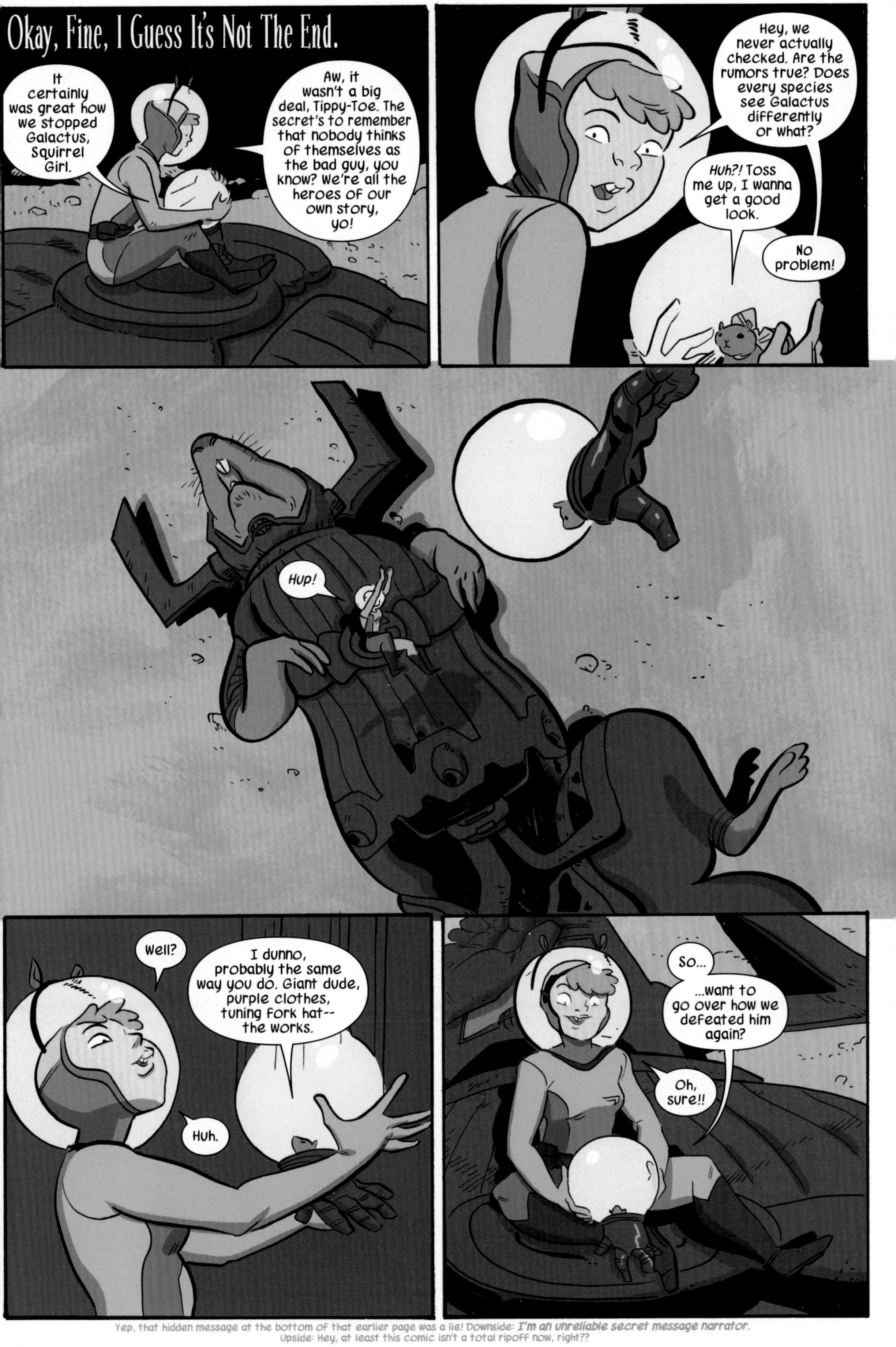
Okay, Fine, I Guess It's Not The End.
It certainly was great how we stopped Galactus, Squirrel Girl.
Aw, it wasn't a big deal, Tippy-Toe. The secret's to remember that nobody thinks of themselves as the bad guy, you know? We're all the heroes of our own story, yo!
Hey, we never actually checked. Are the rumors true? Does every species see Galactus differently or what?
Huh?! Toss me up, I wanna get a good look.
No problem!
Hup!
Well?
I dunno, probably the same way you do. Giant dude, purple clothes, tuning fork hat--the works.
Huh.
So...
...want to go over how we defeated him again?
Oh, sure!!

Yep, that hidden message at the bottom of that earlier page was a lie! Downside: ***I'm an unreliable secret message narrator.***
Upside: Hey, at least this comic isn't a total ripoff now, right??

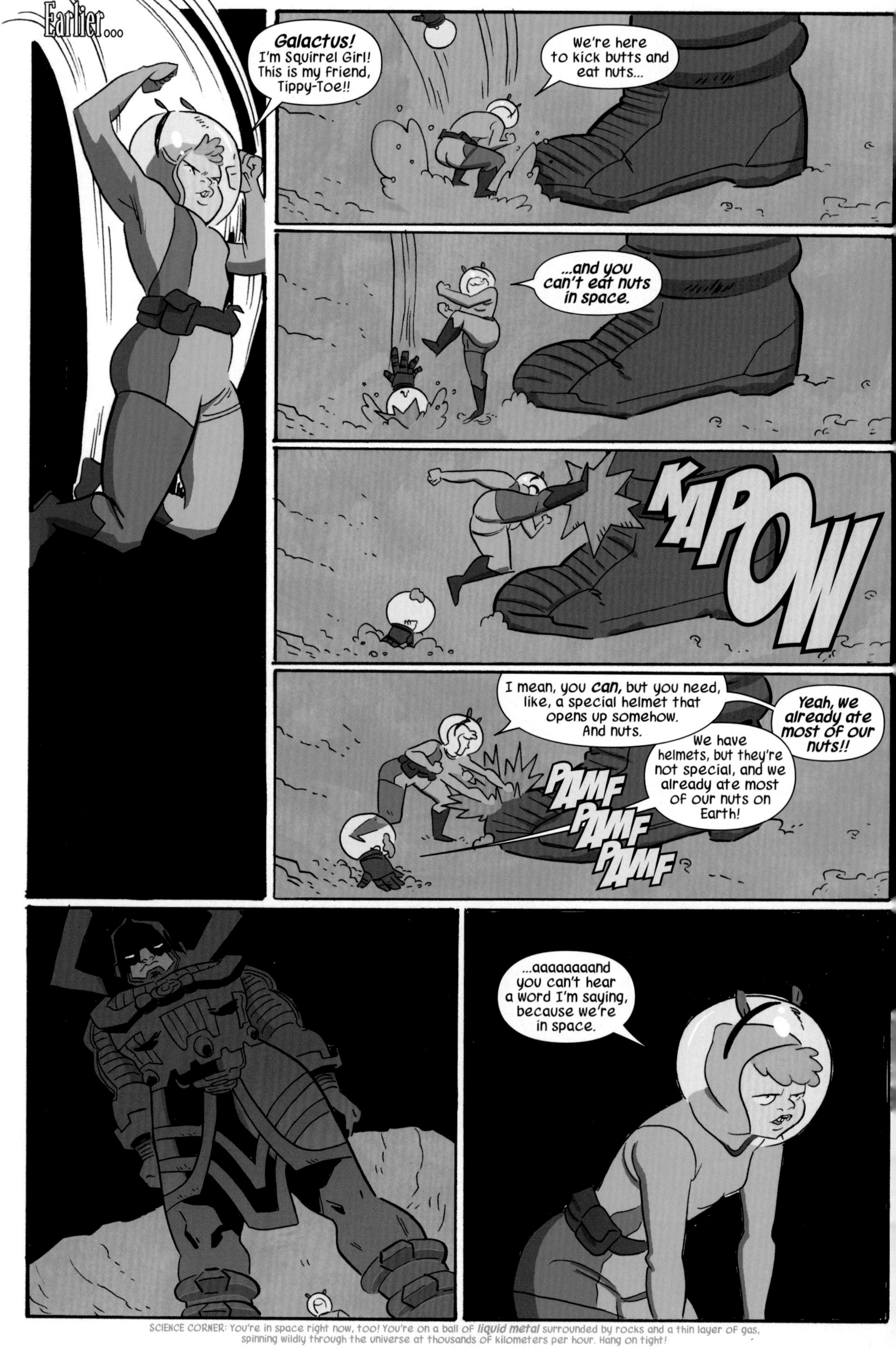
Earlier...
Galactus! I'm Squirrel Girl! This is my friend, Tippy-Toe!!
We're here to kick butts and eat nuts...
...and you can't eat nuts in space.
KAPOW
I mean, you can, but you need, like, a special helmet that opens up somehow. And nuts.
Yeah, we already ate most of our nuts!!
We have helmets, but they're not special, and we already ate most of our nuts on Earth!
PAMF
PAMF
PAMF
...aaaaaaaand you can't hear a word I'm saying, because we're in space.

SCIENCE CORNER: You're in space right now, too! You're on a ball of *liquid metal* surrounded by rocks and a thin layer of gas, spinning wildly through the universe at thousands of kilometers per hour. Hang on tight!

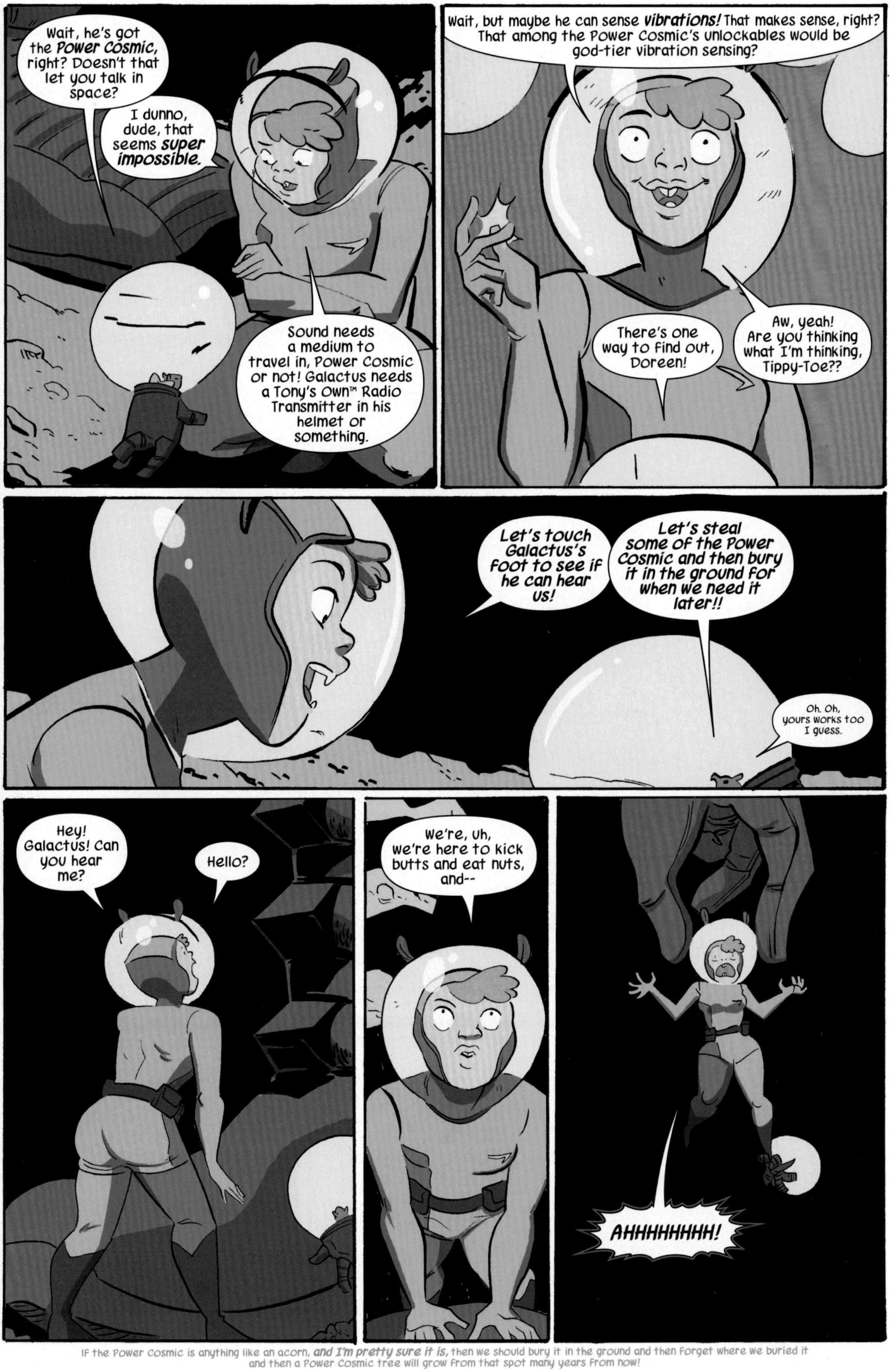
Wait, he's got the Power Cosmic, right? Doesn't that let you talk in space?
I dunno, dude, that seems super impossible.
Sound needs a medium to travel in, Power Cosmic or not! Galactus needs a Tony's Own™ Radio Transmitter in his helmet or something.
Wait, but maybe he can sense vibrations! That makes sense, right? That among the Power Cosmic's unlockables would be god-tier vibration sensing?
There's one way to find out, Doreen!
Aw, yeah! Are you thinking what I'm thinking, Tippy-Toe??
Let's touch Galactus's foot to see if he can hear us!
Let's steal some of the Power Cosmic and then bury it in the ground for when we need it later!!
Oh. Oh, yours works too I guess.
Hey! Galactus! Can you hear me?
Hello?
We're, uh, we're here to kick butts and eat nuts, and--
AHHHHHHHH!

If the Power Cosmic is anything like an acorn, *and I'm pretty sure it is,* then we should bury it in the ground and then forget where we buried it and then a Power Cosmic tree will grow from that spot many years from now!

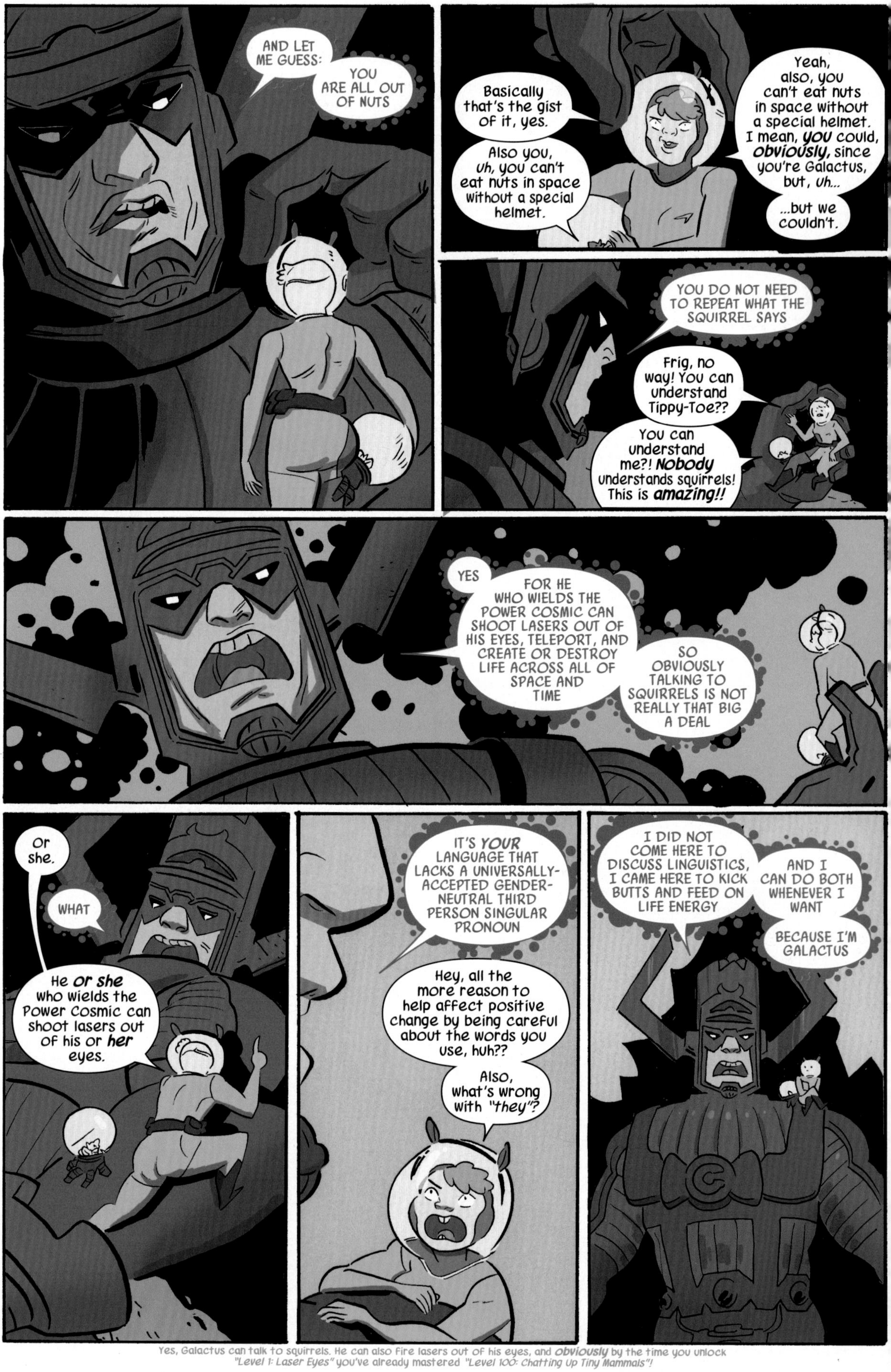
AND LET ME GUESS:
YOU ARE ALL OUT OF NUTS
Basically that's the gist of it, yes.
Also you, uh, you can't eat nuts in space without a special helmet.
Yeah, also, you can't eat nuts in space without a special helmet. I mean, YOU could, obviously, since you're Galactus, but, uh...
...but we couldn't.
YOU DO NOT NEED TO REPEAT WHAT THE SQUIRREL SAYS
Frig, no way! You can understand Tippy-Toe??
You can understand me?! Nobody understands squirrels! This is amazing!!
YES
FOR HE WHO WIELDS THE POWER COSMIC CAN SHOOT LASERS OUT OF HIS EYES, TELEPORT, AND CREATE OR DESTROY LIFE ACROSS ALL OF SPACE AND TIME
SO OBVIOUSLY TALKING TO SQUIRRELS IS NOT REALLY THAT BIG A DEAL
Or she.
WHAT
He or she who wields the Power Cosmic can shoot lasers out of his or her eyes.
IT'S YOUR LANGUAGE THAT LACKS A UNIVERSALLY-ACCEPTED GENDER-NEUTRAL THIRD PERSON SINGULAR PRONOUN
Hey, all the more reason to help affect positive change by being careful about the words you use, huh??
Also, what's wrong with "they"?
I DID NOT COME HERE TO DISCUSS LINGUISTICS, I CAME HERE TO KICK BUTTS AND FEED ON LIFE ENERGY
AND I CAN DO BOTH WHENEVER I WANT
BECAUSE I'M GALACTUS

Yes, Galactus can talk to squirrels. He can also fire lasers out of his eyes, and *obviously* by the time you unlock *"Level 1: Laser Eyes"* you've already mastered *"Level 100: Chatting Up Tiny Mammals"*!

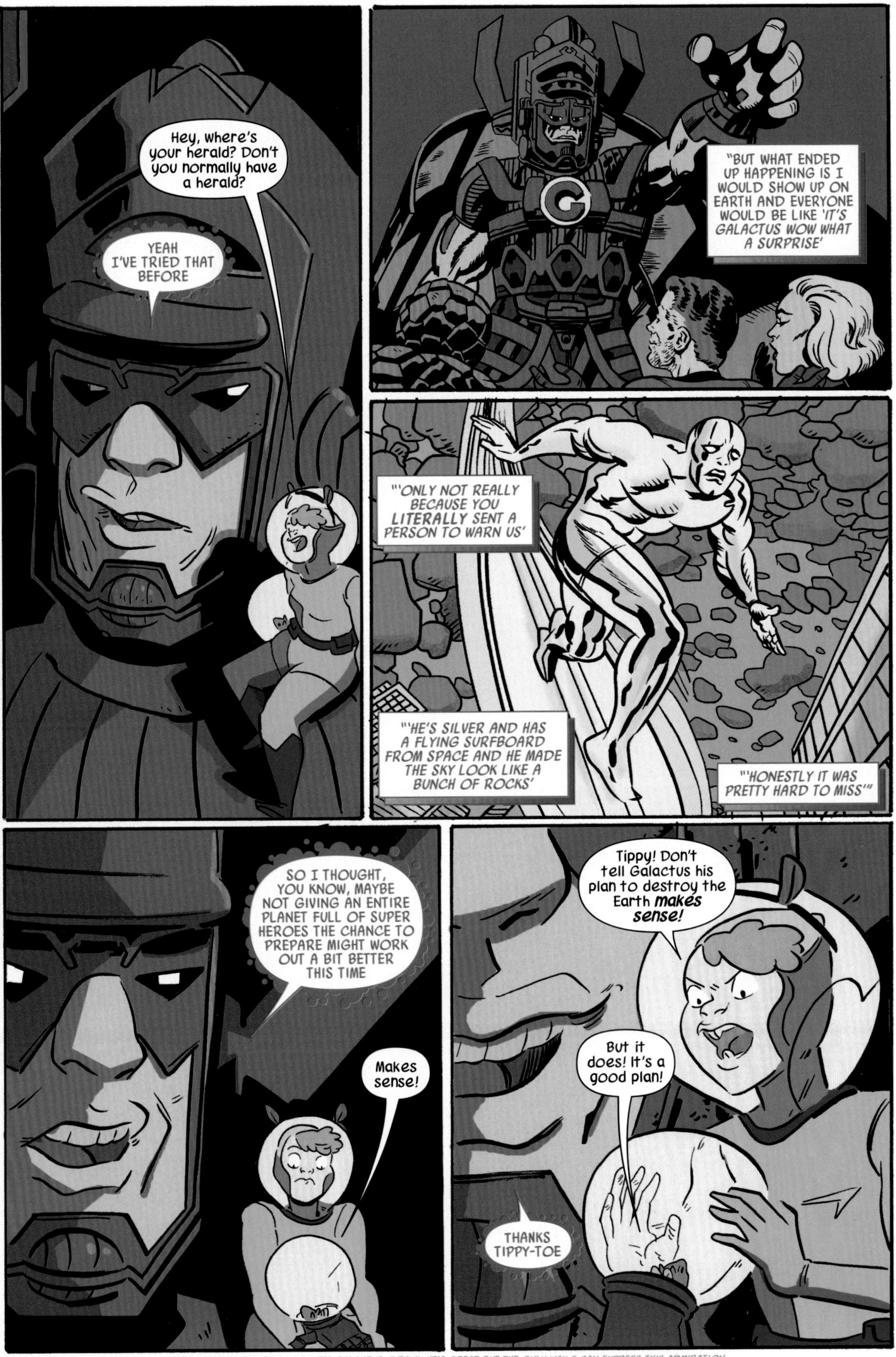
Hey, where's your herald? Don't you normally have a herald?
YEAH I'VE TRIED THAT BEFORE
"BUT WHAT ENDED UP HAPPENING IS I WOULD SHOW UP ON EARTH AND EVERYONE WOULD BE LIKE '*IT'S GALACTUS WOW WHAT A SURPRISE*'
"'*ONLY NOT REALLY BECAUSE YOU **LITERALLY** SENT A PERSON TO WARN US*'
"'*HE'S SILVER AND HAS A FLYING SURFBOARD FROM SPACE AND HE MADE THE SKY LOOK LIKE A BUNCH OF ROCKS*'
"'*HONESTLY IT WAS PRETTY HARD TO MISS*'"
SO I THOUGHT, YOU KNOW, MAYBE NOT GIVING AN ENTIRE PLANET FULL OF SUPER HEROES THE CHANCE TO PREPARE MIGHT WORK OUT A BIT BETTER THIS TIME
Makes sense!
Tippy! Don't tell Galactus his plan to destroy the Earth ***makes sense!***
But it does! It's a good plan!
THANKS TIPPY-TOE

EVERYONE WAS ALL *"OH LOOK IT'S GALACTUS, I THINK HE'S GREAT BUT THE ONLY WAY I CAN EXPRESS THIS ADMIRATION IS TO STYMIE HIS PLANS, NEVERTHELESS I DO SECRETLY REALLY RESPECT WHAT HE'S TRYING TO DO HERE"*

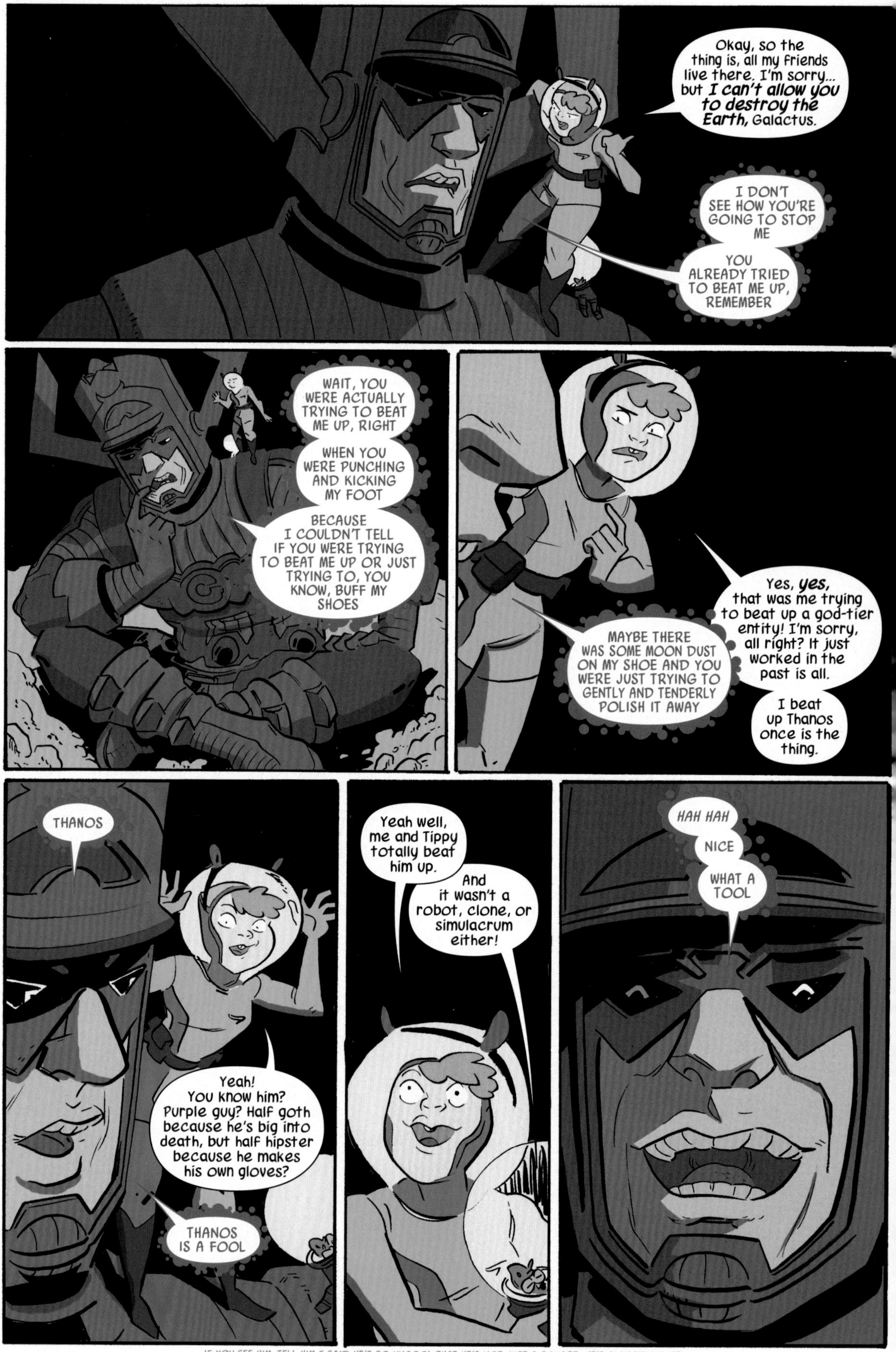
Okay, so the thing is, all my friends live there. I'm sorry... but *I can't allow you to destroy the Earth,* Galactus.
I DON'T SEE HOW YOU'RE GOING TO STOP ME
YOU ALREADY TRIED TO BEAT ME UP, REMEMBER
WAIT, YOU WERE ACTUALLY TRYING TO BEAT ME UP, RIGHT
WHEN YOU WERE PUNCHING AND KICKING MY FOOT
BECAUSE I COULDN'T TELL IF YOU WERE TRYING TO BEAT ME UP OR JUST TRYING TO, YOU KNOW, BUFF MY SHOES
MAYBE THERE WAS SOME MOON DUST ON MY SHOE AND YOU WERE JUST TRYING TO GENTLY AND TENDERLY POLISH IT AWAY
Yes, *yes,* that was me trying to beat up a god-tier entity! I'm sorry, all right? It just worked in the past is all.
I beat up Thanos once is the thing.
THANOS
Yeah! You know him? Purple guy? Half goth because he's big into death, but half hipster because he makes his own gloves?
THANOS IS A FOOL
Yeah well, me and Tippy totally beat him up.
And it wasn't a robot, clone, or simulacrum either!
HAH HAH
NICE
WHAT A TOOL

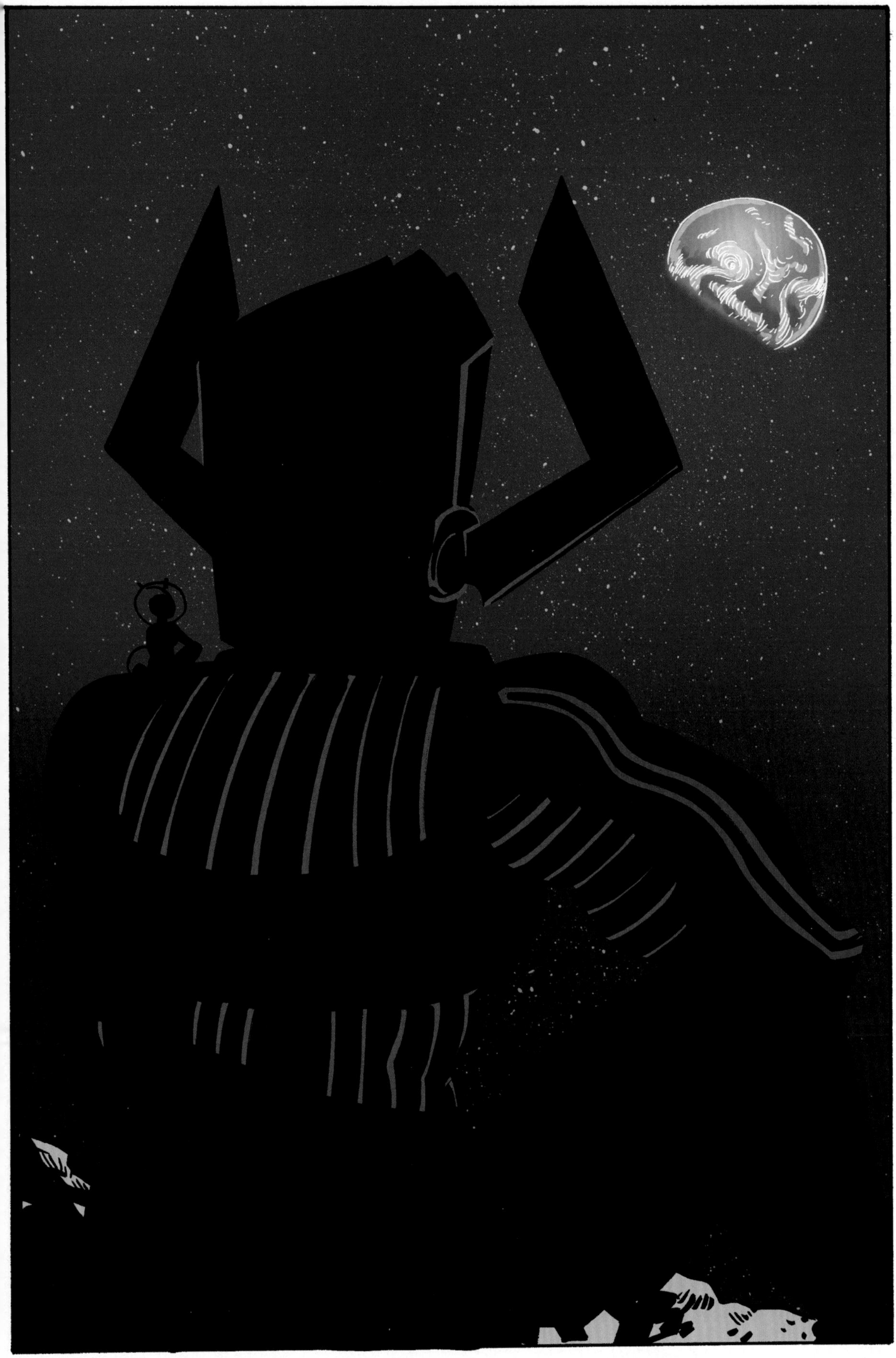

I LIKE YOU, SQUIRREL GIRL. YOU DON'T FEAR ME. IN ALL MY TRAVELS, YOU ARE THE FIRST TO APPROACH ME... AS A PEER

I like you too, Galactus.

Me too!

AND TIPPY-TOE, I FEEL FOR YOU. THOUGH YOUR PLANET IS OVERRUN BY HUMANS, YOU AND YOUR PEOPLE ARE ALONE, UNABLE TO COMMUNICATE WITH THOSE YOU SHARE YOUR PLANET WITH. THIS SOLITUDE, THIS AWFUL, ENDLESS SOLITUDE...

...I KNOW IT WELL. YOU ARE LUCKY TO HAVE SQUIRREL GIRL, AND SHE IS LUCKY TO HAVE YOU

Thank you, Galactus.

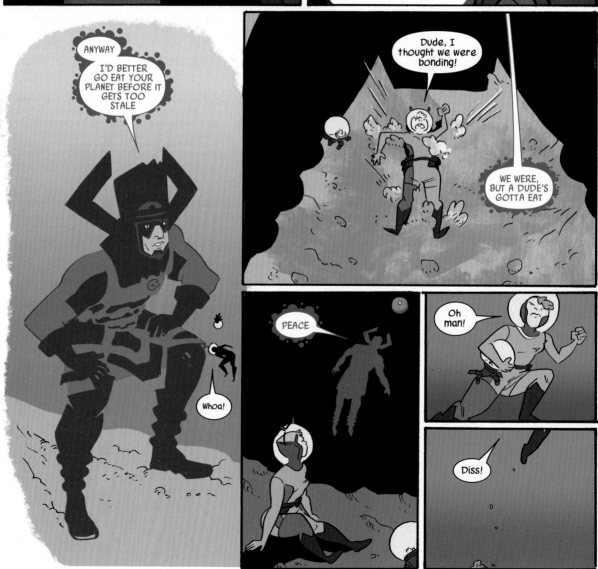

ANYWAY

I'D BETTER GO EAT YOUR PLANET BEFORE IT GETS TOO STALE

Whoa!

Dude, I thought we were bonding!

WE WERE, BUT A DUDE'S GOTTA EAT

PEACE

Oh man!

Diss!

Turns out you *can't* defeat Galactus by just chilling with him on the moon! All right, Tippy, scratch that off the list, and we'll see how well *"Fight him in orbit around the moon"* works out.

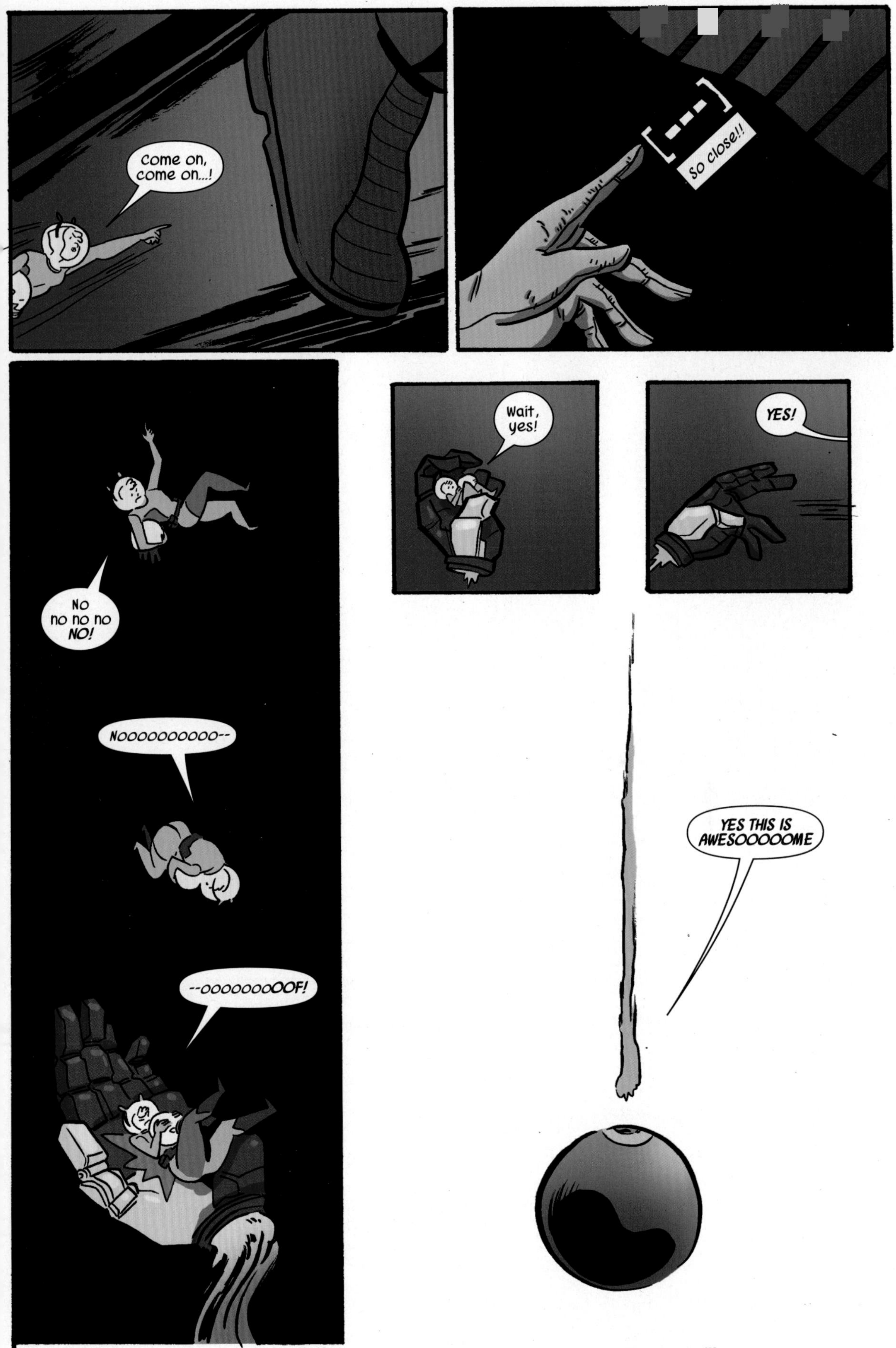
Come on, come on...!
[...]
So close!!
No no no no NO!
NOOOOOOOOOO--
--OOOOOOOOOF!
Wait, yes!
YES!
YES THIS IS AWESOOOOOME

Thanks, Iron Man suit parts! You saved the day. Come on, everyone, let's all give those suit parts...a hand??

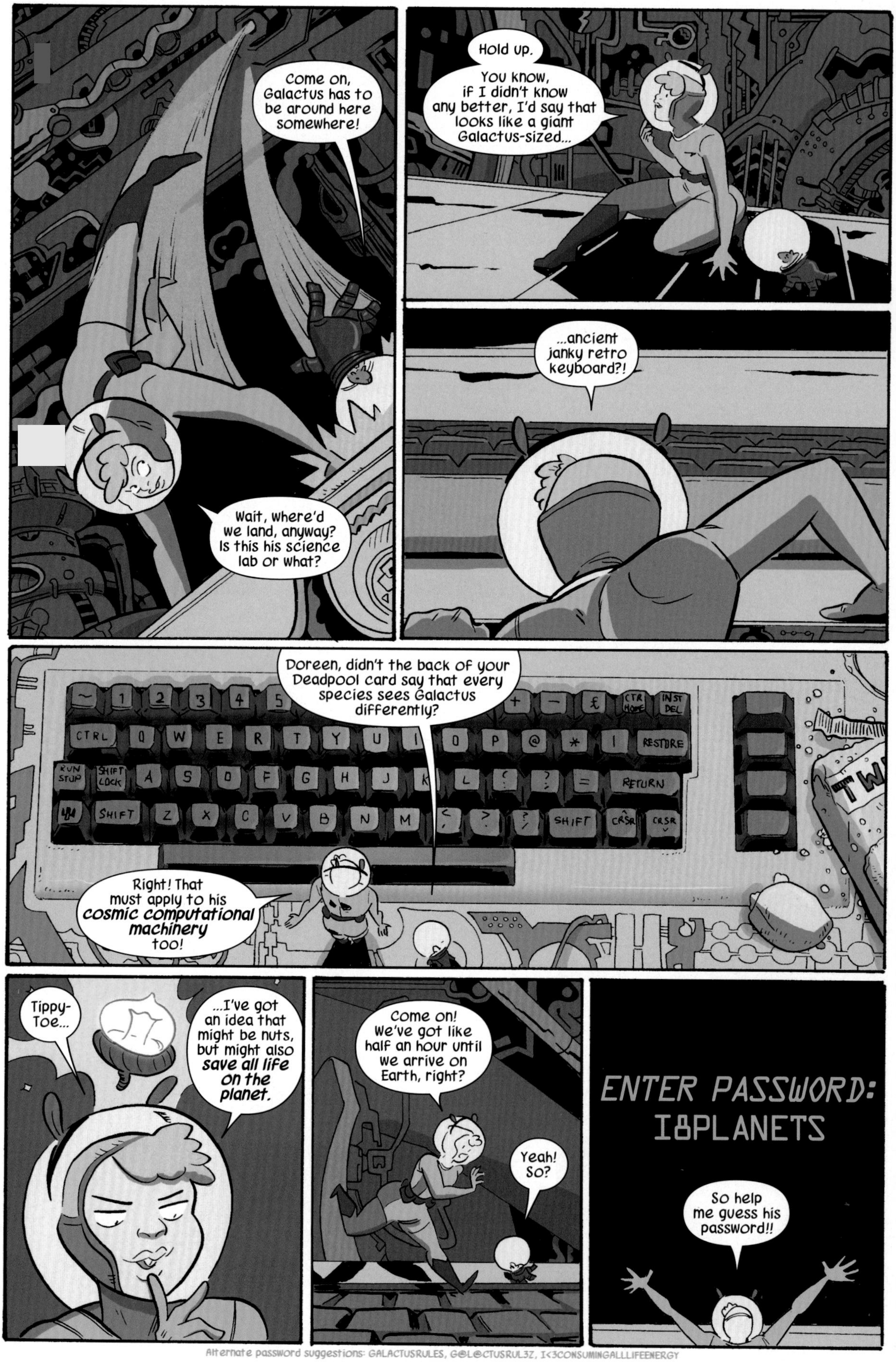

Come on, Galactus has to be around here somewhere!
Wait, where'd we land, anyway? Is this his science lab or what?
Hold up.
You know, if I didn't know any better, I'd say that looks like a giant Galactus-sized...
...ancient janky retro keyboard?!
Doreen, didn't the back of your Deadpool card say that every species sees Galactus differently?
Right! That must apply to his *cosmic computational machinery* too!
Tippy-Toe...
...I've got an idea that might be nuts, but might also *save all life on the planet.*
Come on! We've got like half an hour until we arrive on Earth, right?
Yeah! So?
ENTER PASSWORD:
I8PLANETS
So help me guess his password!!

Alternate password suggestions: GALACTUSRULES, G@L@CTUSRUL3Z, I<3CONSUMINGALLLIFEENERGY

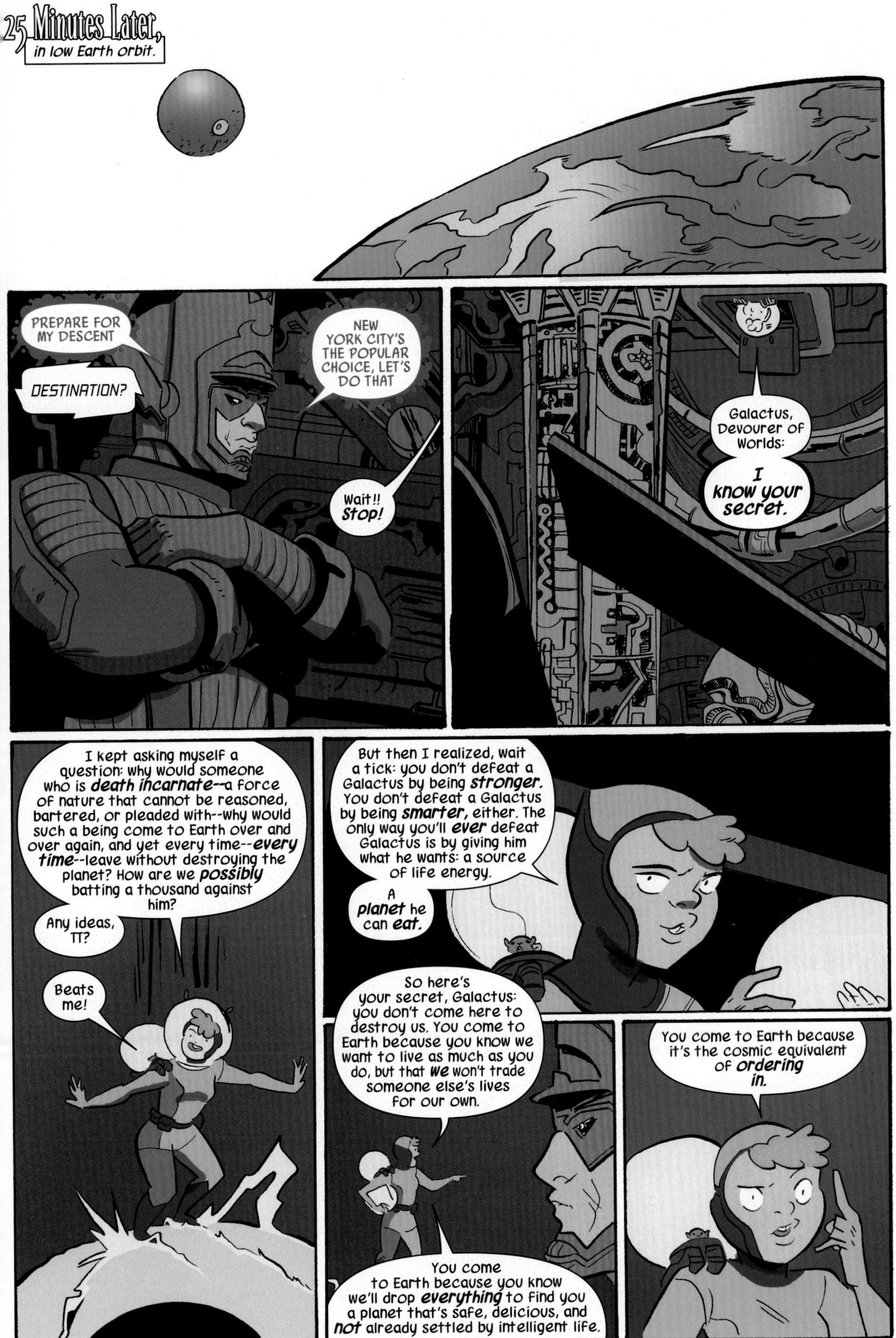
25 Minutes Later,
in low Earth orbit.
PREPARE FOR MY DESCENT
DESTINATION?
NEW YORK CITY'S THE POPULAR CHOICE, LET'S DO THAT
Wait!! Stop!
Galactus, Devourer of Worlds:
I know your secret.
I kept asking myself a question: why would someone who is death incarnate--a force of nature that cannot be reasoned, bartered, or pleaded with--why would such a being come to Earth over and over again, and yet every time--every time--leave without destroying the planet? How are we possibly batting a thousand against him?
Any ideas, TT?
Beats me!
But then I realized, wait a tick: you don't defeat a Galactus by being stronger. You don't defeat a Galactus by being smarter, either. The only way you'll ever defeat Galactus is by giving him what he wants: a source of life energy.
A planet he can eat.
So here's your secret, Galactus: you don't come here to destroy us. You come to Earth because you know we want to live as much as you do, but that we won't trade someone else's lives for our own.
You come to Earth because you know we'll drop everything to find you a planet that's safe, delicious, and not already settled by intelligent life.
You come to Earth because it's the cosmic equivalent of ordering in.

And you *definitely* don't defeat Galactus by having a more audacious fashion sense. Many have tried, all have failed, though honestly many of them looked pretty great while they did so.

SACRILEGE. NOBODY SPEAKS TO GALACTUS THIS WAY. SQUIRREL GIRL, TIPPY-TOE, YOU WILL BOTH BE DESTROYED, WIPED FROM THIS AND ALL OTHER UNIVERSES AND TIMELINES, FOR EVEN CONSIDERING FOR ONE MOMENT THAT--

You could do that, sure. But if you kill us, you won't find the plaaaaaaanet we discovered!

Yeah, we took the liberty of going through your databases, Galactus! And we found one covered--seriously, totally covered-- with nuts!

NUTS

Oh my gosh they're delicious. You've never tried one, right? A lot of god-tier beings haven't. I dunno.

Here. Take a look. Examine it with your cosmic powers.

THIS IS MERELY AN ORGANIC STORAGE UNIT HOLDING A SMALL AMOUNT OF MATTER

Sure! But examine what's inside, Galactus: I think you'll find it's filled with proteins, vitamins, carbohydrates, fats--in other words...

LIFE ENERGY.

Calories.

I mean, yes, life energy.

AND YOU KNOW OF A CELESTIAL BODY SUFFUSED WITH THESE "NUTS"

Found a whole planet of them, buddy. Spare the Earth, and I'll take you to it. There's nobody living there, just continents and continents covered in nuts and trees and more nuts. You'll be able to feed without guilt.

It's seriously the greatest!!

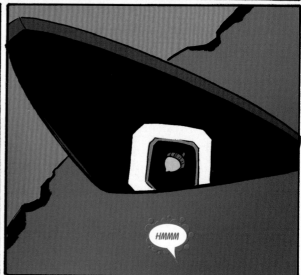

HMMM

Galactus, I don't know what your computers actually look like, but that retro computer interface had ultra-primitive terrible security. Do I thank you, or thank my imagination, or...?

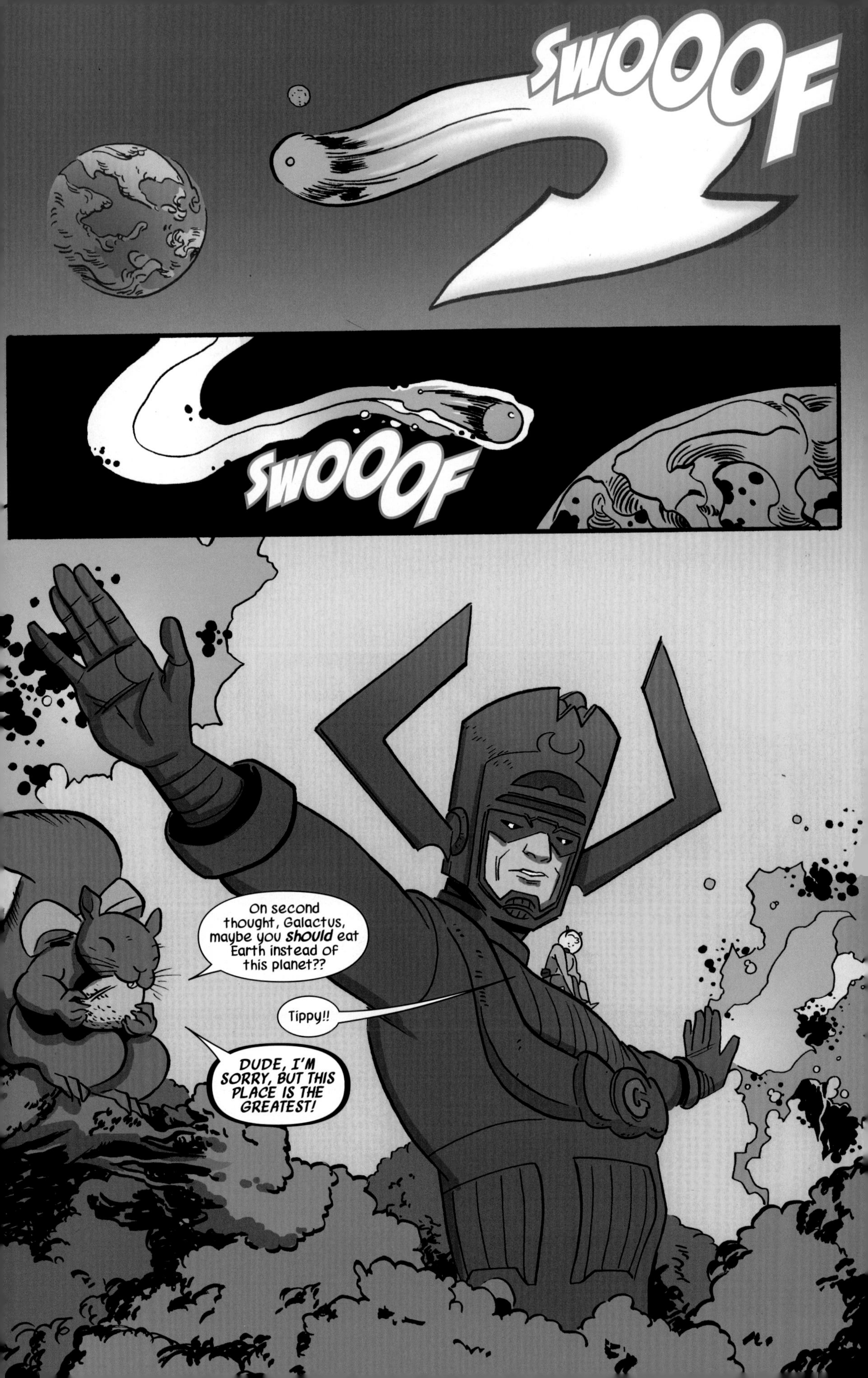
SWOOOF
SWOOOF
On second thought, Galactus, maybe you *should* eat Earth instead of this planet??
Tippy!!
DUDE, I'M SORRY, BUT THIS PLACE IS THE GREATEST!

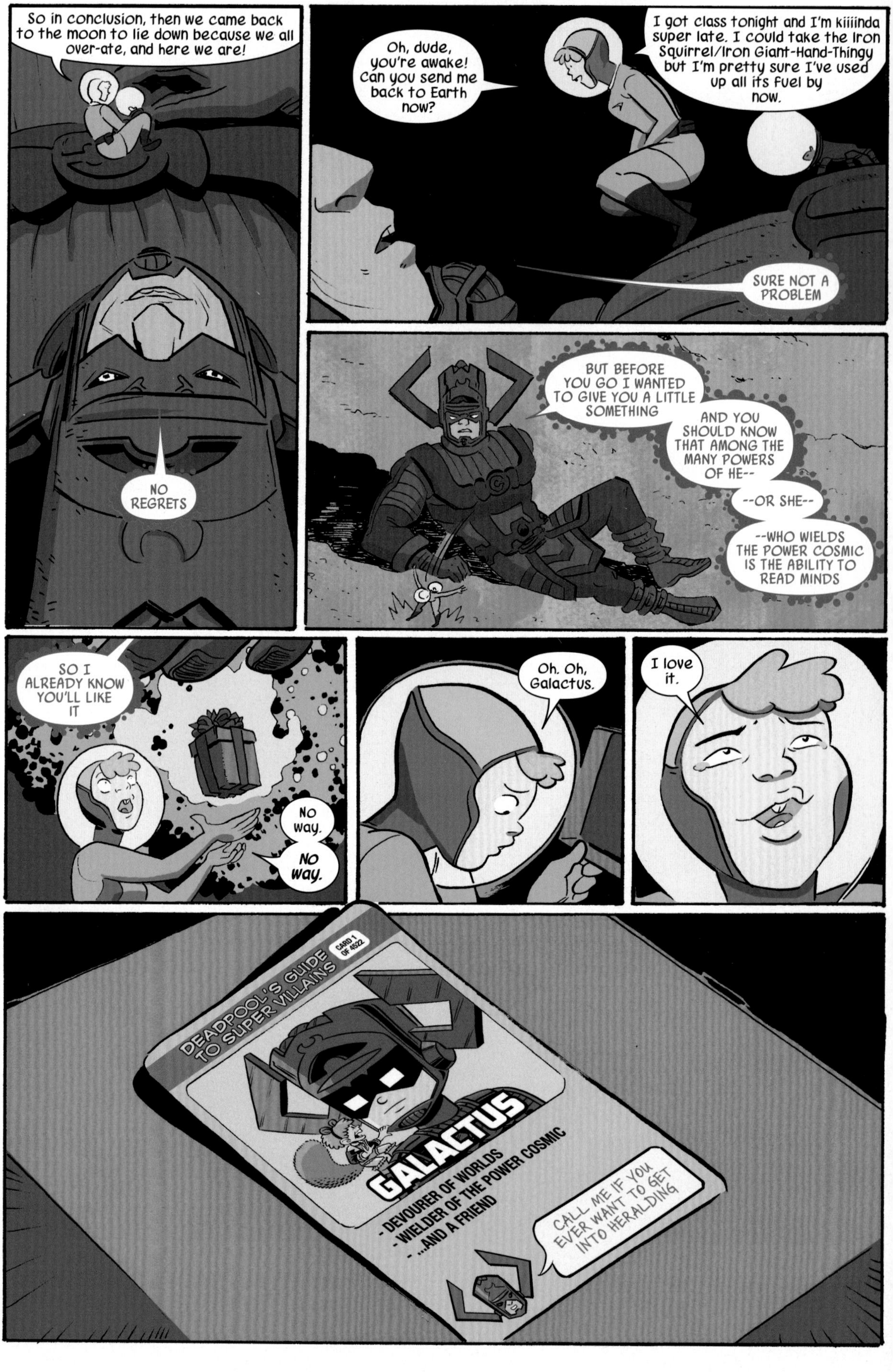

So in conclusion, then we came back to the moon to lie down because we all over-ate, and here we are!
NO REGRETS
Oh, dude, you're awake! Can you send me back to Earth now?
I got class tonight and I'm kiiiinda super late. I could take the Iron Squirrel/Iron Giant-Hand-Thingy but I'm pretty sure I've used up all its fuel by now.
SURE NOT A PROBLEM
BUT BEFORE YOU GO I WANTED TO GIVE YOU A LITTLE SOMETHING
AND YOU SHOULD KNOW THAT AMONG THE MANY POWERS OF HE--
--OR SHE--
--WHO WIELDS THE POWER COSMIC IS THE ABILITY TO READ MINDS
SO I ALREADY KNOW YOU'LL LIKE IT
No way.
No way.
Oh. Oh, Galactus.
I love it.
DEADPOOL'S GUIDE TO SUPER VILLAINS
CARD 1 OF 4522
GALACTUS
- DEVOURER OF WORLDS
- WIELDER OF THE POWER COSMIC
- ...AND A FRIEND
CALL ME IF YOU EVER WANT TO GET INTO HERALDING

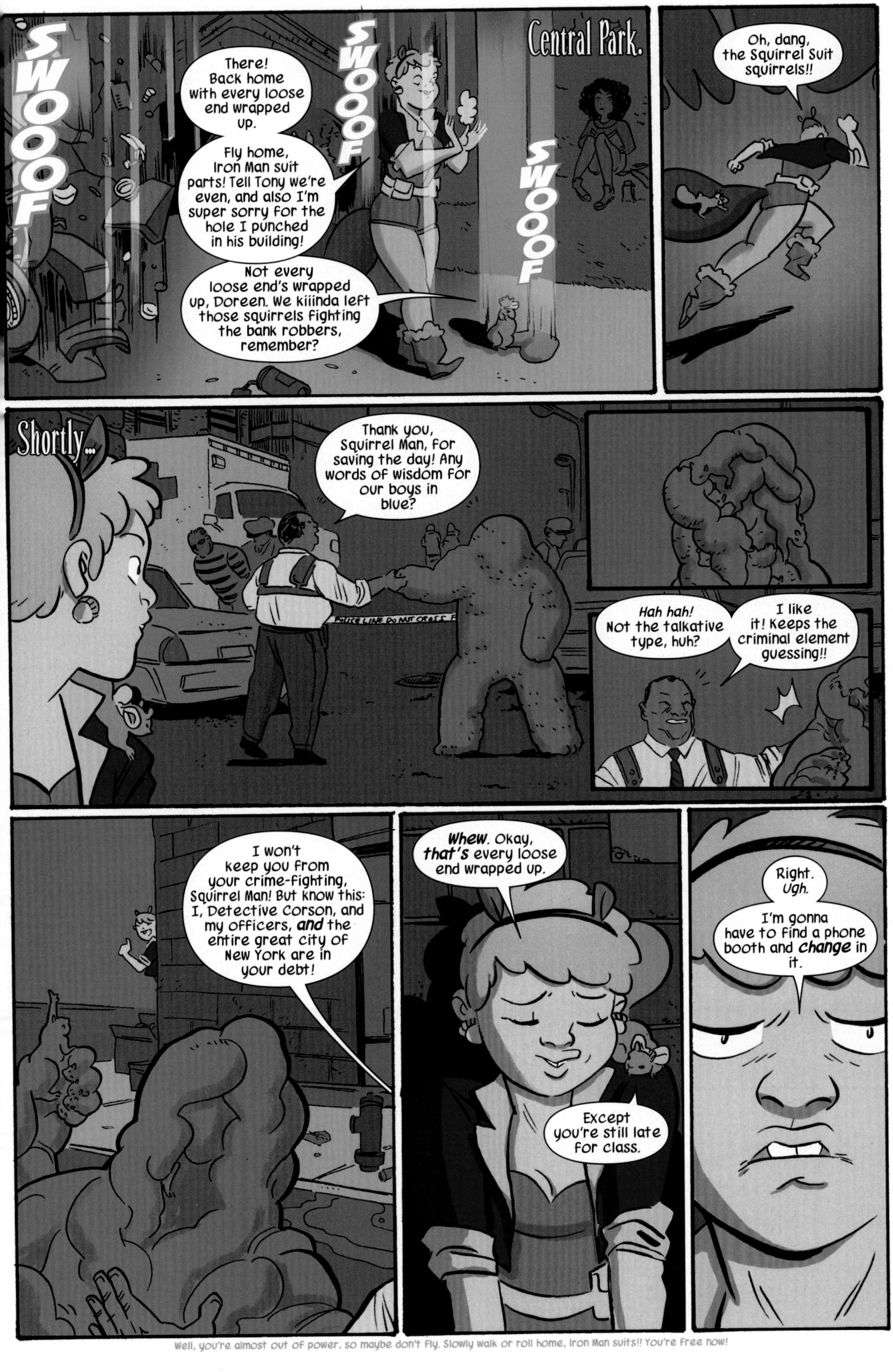
SWOOOF
SWOOOF
Central Park.
There! Back home with every loose end wrapped up.
Fly home, Iron Man suit parts! Tell Tony we're even, and also I'm super sorry for the hole I punched in his building!
SWOOOF
Not every loose end's wrapped up, Doreen. We kiiinda left those squirrels fighting the bank robbers, remember?
Oh, dang, the Squirrel Suit squirrels!!
Shortly...
Thank you, Squirrel Man, for saving the day! Any words of wisdom for our boys in blue?
Hah hah! Not the talkative type, huh?
I like it! Keeps the criminal element guessing!!
I won't keep you from your crime-fighting, Squirrel Man! But know this: I, Detective Corson, and my officers, and the entire great city of New York are in your debt!
Whew. Okay, that's every loose end wrapped up.
Except you're still late for class.
Right. Ugh.
I'm gonna have to find a phone booth and change in it.

Well, you're almost out of power, so maybe don't fly. Slowly walk or roll home, Iron Man suits!! You're free now!

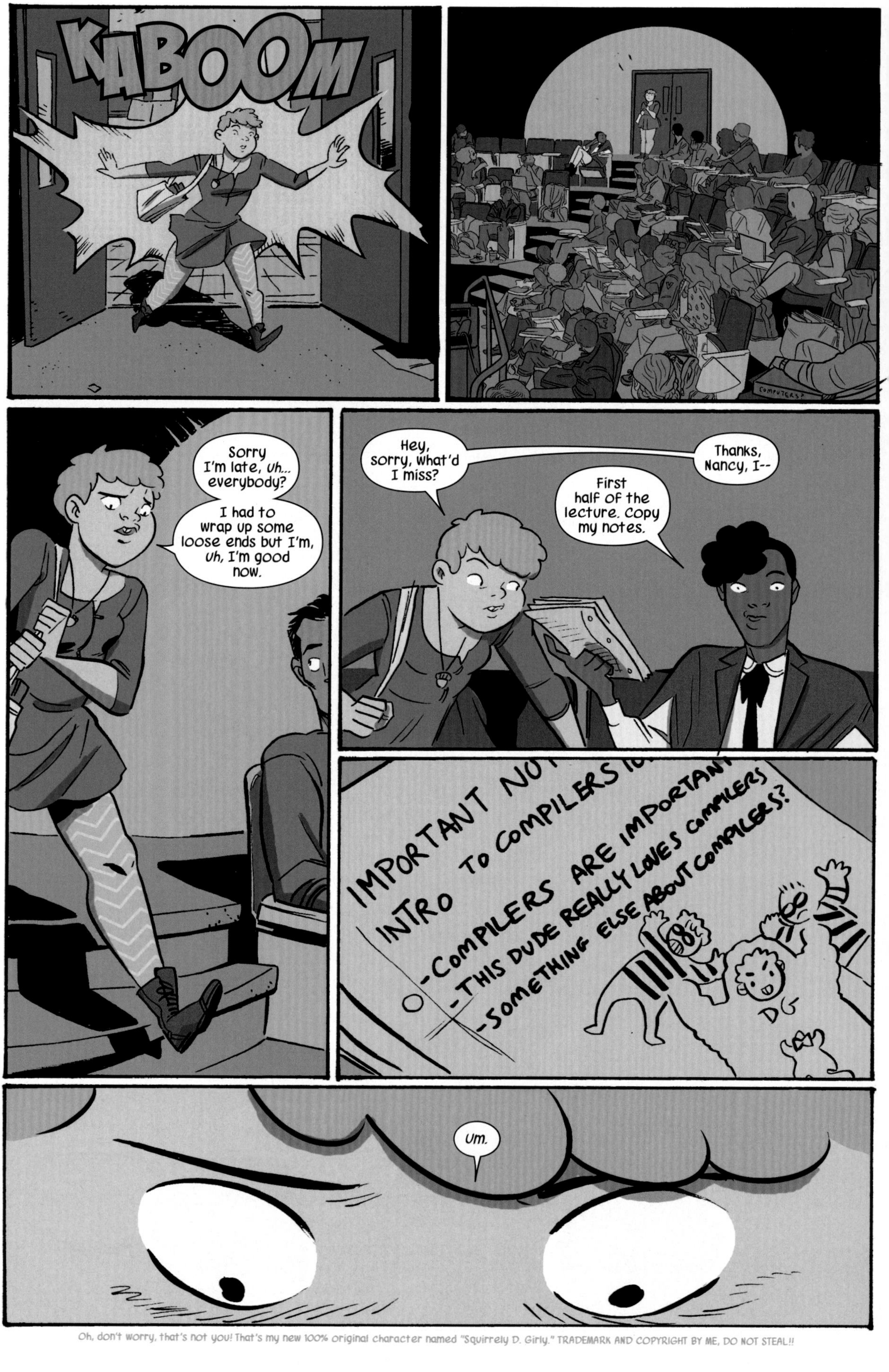
KABOOM
COMPUTERS?
Sorry I'm late, uh... everybody?
I had to wrap up some loose ends but I'm, uh, I'm good now.
Hey, sorry, what'd I miss?
First half of the lecture. Copy my notes.
Thanks, Nancy, I--
IMPORTANT NOT
INTRO TO COMPILERS
-COMPILERS ARE IMPORTANT
-THIS DUDE REALLY LOVES COMPILERS
-SOMETHING ELSE ABOUT COMPILERS?
DG
Um.

Oh, don't worry, that's not you! That's my new 100% original character named "Squirrely D. Girly." TRADEMARK AND COPYRIGHT BY ME, DO NOT STEAL!!

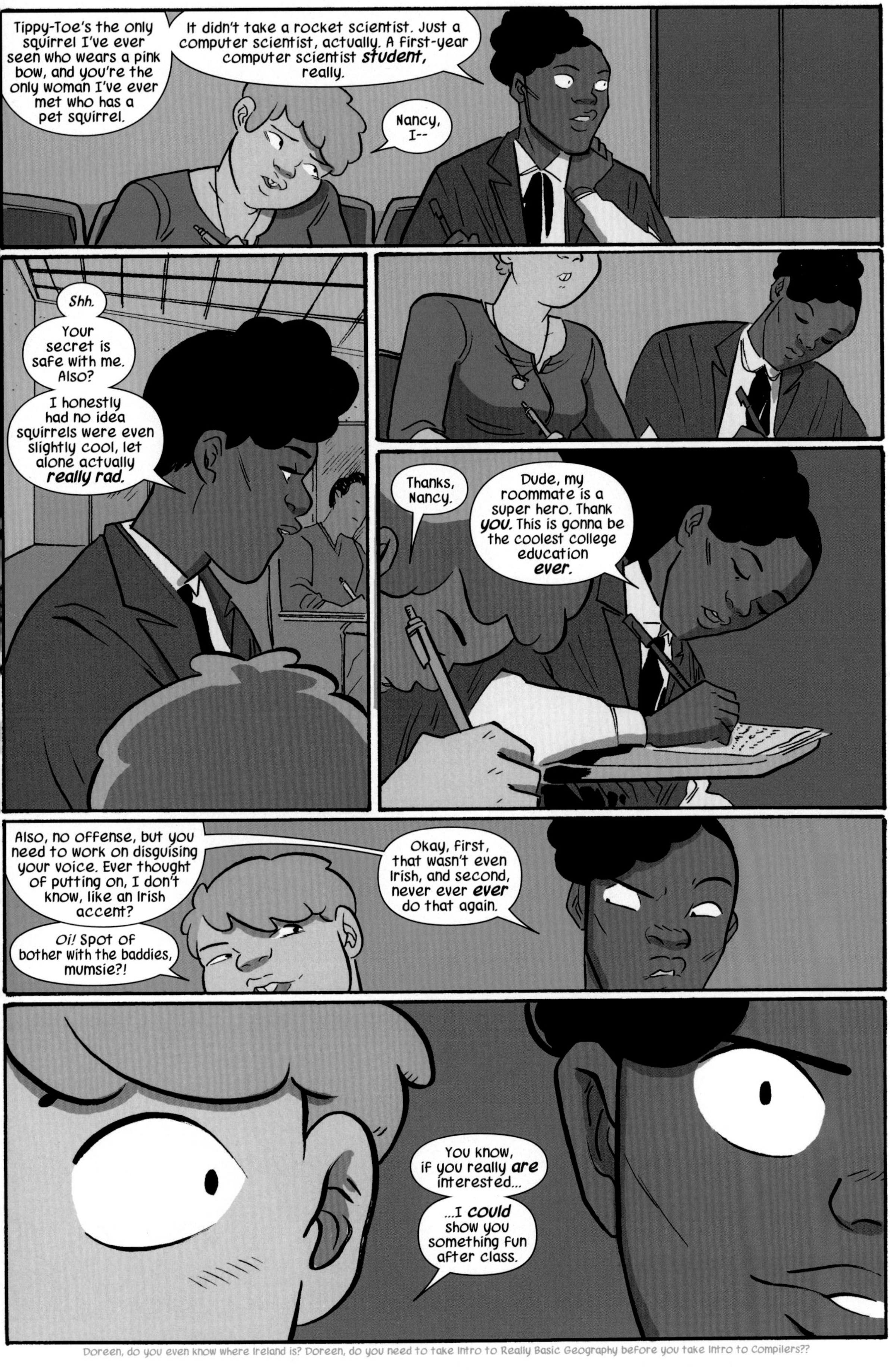
Tippy-Toe's the only squirrel I've ever seen who wears a pink bow, and you're the only woman I've ever met who has a pet squirrel.
It didn't take a rocket scientist. Just a computer scientist, actually. A first-year computer scientist *student,* really.
Nancy, I--
Shh.
Your secret is safe with me. Also?
I honestly had no idea squirrels were even slightly cool, let alone actually ***really rad.***
Thanks, Nancy.
Dude, my roommate is a super hero. Thank ***you.*** This is gonna be the coolest college education ***ever.***
Also, no offense, but you need to work on disguising your voice. Ever thought of putting on, I don't know, like an Irish accent?
Oi! Spot of bother with the baddies, mumsie?!
Okay, first, that wasn't even Irish, and second, never ever ***ever*** do that again.
You know, if you really ***are*** interested...
...I ***could*** show you something fun after class.

Doreen, do you even know where Ireland is? Doreen, do you need to take Intro to Really Basic Geography before you take Intro to Compilers??

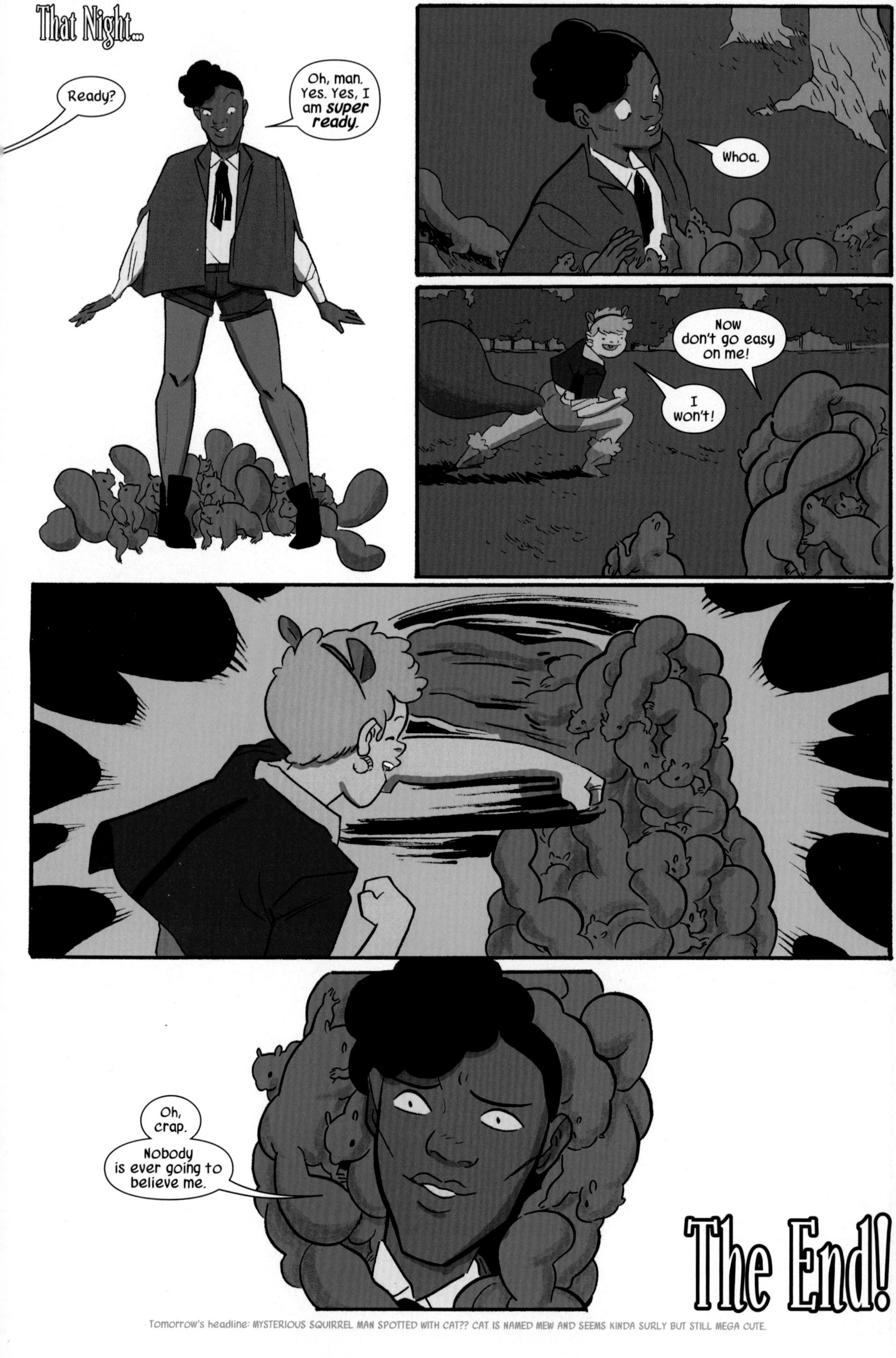
That Night...
Ready?
Oh, man. Yes. Yes, I am super ready.
Whoa.
Now don't go easy on me!
I won't!
Oh, crap.
Nobody is ever going to believe me.
The End!

Tomorrow's headline: MYSTERIOUS SQUIRREL MAN SPOTTED WITH CAT?? CAT IS NAMED MEW AND SEEMS KINDA SURLY BUT STILL MEGA CUTE.

the unbeatable Squirrel Girl #4!

Written by
Ryan North

Art by
Erica Henderson

Trading Card Art by
Chris Giarrusso

Color Art by
Rico Renzi

Lettering and Production by
VC's Clayton Cowles

Cover Artist	Erica Henderson
Special Thanks to	Cassie Hart Kelly
Assistant Editor	Jon Moisan
Editor	Wil Moss
Executive Editor	Tom Brevoort
Editor in Chief	Axel Alonso
Chief Creative Officer	Joe Quesada
Publisher	Dan Buckley
Executive Producer	Alan Fine

Squirrel Girl will return in... Squirrel Girl #5, duh.

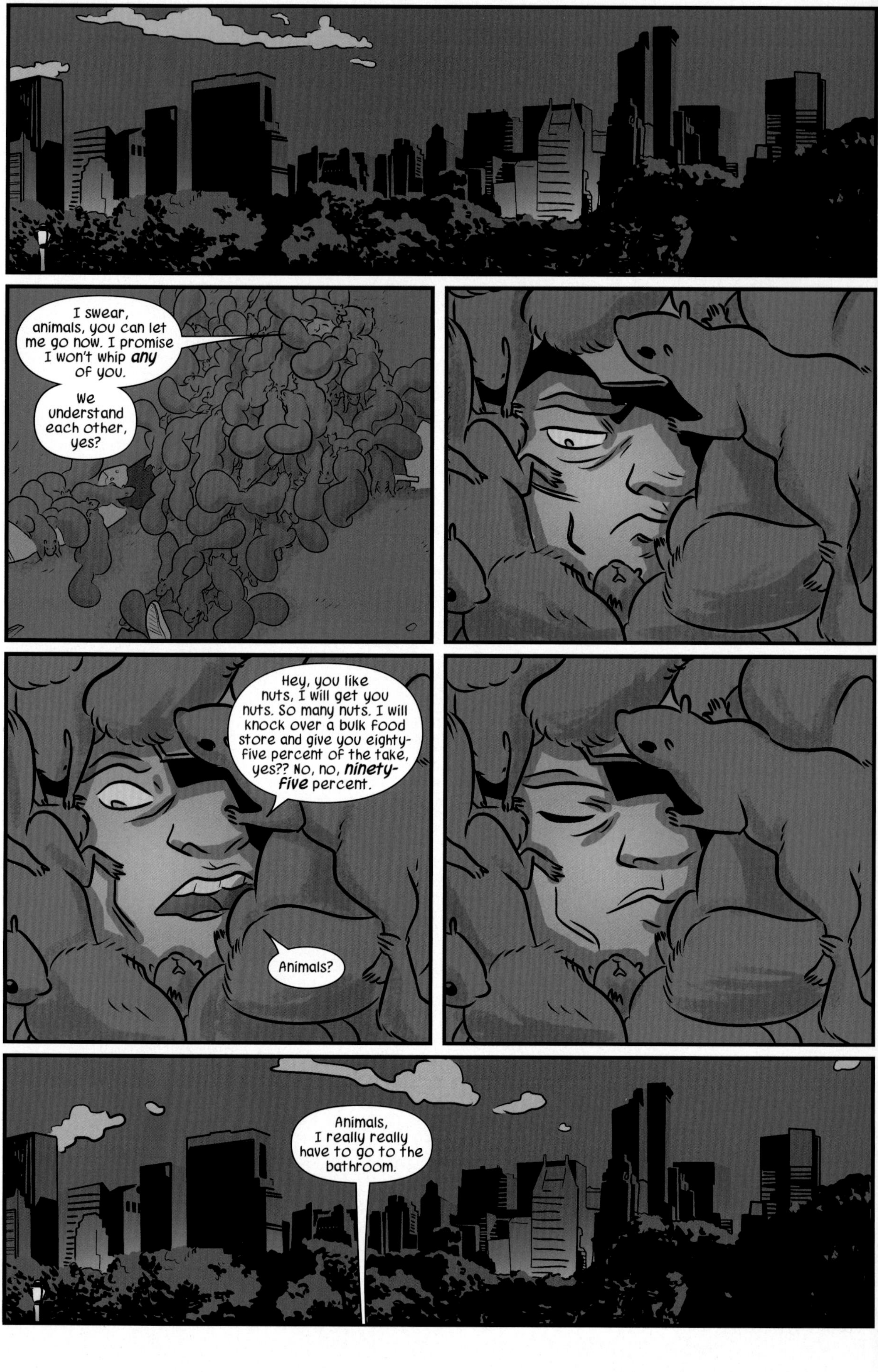
I swear, animals, you can let me go now. I promise I won't whip *any* of you.
We understand each other, yes?
Hey, you like nuts, I will get you nuts. So many nuts. I will knock over a bulk food store and give you eighty-five percent of the take, yes?? No, no, *ninety-five* percent.
Animals?
Animals, I really really have to go to the bathroom.

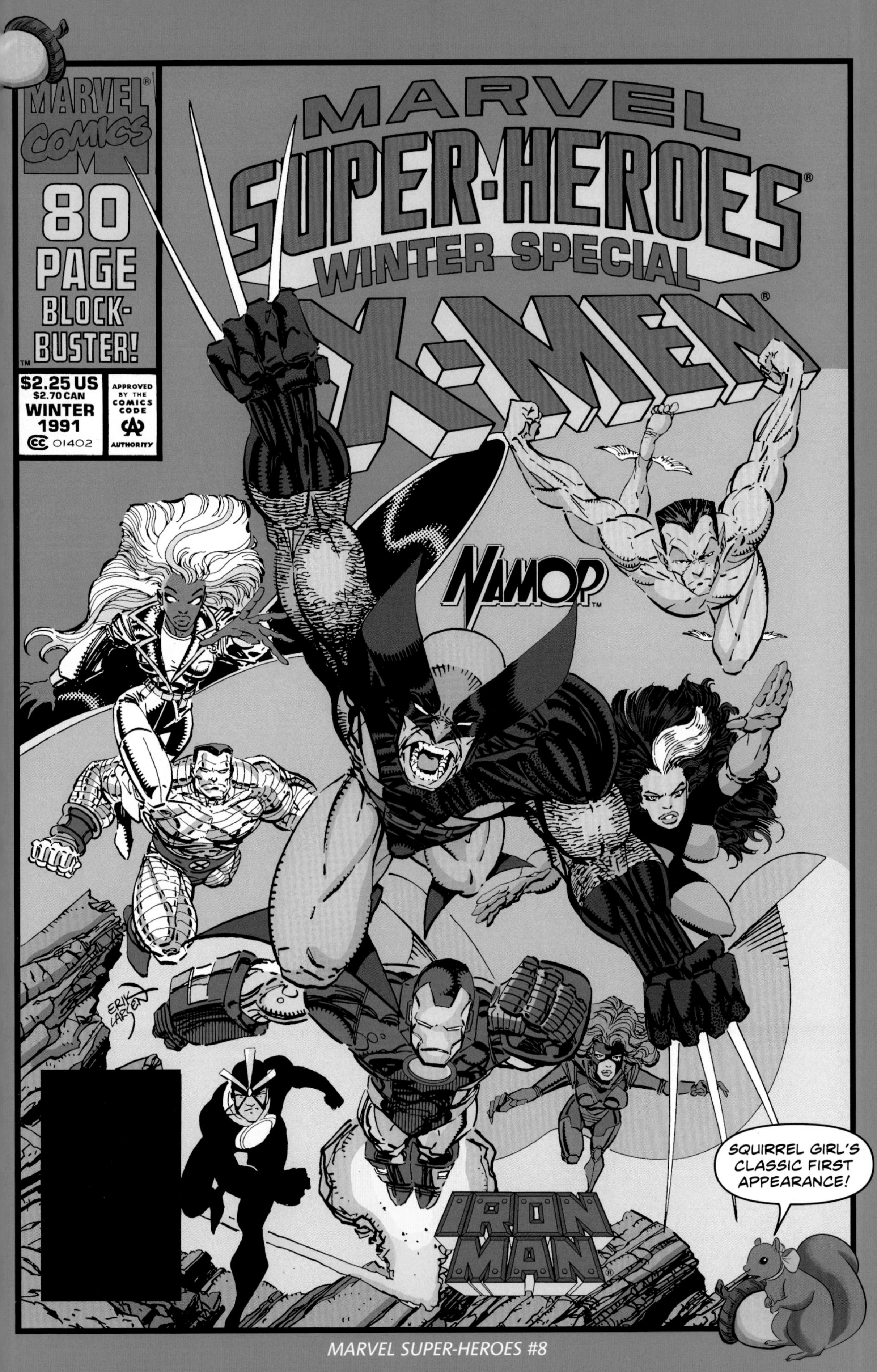

MARVEL SUPER-HEROES #8

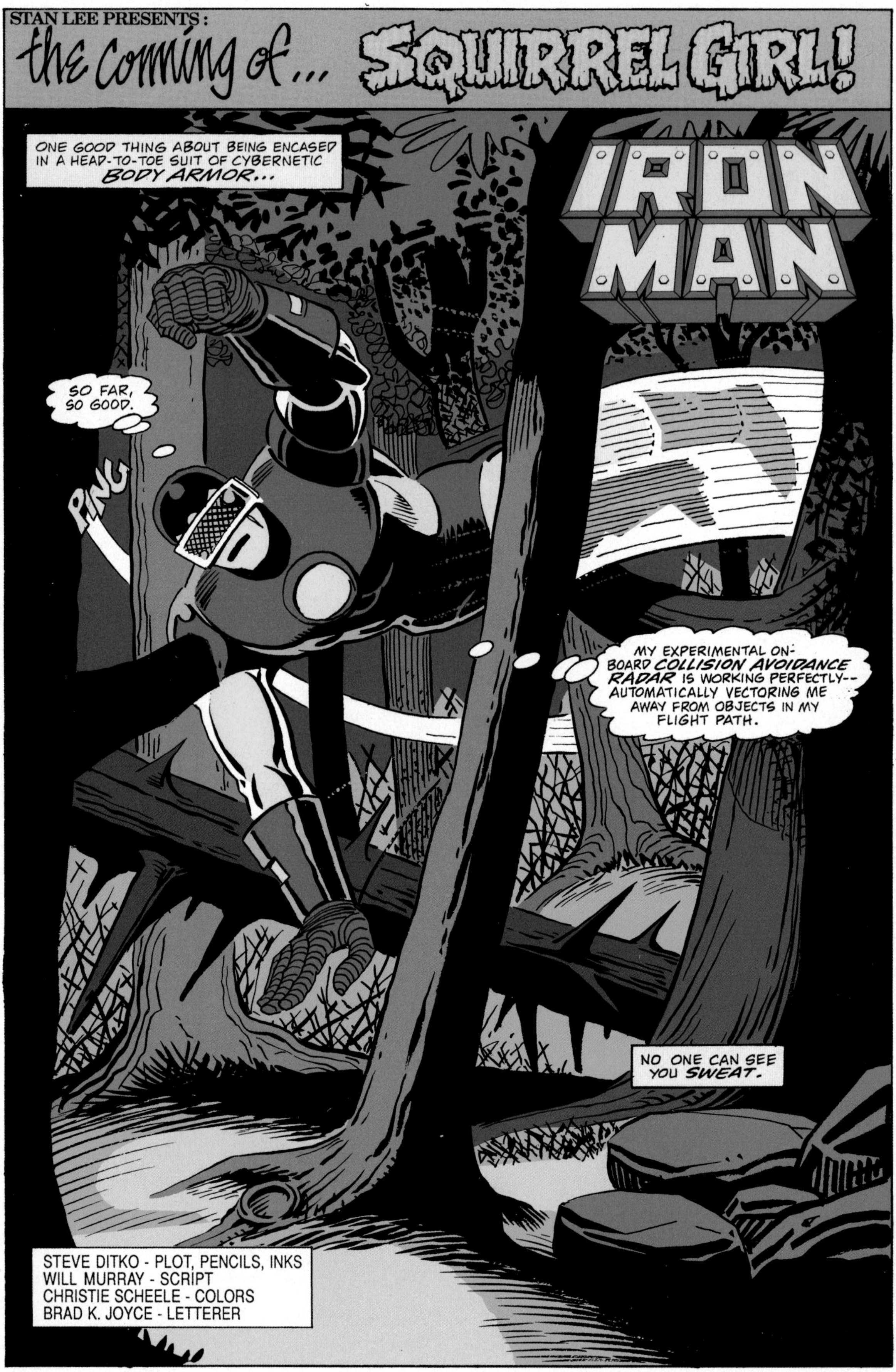
STAN LEE PRESENTS:
the coming of... SQUIRREL GIRL!
ONE GOOD THING ABOUT BEING ENCASED IN A HEAD-TO-TOE SUIT OF CYBERNETIC BODY ARMOR...
IRON MAN
SO FAR, SO GOOD.
PING
MY EXPERIMENTAL ON-BOARD COLLISION AVOIDANCE RADAR IS WORKING PERFECTLY-- AUTOMATICALLY VECTORING ME AWAY FROM OBJECTS IN MY FLIGHT PATH.
NO ONE CAN SEE YOU SWEAT.
STEVE DITKO - PLOT, PENCILS, INKS
WILL MURRAY - SCRIPT
CHRISTIE SCHEELE - COLORS
BRAD K. JOYCE - LETTERER

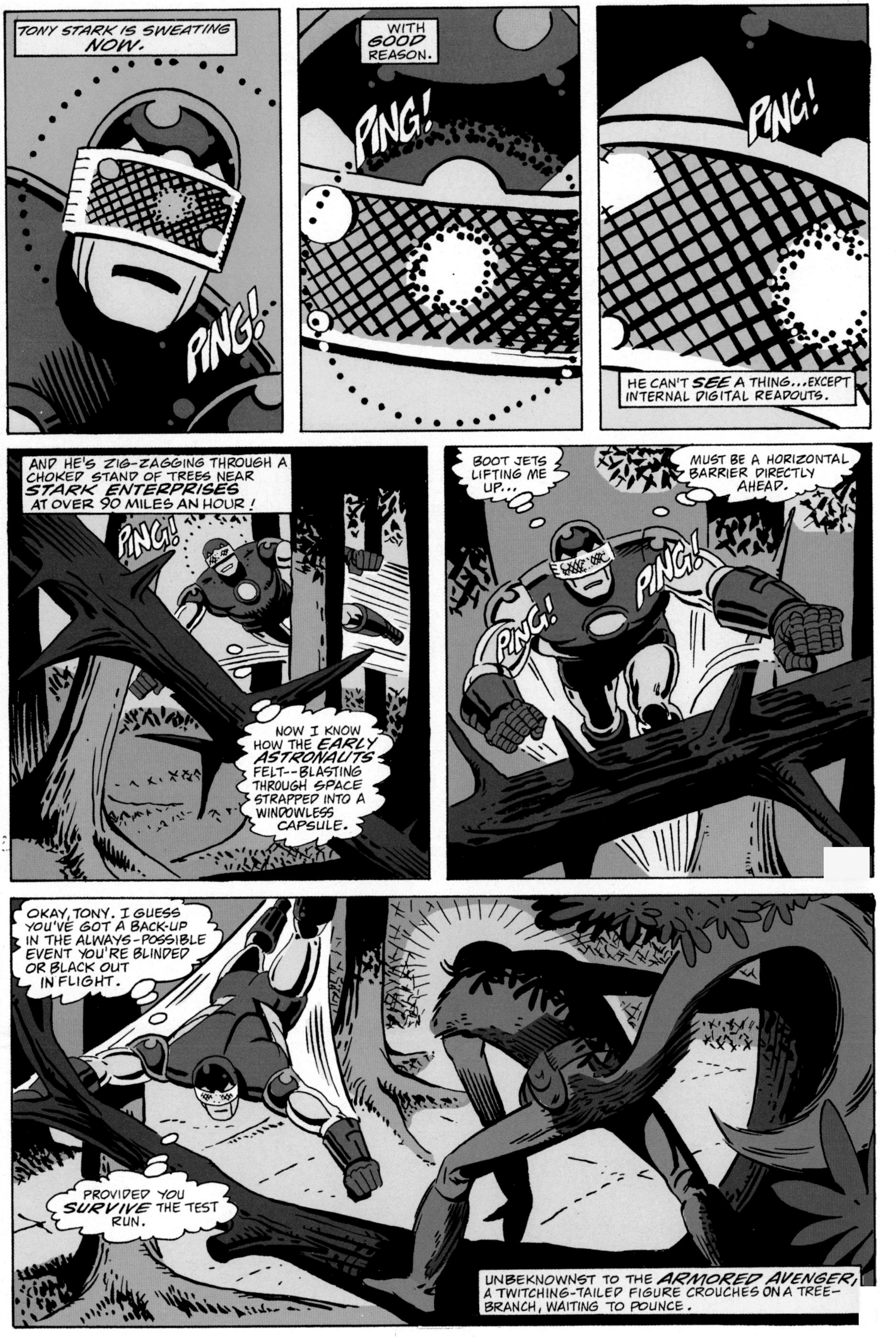

TONY STARK IS SWEATING NOW.
PING!
WITH GOOD REASON.
PING!
PING!
HE CAN'T SEE A THING... EXCEPT INTERNAL DIGITAL READOUTS.
AND HE'S ZIG-ZAGGING THROUGH A CHOKED STAND OF TREES NEAR STARK ENTERPRISES AT OVER 90 MILES AN HOUR!
PING!
NOW I KNOW HOW THE EARLY ASTRONAUTS FELT--BLASTING THROUGH SPACE STRAPPED INTO A WINDOWLESS CAPSULE.
BOOT JETS LIFTING ME UP...
MUST BE A HORIZONTAL BARRIER DIRECTLY AHEAD.
PING!
PING!
OKAY, TONY. I GUESS YOU'VE GOT A BACK-UP IN THE ALWAYS-POSSIBLE EVENT YOU'RE BLINDED OR BLACK OUT IN FLIGHT.
PROVIDED YOU SURVIVE THE TEST RUN.
UNBEKNOWNST TO THE ARMORED AVENGER, A TWITCHING-TAILED FIGURE CROUCHES ON A TREE-BRANCH, WAITING TO POUNCE.

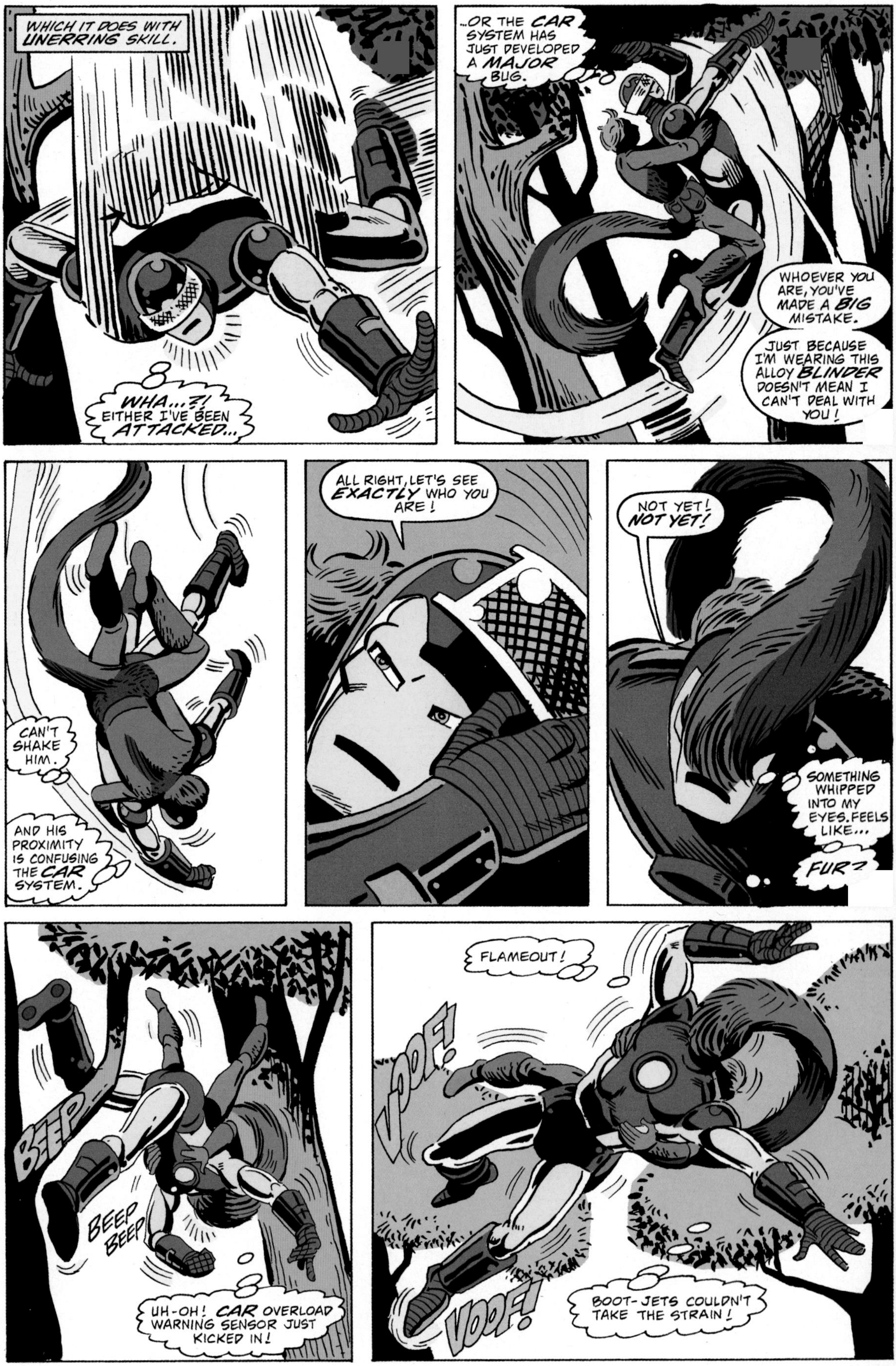
WHICH IT DOES WITH UNERRING SKILL.
WHA...?! EITHER I'VE BEEN ATTACKED...
...OR THE CAR SYSTEM HAS JUST DEVELOPED A MAJOR BUG.
WHOEVER YOU ARE, YOU'VE MADE A BIG MISTAKE.
JUST BECAUSE I'M WEARING THIS ALLOY BLINDER DOESN'T MEAN I CAN'T DEAL WITH YOU!
CAN'T SHAKE HIM.
AND HIS PROXIMITY IS CONFUSING THE CAR SYSTEM.
ALL RIGHT, LET'S SEE EXACTLY WHO YOU ARE!
NOT YET! NOT YET!
SOMETHING WHIPPED INTO MY EYES. FEELS LIKE...
FUR?
BEEP
BEEP BEEP
UH-OH! CAR OVERLOAD WARNING SENSOR JUST KICKED IN!
FLAMEOUT!
VOOF!
VOOF!
BOOT-JETS COULDN'T TAKE THE STRAIN!

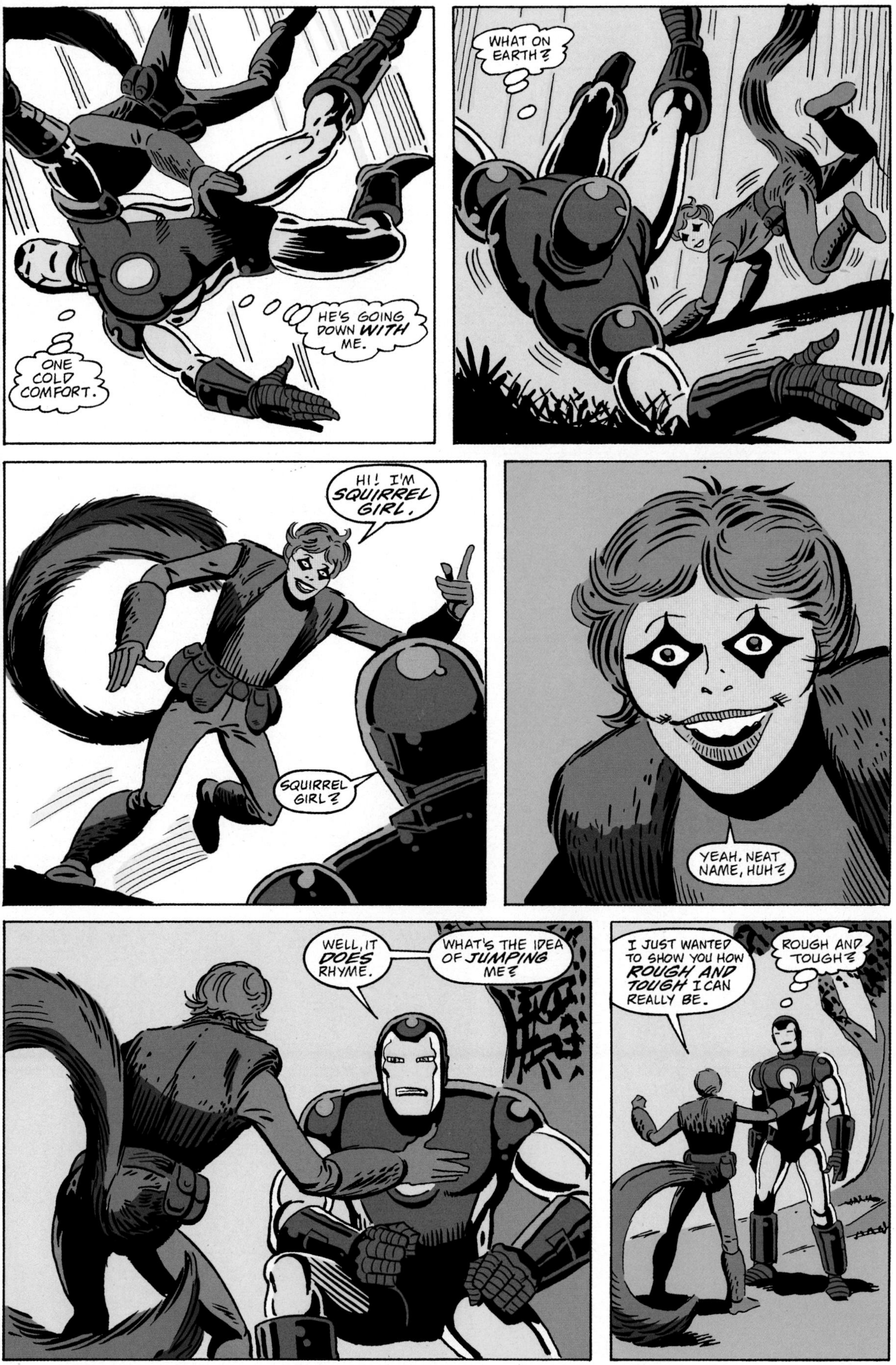
ONE COLD COMFORT.
HE'S GOING DOWN WITH ME.
WHAT ON EARTH?
HI! I'M SQUIRREL GIRL.
SQUIRREL GIRL?
YEAH. NEAT NAME, HUH?
WHAT'S THE IDEA OF JUMPING ME?
WELL, IT DOES RHYME.
I JUST WANTED TO SHOW YOU HOW ROUGH AND TOUGH I CAN REALLY BE.
ROUGH AND TOUGH?

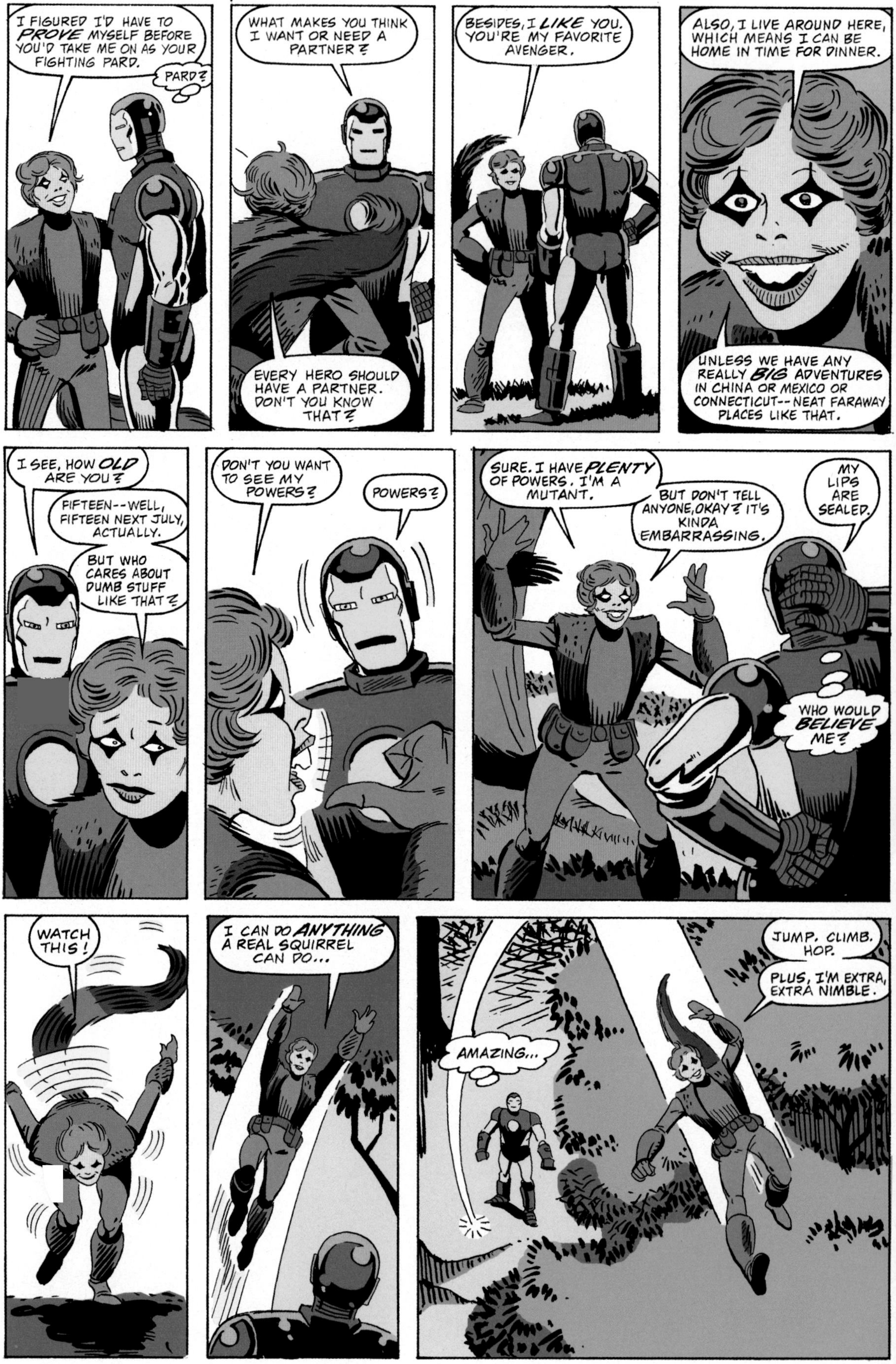
I FIGURED I'D HAVE TO PROVE MYSELF BEFORE YOU'D TAKE ME ON AS YOUR FIGHTING PARD.
PARD?
WHAT MAKES YOU THINK I WANT OR NEED A PARTNER?
EVERY HERO SHOULD HAVE A PARTNER. DON'T YOU KNOW THAT?
BESIDES, I LIKE YOU. YOU'RE MY FAVORITE AVENGER.
ALSO, I LIVE AROUND HERE, WHICH MEANS I CAN BE HOME IN TIME FOR DINNER.
UNLESS WE HAVE ANY REALLY BIG ADVENTURES IN CHINA OR MEXICO OR CONNECTICUT--NEAT FARAWAY PLACES LIKE THAT.
I SEE. HOW OLD ARE YOU?
FIFTEEN--WELL, FIFTEEN NEXT JULY, ACTUALLY.
BUT WHO CARES ABOUT DUMB STUFF LIKE THAT?
DON'T YOU WANT TO SEE MY POWERS?
POWERS?
SURE. I HAVE PLENTY OF POWERS. I'M A MUTANT.
BUT DON'T TELL ANYONE, OKAY? IT'S KINDA EMBARRASSING.
MY LIPS ARE SEALED.
WHO WOULD BELIEVE ME?
WATCH THIS!
I CAN DO ANYTHING A REAL SQUIRREL CAN DO...
AMAZING...
JUMP. CLIMB. HOP.
PLUS, I'M EXTRA, EXTRA NIMBLE.

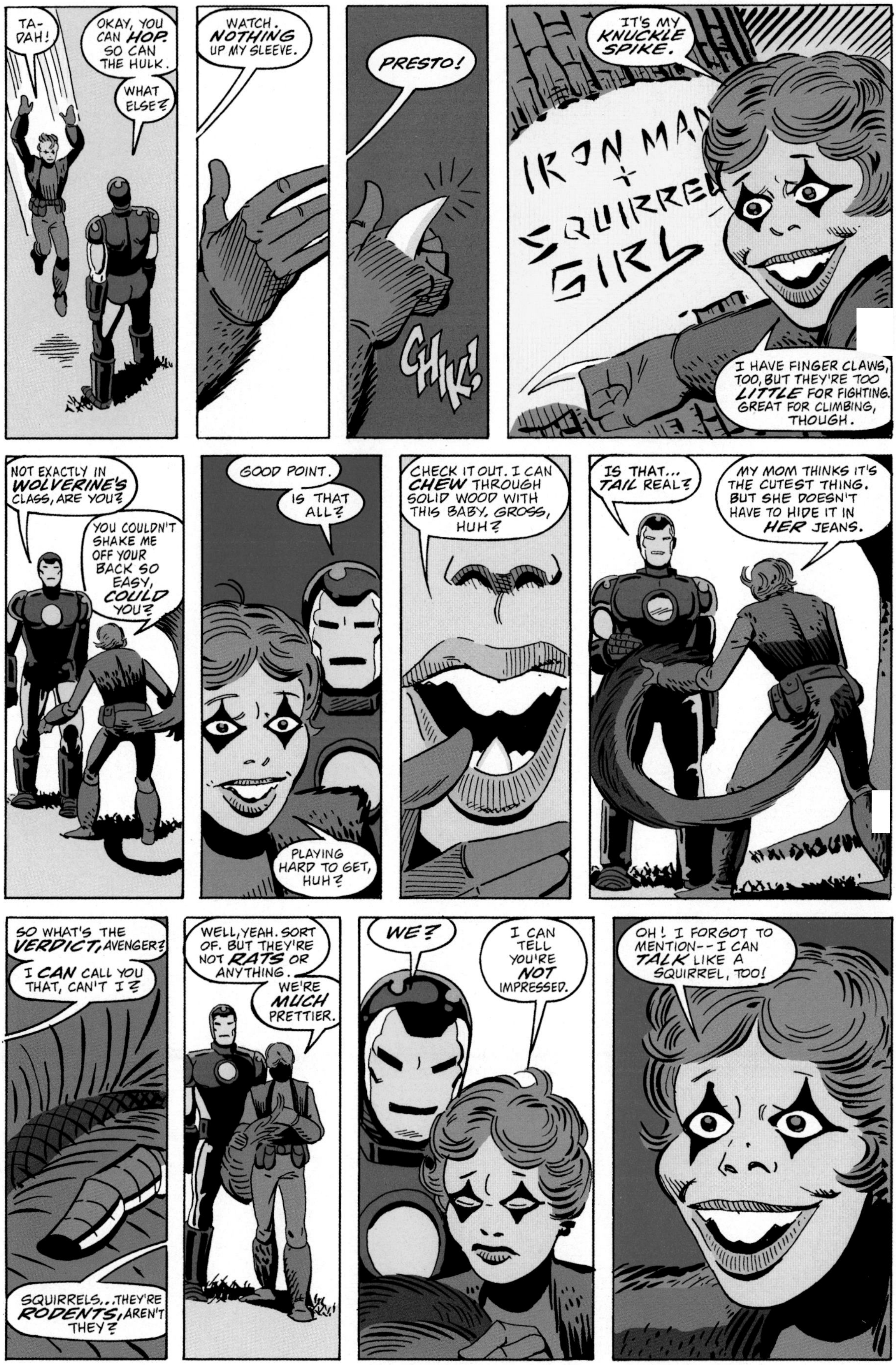
TA-DAH!
OKAY, YOU CAN HOP. SO CAN THE HULK.
WHAT ELSE?
WATCH. NOTHING UP MY SLEEVE.
PRESTO!
CHIK!
IT'S MY KNUCKLE SPIKE.
IRON MAN + SQUIRREL GIRL
I HAVE FINGER CLAWS, TOO, BUT THEY'RE TOO LITTLE FOR FIGHTING. GREAT FOR CLIMBING, THOUGH.
NOT EXACTLY IN WOLVERINE'S CLASS, ARE YOU?
YOU COULDN'T SHAKE ME OFF YOUR BACK SO EASY, COULD YOU?
GOOD POINT.
IS THAT ALL?
PLAYING HARD TO GET, HUH?
CHECK IT OUT. I CAN CHEW THROUGH SOLID WOOD WITH THIS BABY. GROSS, HUH?
IS THAT... TAIL REAL?
MY MOM THINKS IT'S THE CUTEST THING. BUT SHE DOESN'T HAVE TO HIDE IT IN HER JEANS.
SO WHAT'S THE VERDICT, AVENGER?
I CAN CALL YOU THAT, CAN'T I?
SQUIRRELS... THEY'RE RODENTS, AREN'T THEY?
WELL, YEAH. SORT OF. BUT THEY'RE NOT RATS OR ANYTHING.
WE'RE MUCH PRETTIER.
WE?
I CAN TELL YOU'RE NOT IMPRESSED.
OH! I FORGOT TO MENTION-- I CAN TALK LIKE A SQUIRREL, TOO!

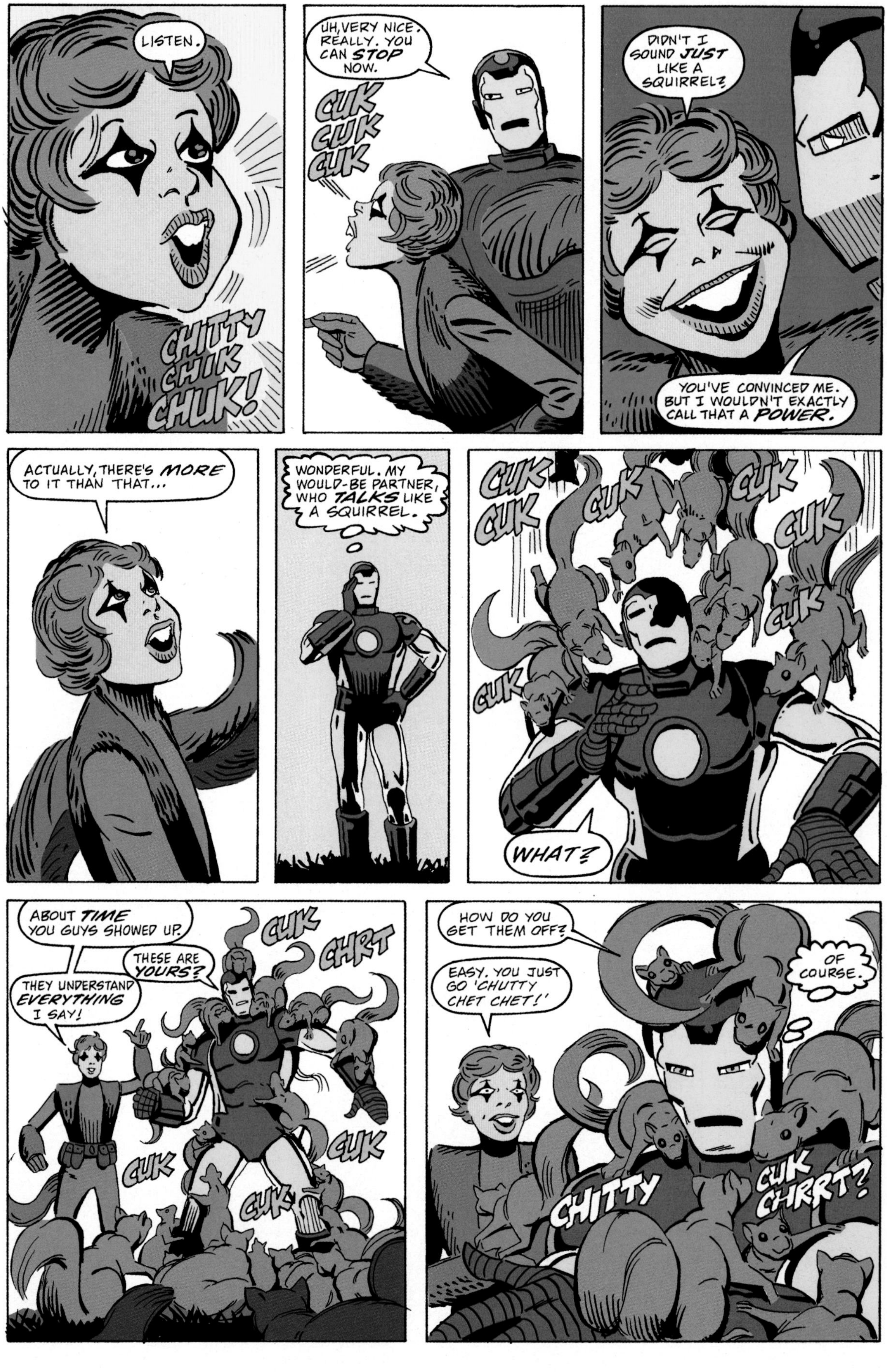
LISTEN.
CHITTY CHIK CHUK!
UH, VERY NICE. REALLY. YOU CAN STOP NOW.
CUK CUK CUK
DIDN'T I SOUND JUST LIKE A SQUIRREL?
YOU'VE CONVINCED ME. BUT I WOULDN'T EXACTLY CALL THAT A POWER.
ACTUALLY, THERE'S MORE TO IT THAN THAT...
WONDERFUL. MY WOULD-BE PARTNER, WHO TALKS LIKE A SQUIRREL.
CUK CUK
CUK
CUK
CUK
CUK
CUK
WHAT?
ABOUT TIME YOU GUYS SHOWED UP.
THEY UNDERSTAND EVERYTHING I SAY!
THESE ARE YOURS?
CUK
CHRT
CUK
CUK
CUK
HOW DO YOU GET THEM OFF?
EASY. YOU JUST GO 'CHUTTY CHET CHET!'
OF COURSE.
CHITTY
CUK CHRRT?

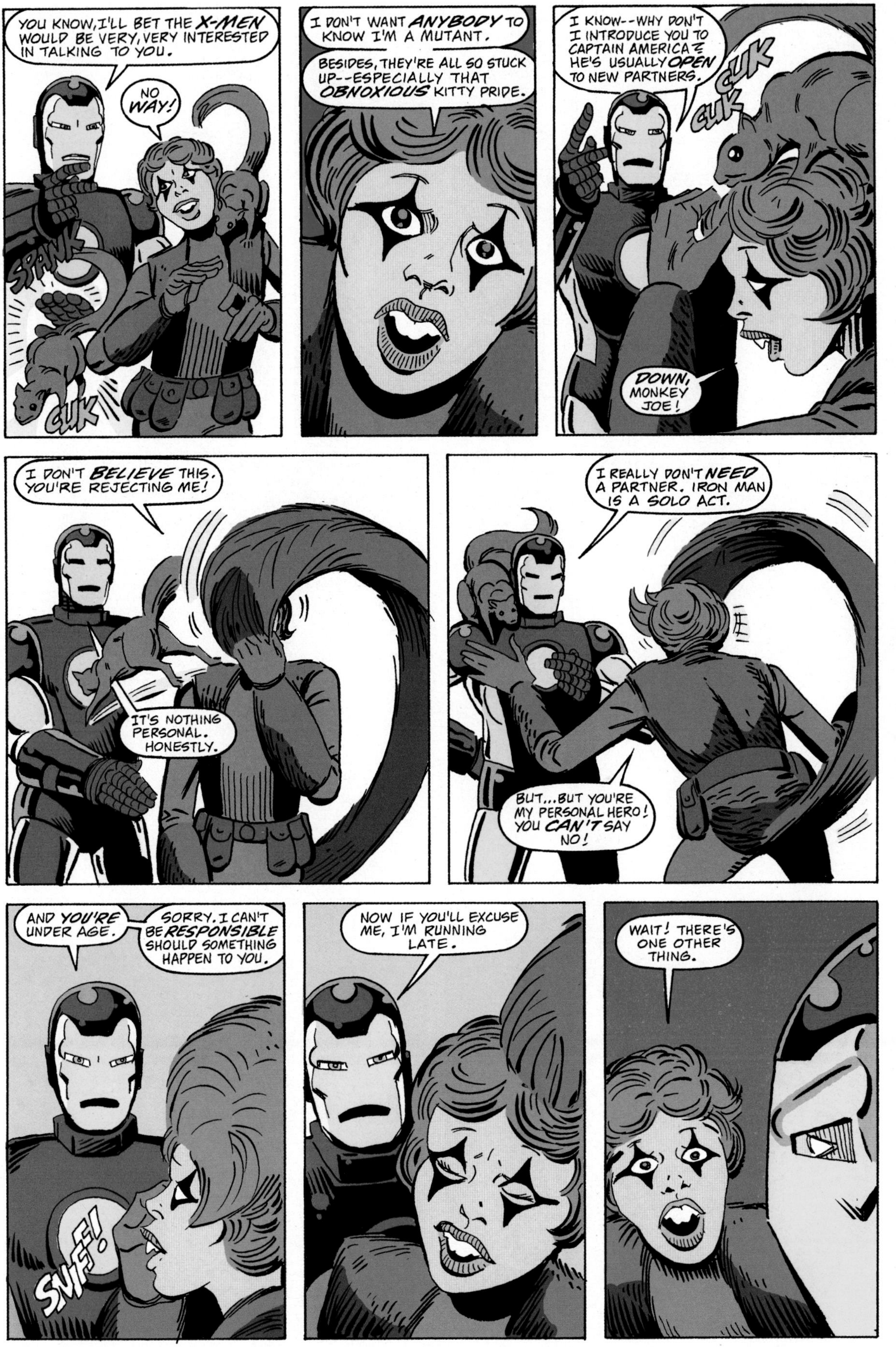
YOU KNOW, I'LL BET THE X-MEN WOULD BE VERY, VERY INTERESTED IN TALKING TO YOU.
NO WAY!
SPANK
CUK
I DON'T WANT ANYBODY TO KNOW I'M A MUTANT.
BESIDES, THEY'RE ALL SO STUCK UP--ESPECIALLY THAT OBNOXIOUS KITTY PRIDE.
I KNOW--WHY DON'T I INTRODUCE YOU TO CAPTAIN AMERICA? HE'S USUALLY OPEN TO NEW PARTNERS.
CUK CUK
DOWN, MONKEY JOE!
I DON'T BELIEVE THIS. YOU'RE REJECTING ME!
IT'S NOTHING PERSONAL. HONESTLY.
I REALLY DON'T NEED A PARTNER. IRON MAN IS A SOLO ACT.
BUT...BUT YOU'RE MY PERSONAL HERO! YOU CAN'T SAY NO!
AND YOU'RE UNDER AGE.
SORRY. I CAN'T BE RESPONSIBLE SHOULD SOMETHING HAPPEN TO YOU.
SNIFF!
NOW IF YOU'LL EXCUSE ME, I'M RUNNING LATE.
WAIT! THERE'S ONE OTHER THING.

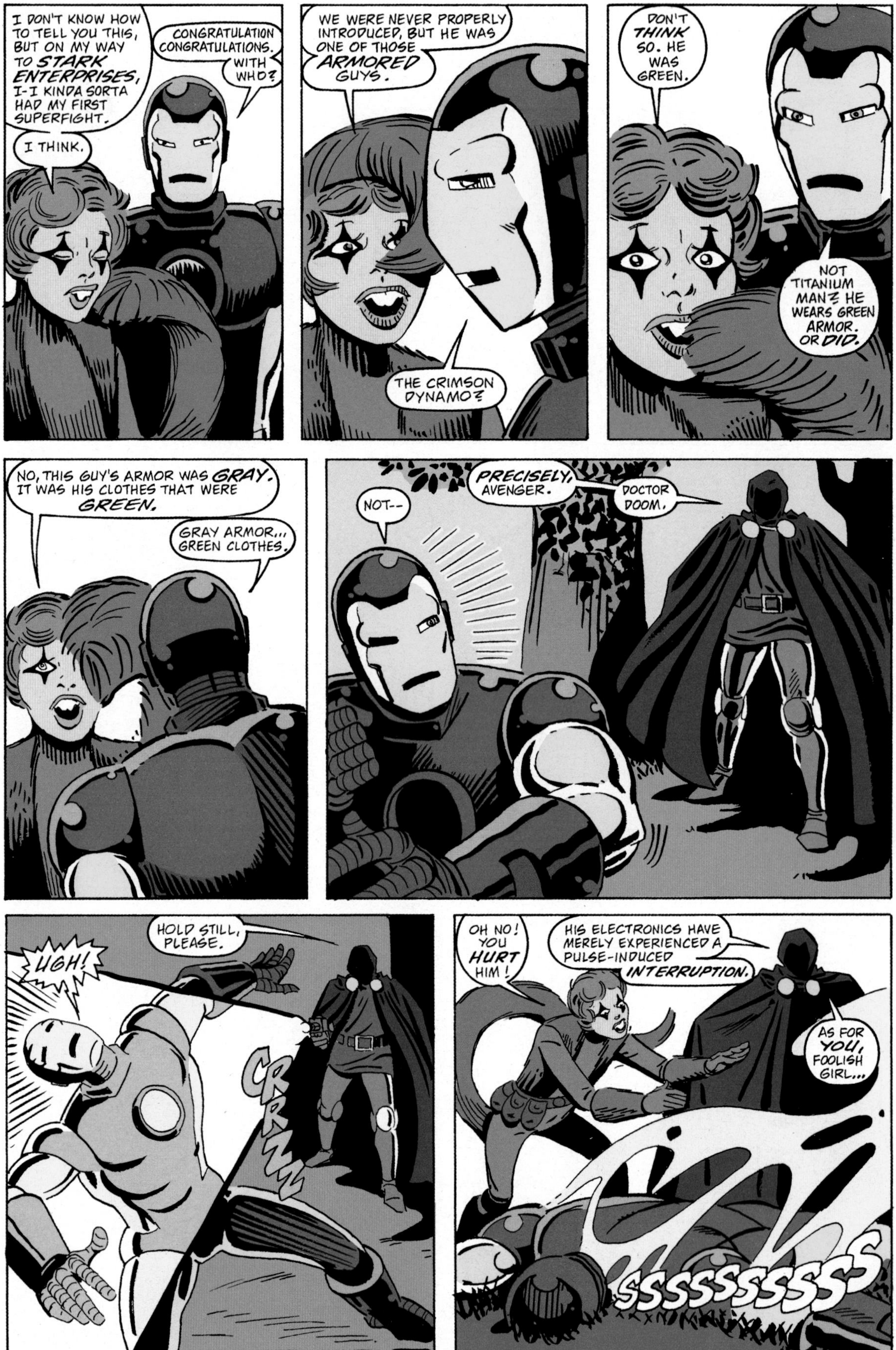

I DON'T KNOW HOW TO TELL YOU THIS, BUT ON MY WAY TO STARK ENTERPRISES, I-I KINDA SORTA HAD MY FIRST SUPERFIGHT.
CONGRATULATION CONGRATULATIONS. WITH WHO?
I THINK.
WE WERE NEVER PROPERLY INTRODUCED, BUT HE WAS ONE OF THOSE ARMORED GUYS.
THE CRIMSON DYNAMO?
DON'T THINK SO. HE WAS GREEN.
NOT TITANIUM MAN? HE WEARS GREEN ARMOR. OR DID.
NO, THIS GUY'S ARMOR WAS GRAY. IT WAS HIS CLOTHES THAT WERE GREEN.
GRAY ARMOR... GREEN CLOTHES.
NOT--
PRECISELY, AVENGER.
DOCTOR DOOM.
HOLD STILL, PLEASE.
UGH!
CRRNN
OH NO! YOU HURT HIM!
HIS ELECTRONICS HAVE MERELY EXPERIENCED A PULSE-INDUCED INTERRUPTION.
AS FOR YOU, FOOLISH GIRL...
SSSSSSSSSS

DO YOU NOT UNDERSTAND THAT **NO ONE** MAY ATTACK THE ROYAL PERSONAGE OF VICTOR VON DOOM WITH IMPUNITY?

LOOK, IF I HAD KNOWN THAT WAS **YOU,** I WOULD NEVER HAVE JUMPED YOU LIKE THAT.

I WAS ONLY TRYING TO **IMPRESS** IRON MAN SO HE'D BE MY PARTNER. YOU KNOW?

INSTEAD, YOU SHALL HENCEFORTH BE KNOWN AS THE **UNWITTING** INSTRUMENT OF HIS DOWNFALL.

BROIIIE

FOR I HAD NO **QUARREL** WITH IRON MAN THIS DAY, HAVING BEEN ENROUTE TO A RENDEZVOUS WHICH NEED NOT **CONCERN** YOU.

YIKES! WHAT'S THAT THING?

BEHOLD, THE DOOMSHIP. AN INFILTRATION CRAFT SO LIGHTWEIGHT, SO DELICATELY BALANCED, IF NEED BE IT CAN CROSS A CONTINENT ON THE POWER OF A COMMON CAR BATTERY.

HUUMMMMMMMM

IT'S **HUMONGOUS!**

STRUGGLE NOT. FOR THE ANTI-GRAVITY LIFTER IS **IRRESISTIBLE.**

EVEN NOW, IT IS **READING** OUR AGGREGATE WEIGHT, MAKING FINE ADJUSTMENTS FOR THE **BURDEN** YOU REPRESENT. I USE THE TERM **ADVISEDLY.**

:GULP!: ANY **CHANCE** YOU'LL TAKE AN APOLOGY?

NONE.

SILENTLY, THE VENTRAL DOORS SLIDE CLOSED.

AND THE DOOMSHIP **GHOSTS** THROUGH THE TREETOPS LIKE AN ALUMINUM WRAITH.

SOON...

OH, MY **HEAD,** WHERE AM I?

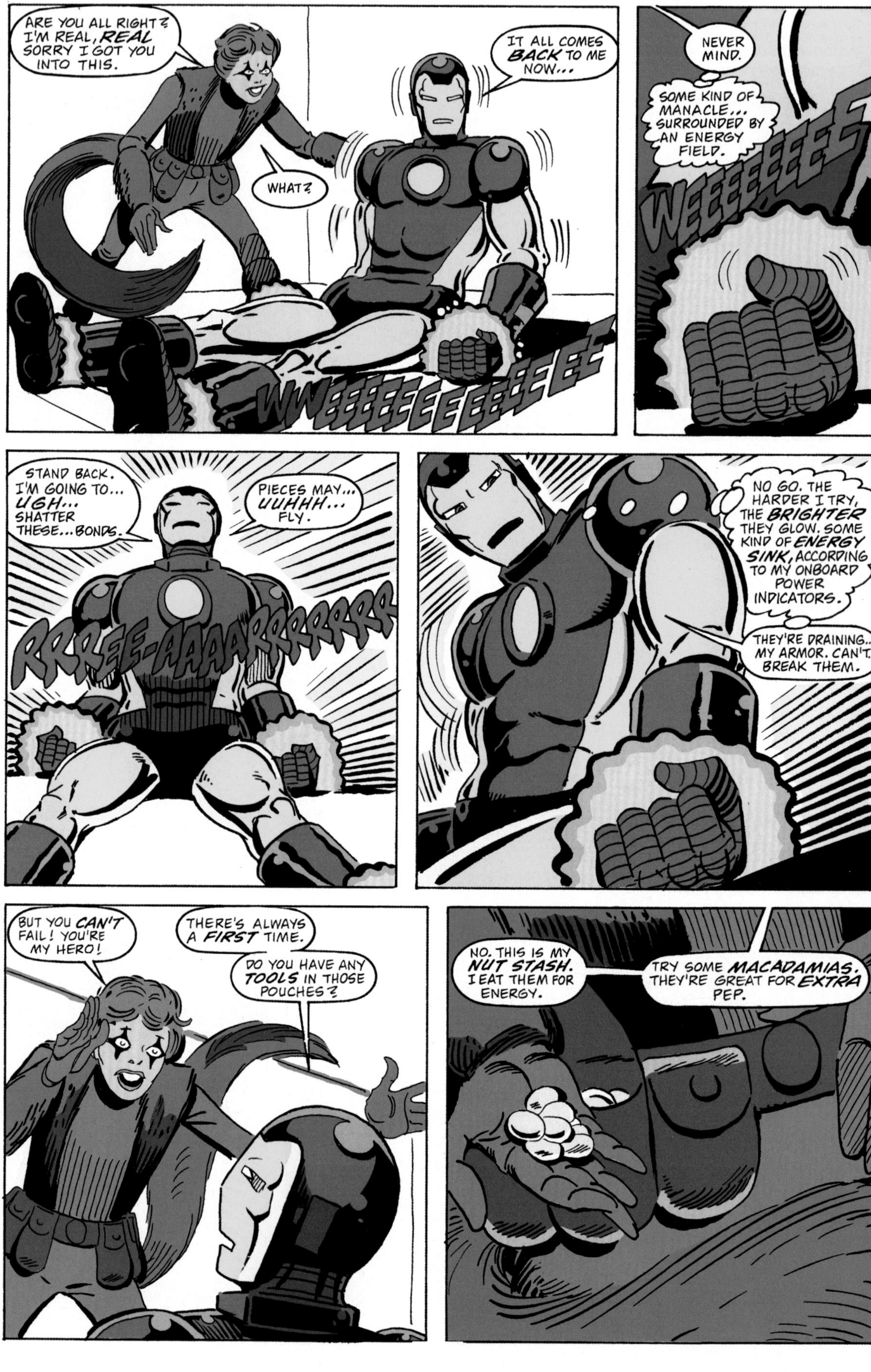

ARE YOU ALL RIGHT? I'M REAL, *REAL* SORRY I GOT YOU INTO THIS.
IT ALL COMES *BACK* TO ME NOW...
WHAT?
WWEEEEEEEEEEEEEE
NEVER MIND.
SOME KIND OF MANACLE... SURROUNDED BY AN ENERGY FIELD.
WEEEEEEEE
STAND BACK. I'M GOING TO... *UGH...* SHATTER THESE... BONDS.
PIECES MAY... *UUHHH...* FLY.
RRREE-AAAARRRRRRR
NO GO. THE HARDER I TRY, THE *BRIGHTER* THEY GLOW. SOME KIND OF *ENERGY SINK*, ACCORDING TO MY ONBOARD POWER INDICATORS.
THEY'RE DRAINING... MY ARMOR. CAN'T... BREAK THEM.
BUT YOU *CAN'T* FAIL! YOU'RE MY HERO!
THERE'S ALWAYS A *FIRST* TIME.
DO YOU HAVE ANY *TOOLS* IN THOSE POUCHES?
NO. THIS IS MY *NUT STASH*. I EAT THEM FOR ENERGY.
TRY SOME *MACADAMIAS*. THEY'RE GREAT FOR *EXTRA* PEP.

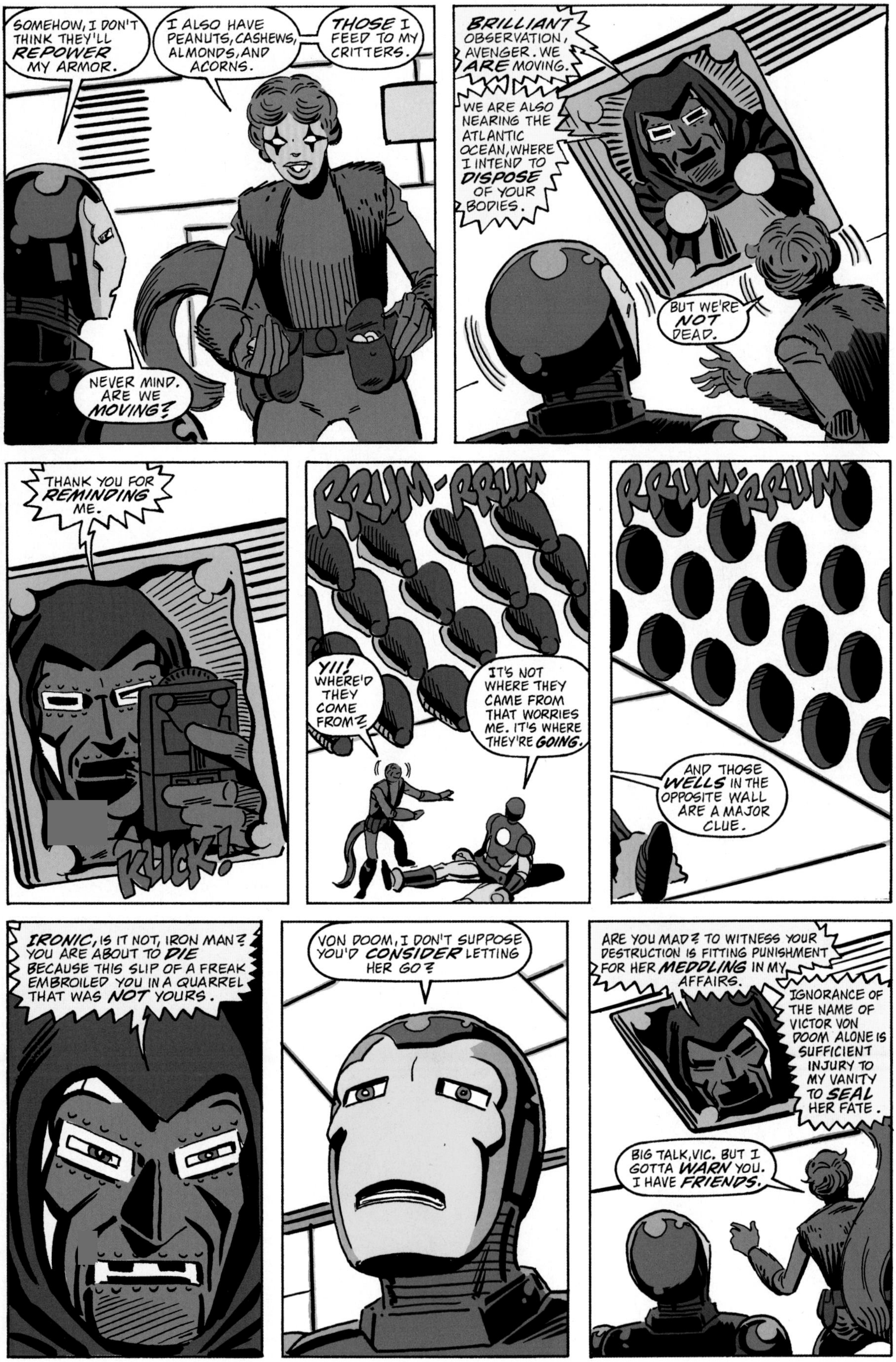
SOMEHOW, I DON'T THINK THEY'LL REPOWER MY ARMOR.
I ALSO HAVE PEANUTS, CASHEWS, ALMONDS, AND ACORNS.
THOSE I FEED TO MY CRITTERS.
NEVER MIND. ARE WE MOVING?
BRILLIANT OBSERVATION, AVENGER. WE ARE MOVING.
WE ARE ALSO NEARING THE ATLANTIC OCEAN, WHERE I INTEND TO DISPOSE OF YOUR BODIES.
BUT WE'RE NOT DEAD.
THANK YOU FOR REMINDING ME.
KLICK!
RRUM-RRUM
YII! WHERE'D THEY COME FROM?
IT'S NOT WHERE THEY CAME FROM THAT WORRIES ME. IT'S WHERE THEY'RE GOING.
RRUM-RRUM
AND THOSE WELLS IN THE OPPOSITE WALL ARE A MAJOR CLUE.
IRONIC, IS IT NOT, IRON MAN? YOU ARE ABOUT TO DIE BECAUSE THIS SLIP OF A FREAK EMBROILED YOU IN A QUARREL THAT WAS NOT YOURS.
VON DOOM, I DON'T SUPPOSE YOU'D CONSIDER LETTING HER GO?
ARE YOU MAD? TO WITNESS YOUR DESTRUCTION IS FITTING PUNISHMENT FOR HER MEDDLING IN MY AFFAIRS.
IGNORANCE OF THE NAME OF VICTOR VON DOOM ALONE IS SUFFICIENT INJURY TO MY VANITY TO SEAL HER FATE.
BIG TALK, VIC. BUT I GOTTA WARN YOU. I HAVE FRIENDS.

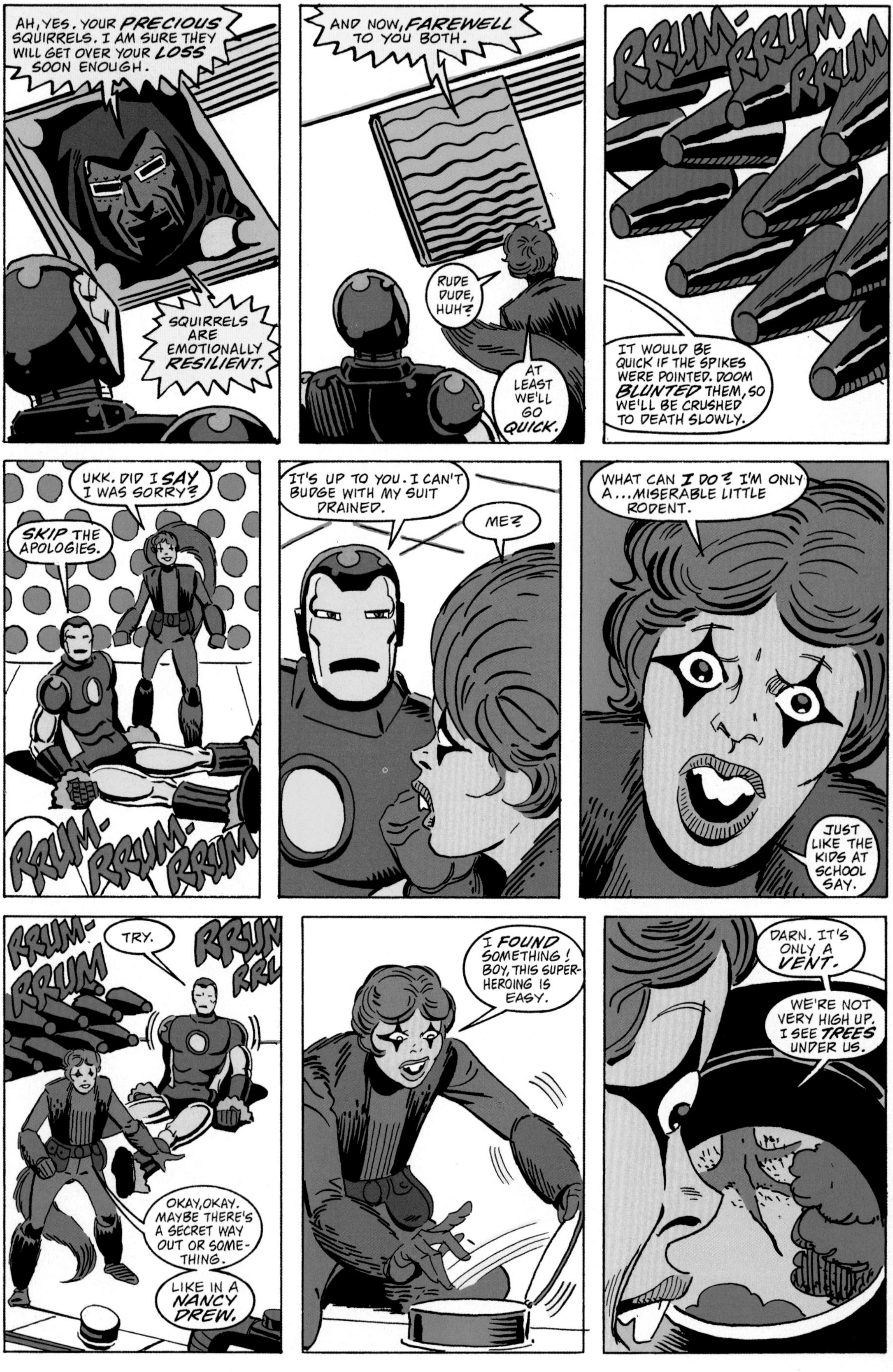
AH, YES. YOUR PRECIOUS SQUIRRELS. I AM SURE THEY WILL GET OVER YOUR LOSS SOON ENOUGH.
SQUIRRELS ARE EMOTIONALLY RESILIENT.
AND NOW, FAREWELL TO YOU BOTH.
RUDE DUDE, HUH?
AT LEAST WE'LL GO QUICK.
RRUM-RRUM-RRUM
IT WOULD BE QUICK IF THE SPIKES WERE POINTED. DOOM BLUNTED THEM, SO WE'LL BE CRUSHED TO DEATH SLOWLY.
UKK. DID I SAY I WAS SORRY?
SKIP THE APOLOGIES.
RRUM-RRUM-RRUM
IT'S UP TO YOU. I CAN'T BUDGE WITH MY SUIT DRAINED.
ME?
WHAT CAN I DO? I'M ONLY A...MISERABLE LITTLE RODENT.
JUST LIKE THE KIDS AT SCHOOL SAY.
RRUM-RRUM
TRY.
OKAY, OKAY. MAYBE THERE'S A SECRET WAY OUT OR SOMETHING.
LIKE IN A NANCY DREW.
I FOUND SOMETHING! BOY, THIS SUPER-HEROING IS EASY.
DARN. IT'S ONLY A VENT.
WE'RE NOT VERY HIGH UP. I SEE TREES UNDER US.

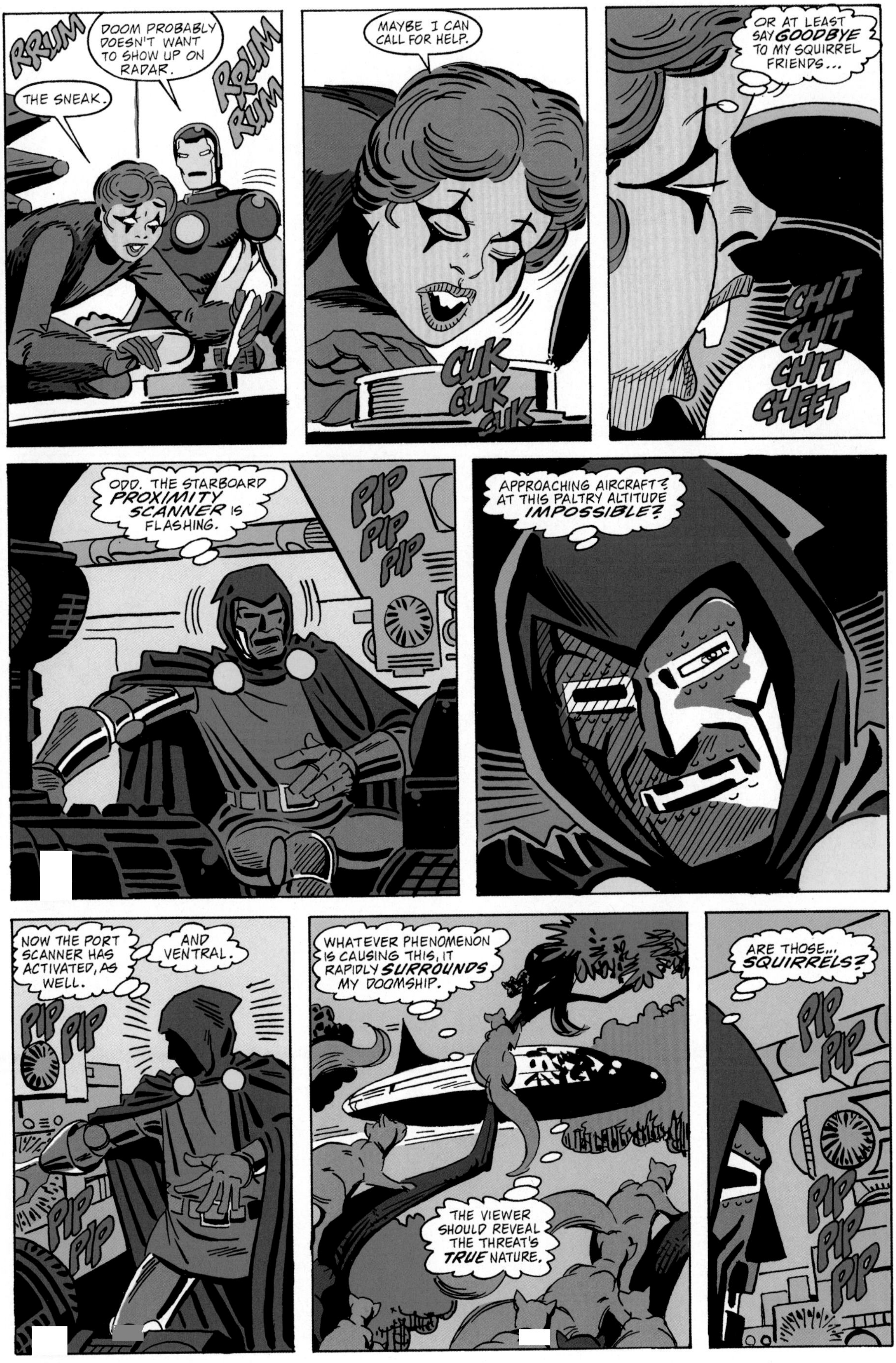
RRUM
DOOM PROBABLY DOESN'T WANT TO SHOW UP ON RADAR.
THE SNEAK.
RRUM RRUM
MAYBE I CAN CALL FOR HELP.
CUK CUK CUK
OR AT LEAST SAY GOODBYE TO MY SQUIRREL FRIENDS...
CHIT CHIT CHIT CHEET
ODD. THE STARBOARD PROXIMITY SCANNER IS FLASHING.
PIP PIP PIP
APPROACHING AIRCRAFT? AT THIS PALTRY ALTITUDE IMPOSSIBLE?
NOW THE PORT SCANNER HAS ACTIVATED, AS WELL.
AND VENTRAL.
PIP PIP
PIP PIP
WHATEVER PHENOMENON IS CAUSING THIS, IT RAPIDLY SURROUNDS MY DOOMSHIP.
THE VIEWER SHOULD REVEAL THE THREAT'S TRUE NATURE.
ARE THOSE... SQUIRRELS?
PIP PIP
PIP PIP PIP

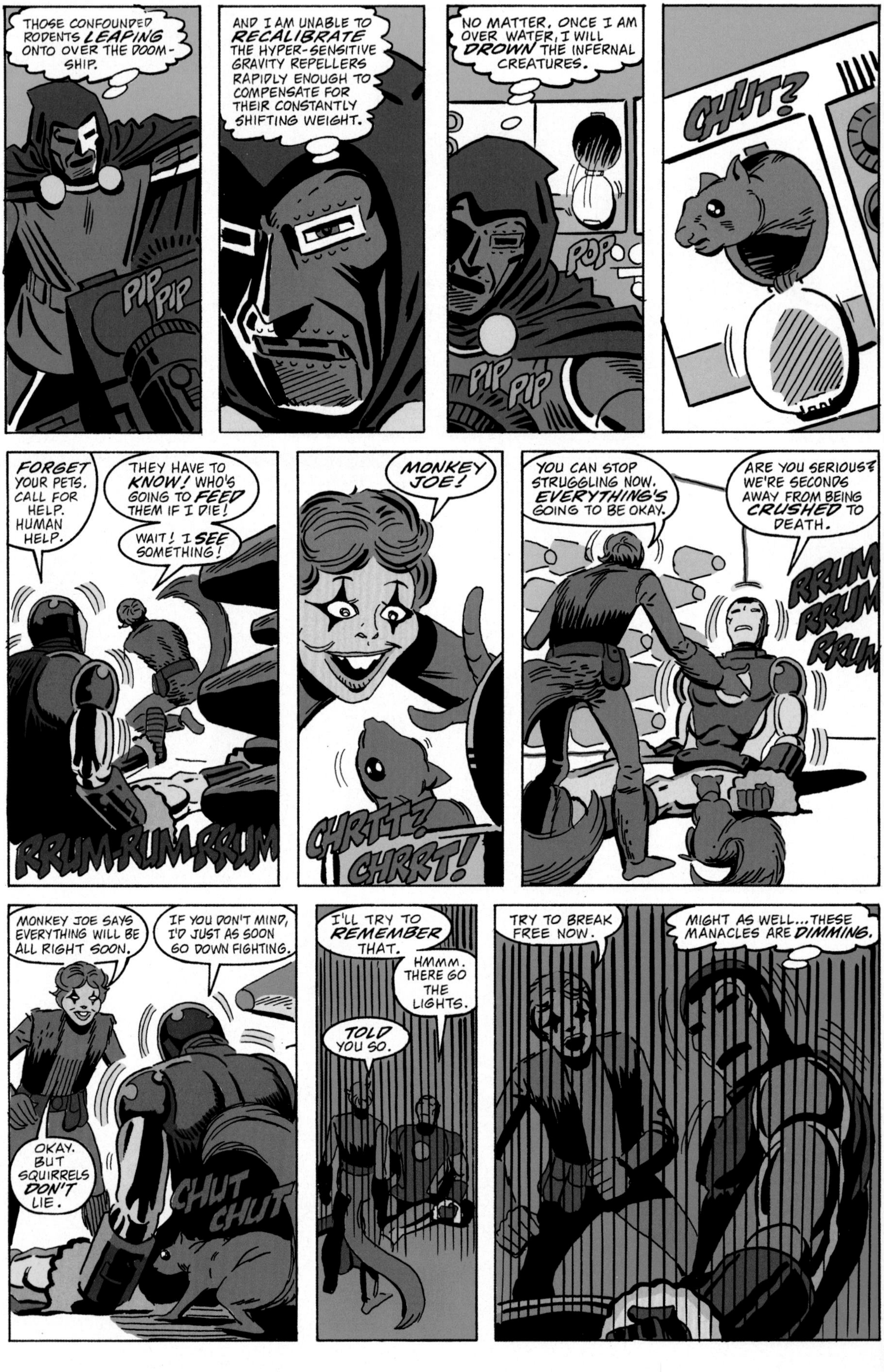

THOSE CONFOUNDED RODENTS LEAPING ONTO OVER THE DOOMSHIP.
PIP PIP
AND I AM UNABLE TO RECALIBRATE THE HYPER-SENSITIVE GRAVITY REPELLERS RAPIDLY ENOUGH TO COMPENSATE FOR THEIR CONSTANTLY SHIFTING WEIGHT.
NO MATTER. ONCE I AM OVER WATER, I WILL DROWN THE INFERNAL CREATURES.
POP
PIP PIP
CHUT?
FORGET YOUR PETS. CALL FOR HELP. HUMAN HELP.
THEY HAVE TO KNOW! WHO'S GOING TO FEED THEM IF I DIE!
WAIT! I SEE SOMETHING!
RRUM-RUM-RRUM
MONKEY JOE!
CHRTT? CHRRT!
YOU CAN STOP STRUGGLING NOW. EVERYTHING'S GOING TO BE OKAY.
ARE YOU SERIOUS? WE'RE SECONDS AWAY FROM BEING CRUSHED TO DEATH.
RRUM RRUM RRUM
MONKEY JOE SAYS EVERYTHING WILL BE ALL RIGHT SOON.
IF YOU DON'T MIND, I'D JUST AS SOON GO DOWN FIGHTING.
OKAY. BUT SQUIRRELS DON'T LIE.
CHUT CHUT
I'LL TRY TO REMEMBER THAT.
HMMM. THERE GO THE LIGHTS.
TOLD YOU SO.
TRY TO BREAK FREE NOW.
MIGHT AS WELL... THESE MANACLES ARE DIMMING.

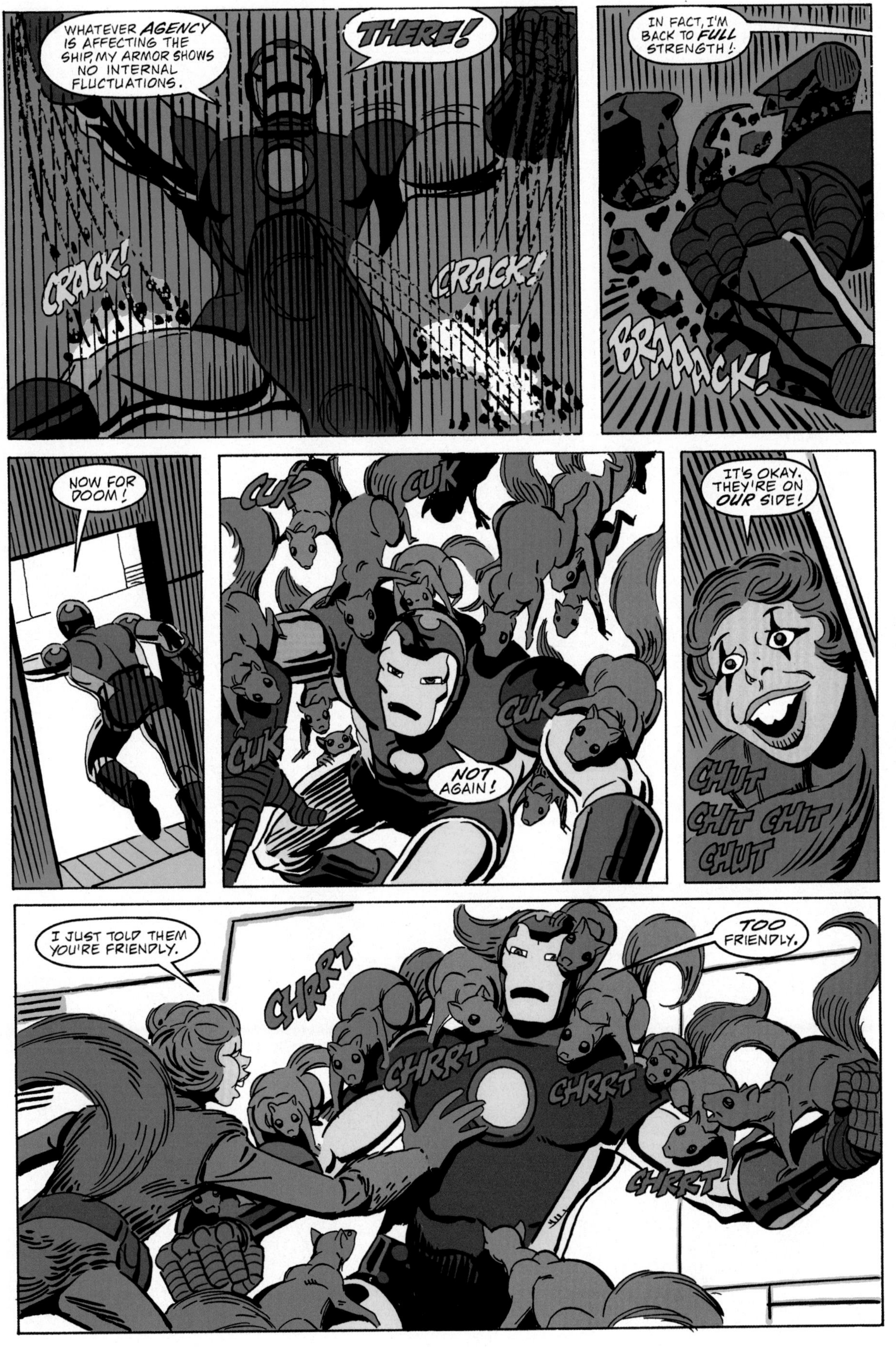
WHATEVER AGENCY IS AFFECTING THE SHIP, MY ARMOR SHOWS NO INTERNAL FLUCTUATIONS.
THERE!
CRACK!
CRACK!
IN FACT, I'M BACK TO FULL STRENGTH!
BRAAACK!
NOW FOR DOOM!
CUK
CUK
CUK
CUK
NOT AGAIN!
IT'S OKAY. THEY'RE ON OUR SIDE!
CHUT
CHIT CHIT
CHUT
I JUST TOLD THEM YOU'RE FRIENDLY.
TOO FRIENDLY.
CHRRT
CHRRT
CHRRT
CHRRT

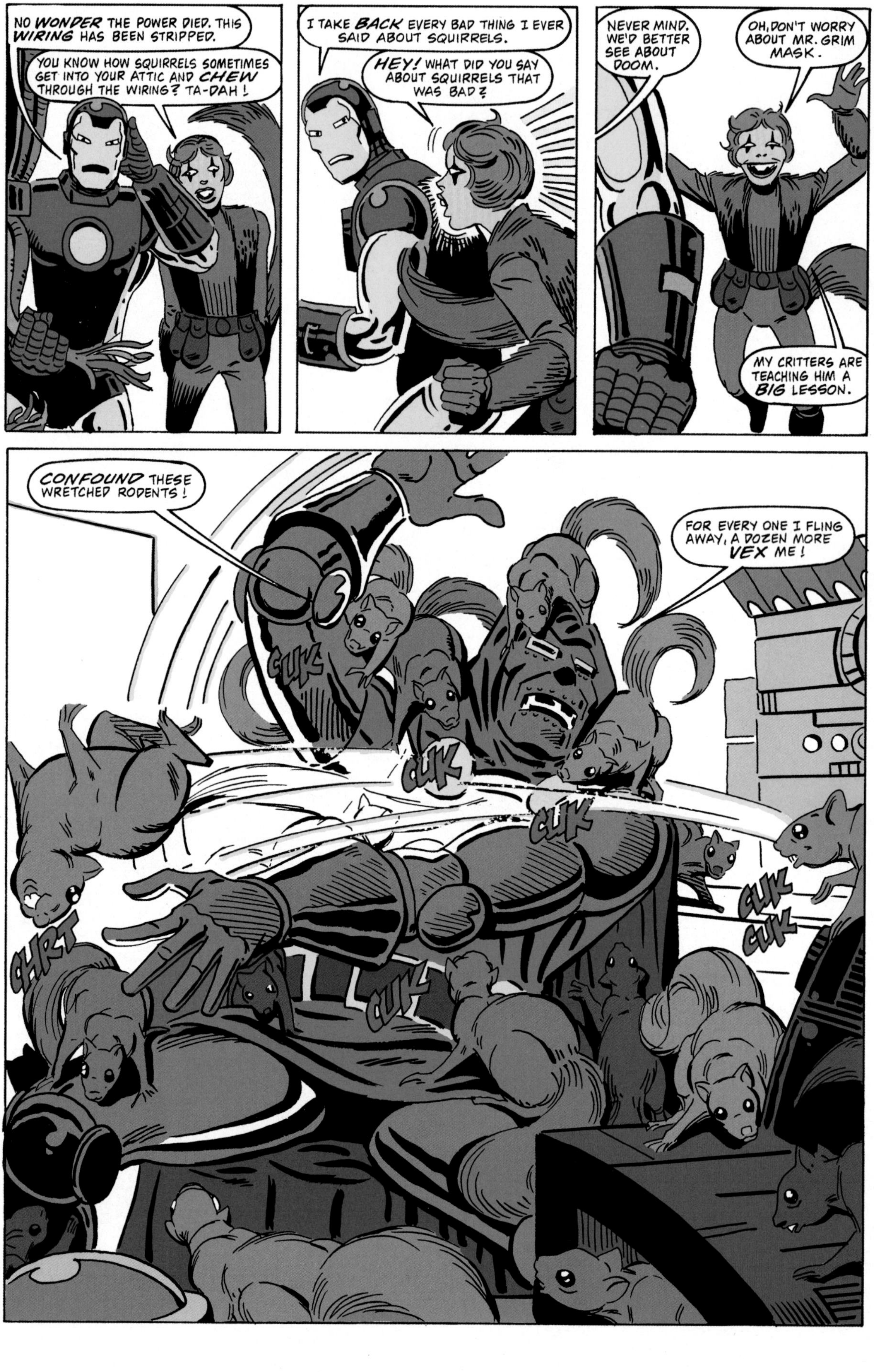
NO WONDER THE POWER DIED. THIS WIRING HAS BEEN STRIPPED.
YOU KNOW HOW SQUIRRELS SOMETIMES GET INTO YOUR ATTIC AND CHEW THROUGH THE WIRING? TA-DAH!
I TAKE BACK EVERY BAD THING I EVER SAID ABOUT SQUIRRELS.
HEY! WHAT DID YOU SAY ABOUT SQUIRRELS THAT WAS BAD?
NEVER MIND. WE'D BETTER SEE ABOUT DOOM.
OH, DON'T WORRY ABOUT MR. GRIM MASK.
MY CRITTERS ARE TEACHING HIM A BIG LESSON.
CONFOUND THESE WRETCHED RODENTS!
FOR EVERY ONE I FLING AWAY, A DOZEN MORE VEX ME!
CUK
CUK
CUK
CUK CUK
CHRT
CUK

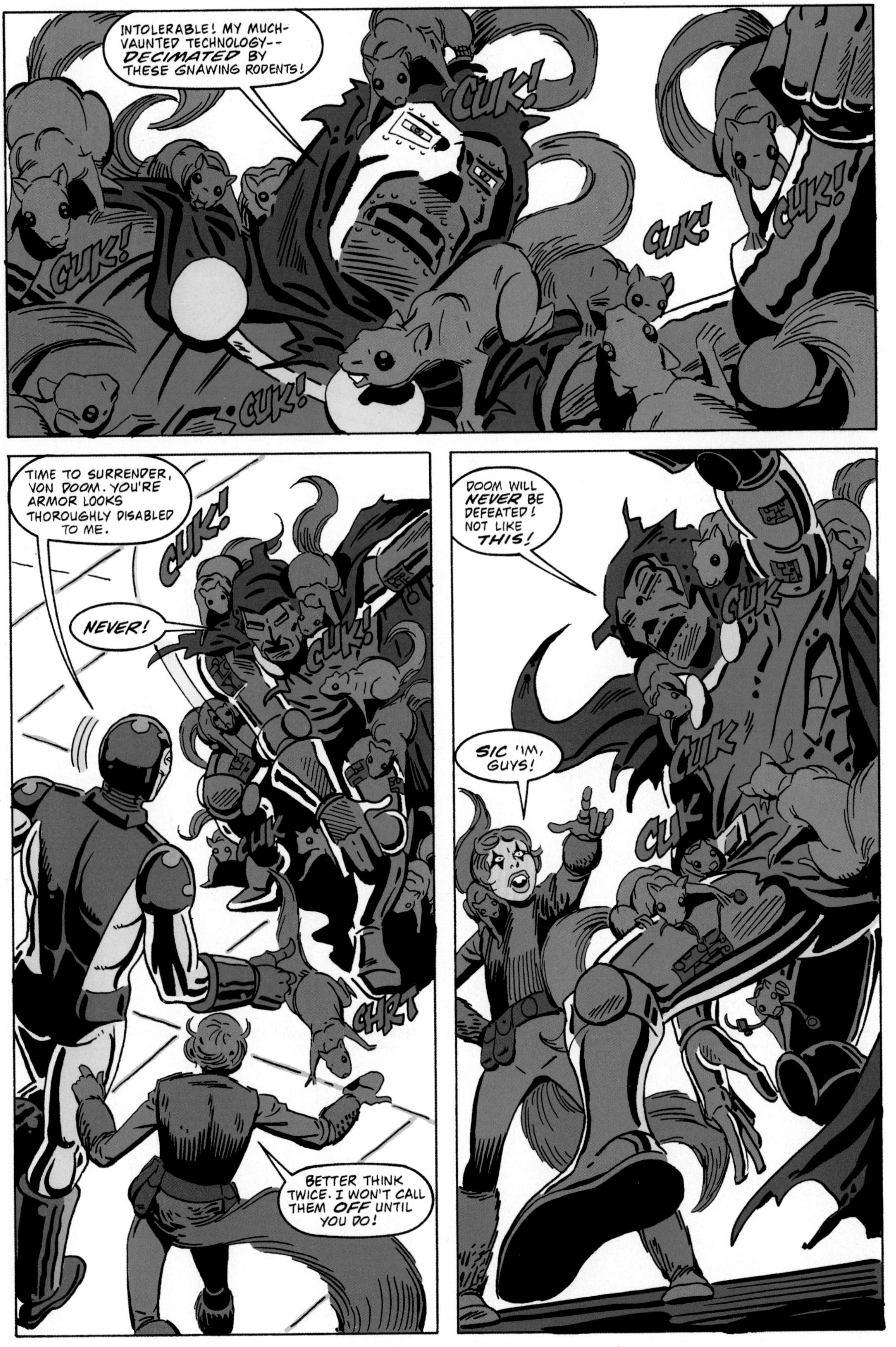

INTOLERABLE! MY MUCH-VAUNTED TECHNOLOGY-- DECIMATED BY THESE GNAWING RODENTS!
CUK!
CUK!
CUK!
CUK!
CUK!
TIME TO SURRENDER, VON DOOM. YOU'RE ARMOR LOOKS THOROUGHLY DISABLED TO ME.
CUK!
NEVER!
CUK!
CUK
CHRT
BETTER THINK TWICE. I WON'T CALL THEM OFF UNTIL YOU DO!
DOOM WILL NEVER BE DEFEATED! NOT LIKE THIS!
CUK
SIC 'IM, GUYS!
CUK
CUK

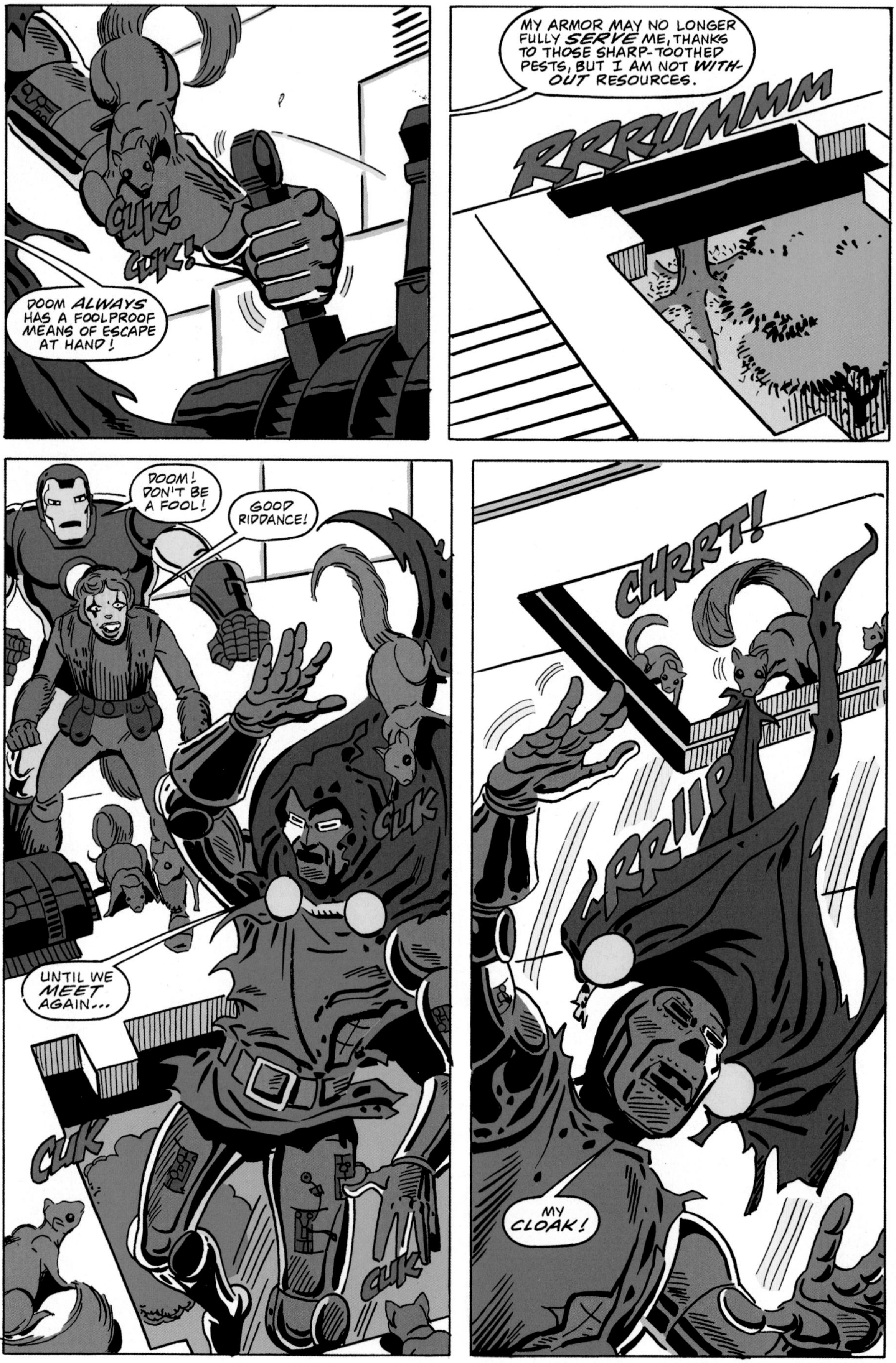
CLIK!
CLIK!
DOOM ALWAYS HAS A FOOLPROOF MEANS OF ESCAPE AT HAND!
MY ARMOR MAY NO LONGER FULLY SERVE ME, THANKS TO THOSE SHARP-TOOTHED PESTS, BUT I AM NOT WITH-OUT RESOURCES.
RRRUMMM
DOOM! DON'T BE A FOOL!
GOOD RIDDANCE!
CLIK
UNTIL WE MEET AGAIN...
CLIK
CLIK
CHRRT!
RRIIP
MY CLOAK!

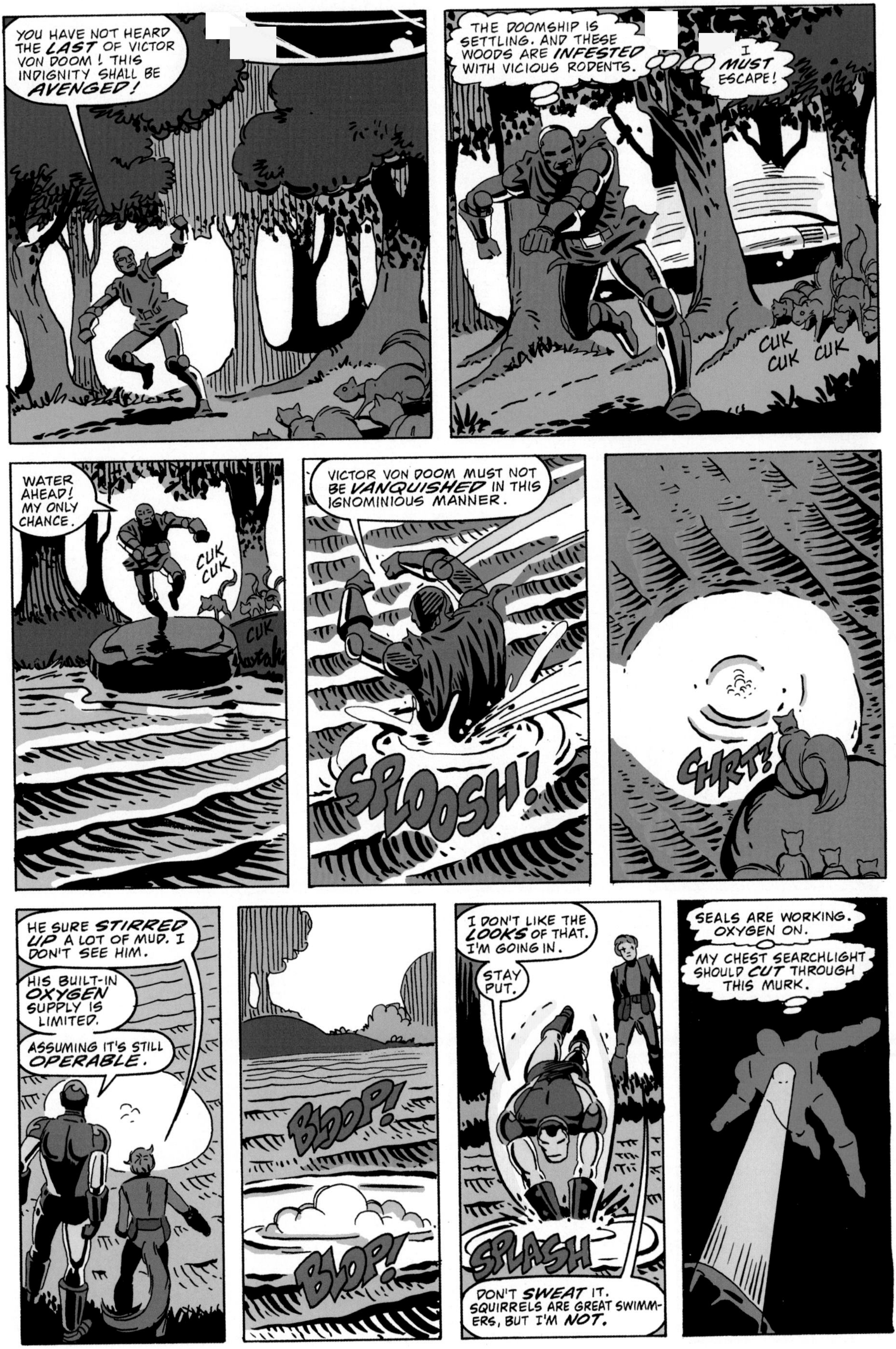

YOU HAVE NOT HEARD THE LAST OF VICTOR VON DOOM! THIS INDIGNITY SHALL BE AVENGED!
THE DOOMSHIP IS SETTLING. AND THESE WOODS ARE INFESTED WITH VICIOUS RODENTS.
I MUST ESCAPE!
CUK CUK CUK
WATER AHEAD! MY ONLY CHANCE.
CUK CUK
CUK
VICTOR VON DOOM MUST NOT BE VANQUISHED IN THIS IGNOMINIOUS MANNER.
SPLOOSH!
CHRT?
HE SURE STIRRED UP A LOT OF MUD. I DON'T SEE HIM.
HIS BUILT-IN OXYGEN SUPPLY IS LIMITED.
ASSUMING IT'S STILL OPERABLE.
BLOOP!
BLOP!
I DON'T LIKE THE LOOKS OF THAT. I'M GOING IN.
STAY PUT.
SPLASH
DON'T SWEAT IT. SQUIRRELS ARE GREAT SWIMMERS, BUT I'M NOT.
SEALS ARE WORKING. OXYGEN ON.
MY CHEST SEARCHLIGHT SHOULD CUT THROUGH THIS MURK.

THERE'S DOOM'S MASK...

AND THERE *HE* GOES-- BURROWING INTO THE MUD LIKE A CLAM.

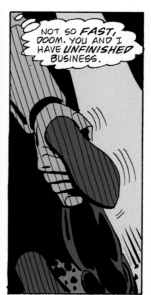

NOT SO *FAST*, DOOM. YOU AND I HAVE *UNFINISHED* BUSINESS.

NO GOOD! HIS ARMOR'S TOO SLIPPERY--SOME KIND OF *SILICON* COATING.

MUD. NOTHING BUT MUD.

GOT *AWAY*, HUH?

AFRAID SO.

SPLASH

SPLOOP!

CUK CUK

THANKS, MONKEY JOE. *GOOD* SQUIRREL.

CHRRT!

HERE. YOU SHOULD *HAVE* THIS.

MAYBE THERE ARE SOME NEAT *SECRETS* INSIDE.

THANKS.

I-I GUESS I KINDA MADE A MESS OF THINGS, HUH?

OH, I DON'T KNOW ABOUT THAT.

YOU MANAGED TO HAND DR. DOOM ONE OF THE MOST *INGLORIOUS* DEFEATS OF HIS CAREER.

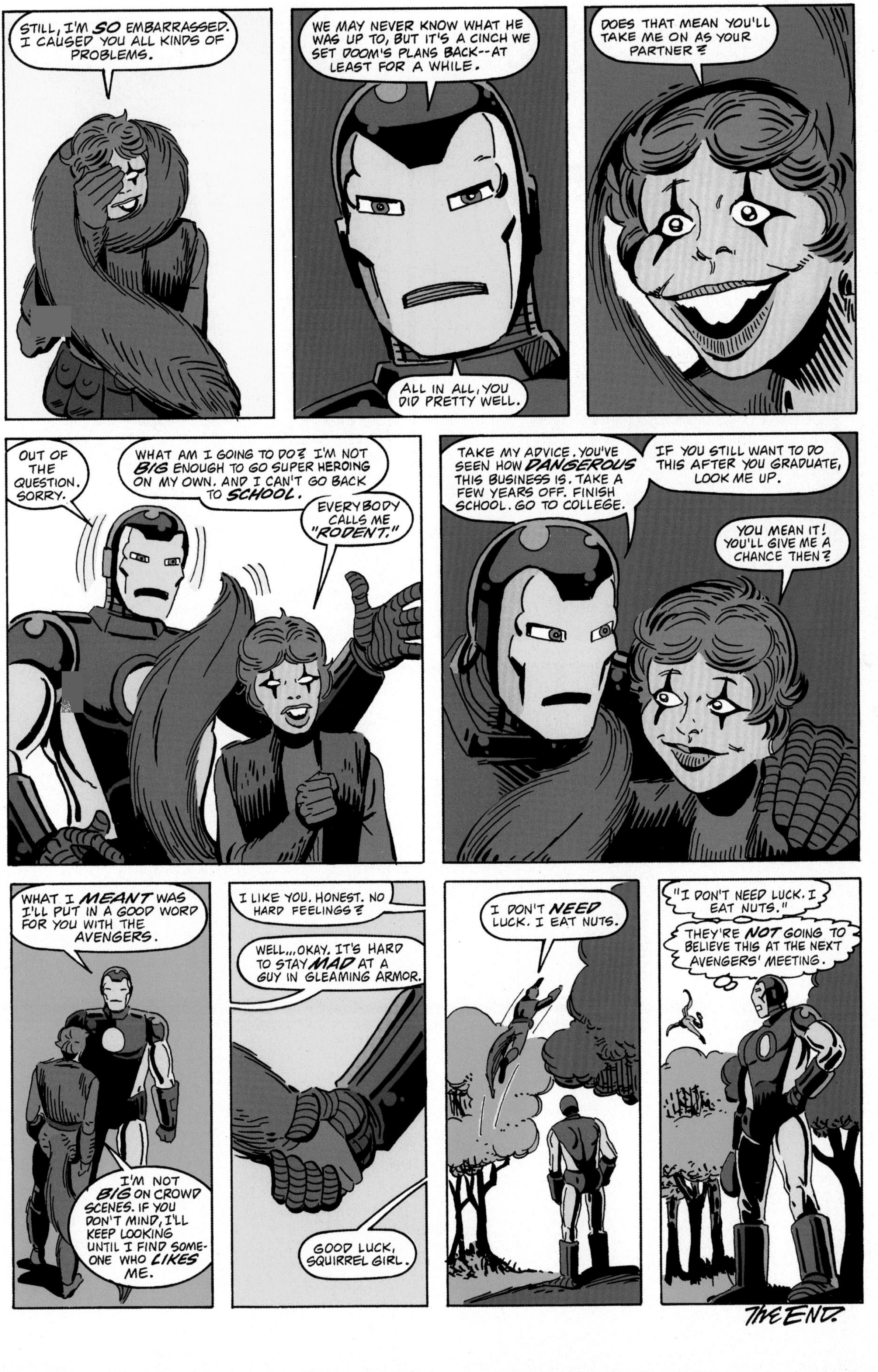
STILL, I'M SO EMBARRASSED. I CAUSED YOU ALL KINDS OF PROBLEMS.
WE MAY NEVER KNOW WHAT HE WAS UP TO, BUT IT'S A CINCH WE SET DOOM'S PLANS BACK--AT LEAST FOR A WHILE.
ALL IN ALL, YOU DID PRETTY WELL.
DOES THAT MEAN YOU'LL TAKE ME ON AS YOUR PARTNER?
OUT OF THE QUESTION. SORRY.
WHAT AM I GOING TO DO? I'M NOT BIG ENOUGH TO GO SUPER HEROING ON MY OWN. AND I CAN'T GO BACK TO SCHOOL.
EVERYBODY CALLS ME "RODENT."
TAKE MY ADVICE. YOU'VE SEEN HOW DANGEROUS THIS BUSINESS IS. TAKE A FEW YEARS OFF. FINISH SCHOOL. GO TO COLLEGE.
IF YOU STILL WANT TO DO THIS AFTER YOU GRADUATE, LOOK ME UP.
YOU MEAN IT! YOU'LL GIVE ME A CHANCE THEN?
WHAT I MEANT WAS I'LL PUT IN A GOOD WORD FOR YOU WITH THE AVENGERS.
I'M NOT BIG ON CROWD SCENES. IF YOU DON'T MIND, I'LL KEEP LOOKING UNTIL I FIND SOME-ONE WHO LIKES ME.
I LIKE YOU. HONEST. NO HARD FEELINGS?
WELL...OKAY. IT'S HARD TO STAY MAD AT A GUY IN GLEAMING ARMOR.
GOOD LUCK, SQUIRREL GIRL.
I DON'T NEED LUCK. I EAT NUTS.
"I DON'T NEED LUCK. I EAT NUTS."
THEY'RE NOT GOING TO BELIEVE THIS AT THE NEXT AVENGERS' MEETING.
THE END.

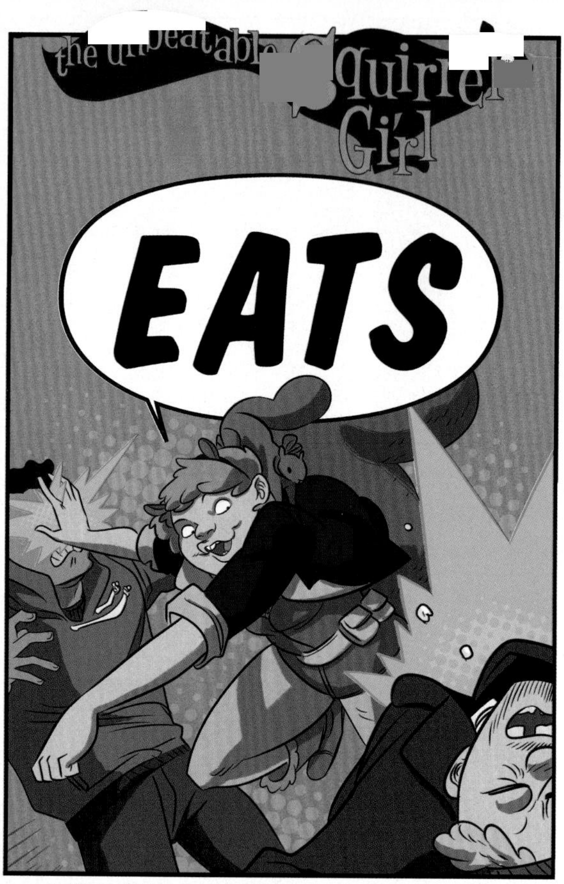
EATS
Squirrel Girl is saying "EATS," but what could she be eating? If only there were also a reprinting of issue #2 whose cover clarified this matter in some way!

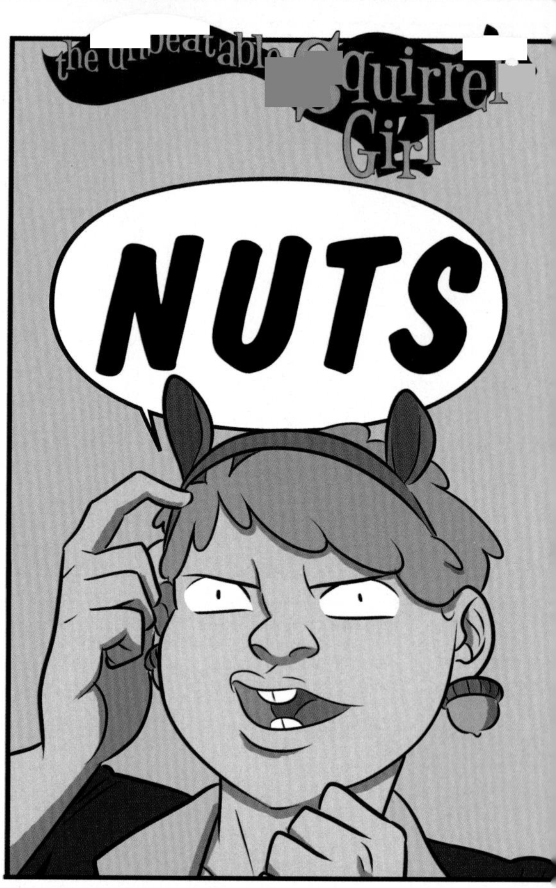
NUTS
Oh, Squirrel Girl is eating nuts! Okay, that makes sense. That's really appropriate actually.

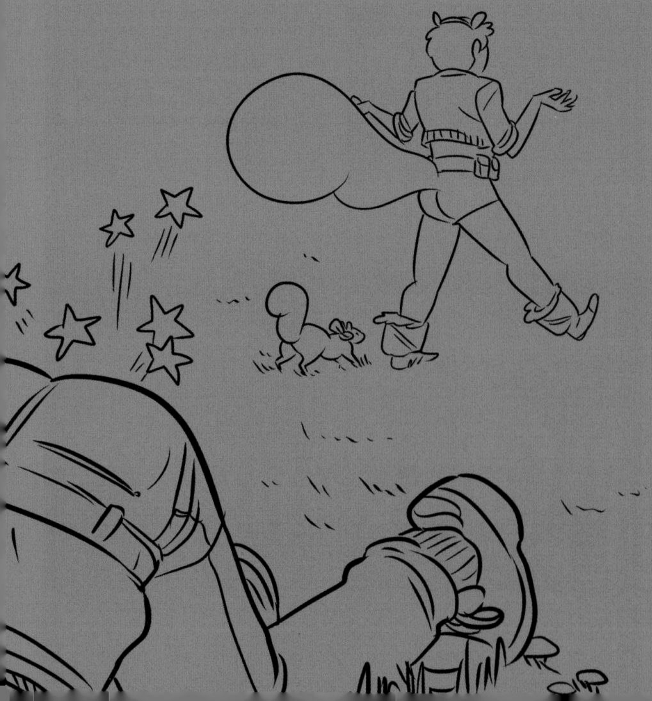

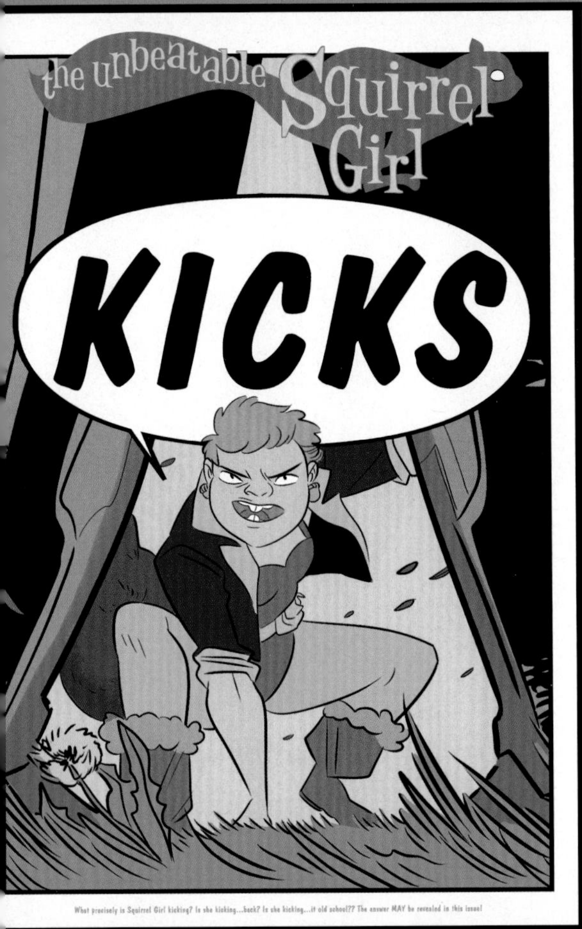
the unbeatable Squirrel Girl
KICKS
What precisely is Squirrel Girl kicking? Is she kicking...back? Is she kicking...it old school?? The answer MAY be revealed in this issue!

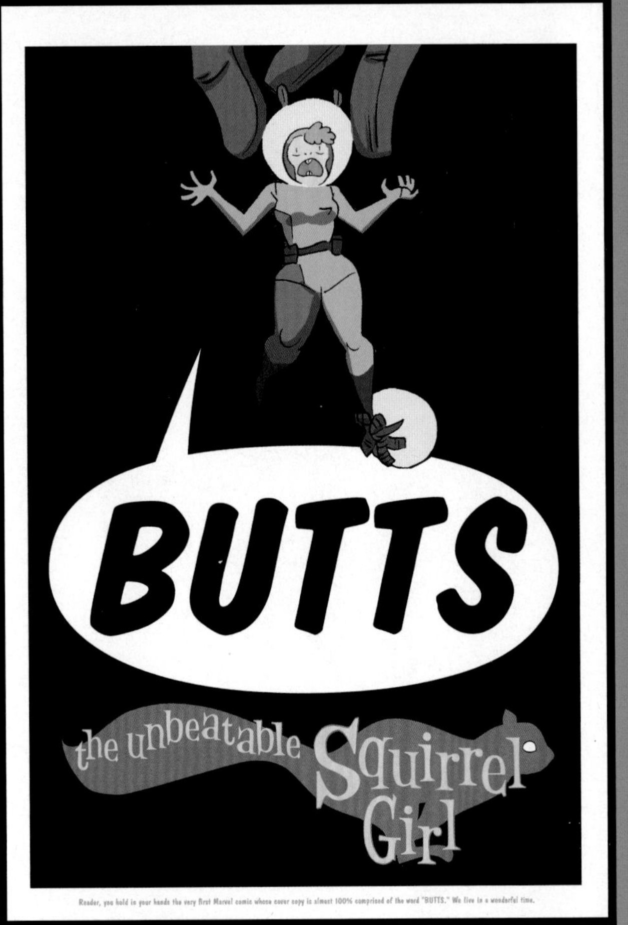
BUTTS
the unbeatable Squirrel Girl
Reader, you hold in your hands the very first Marvel comic whose cover copy is almost 100% comprised of the word "BUTTS." We live in a wonderful time.

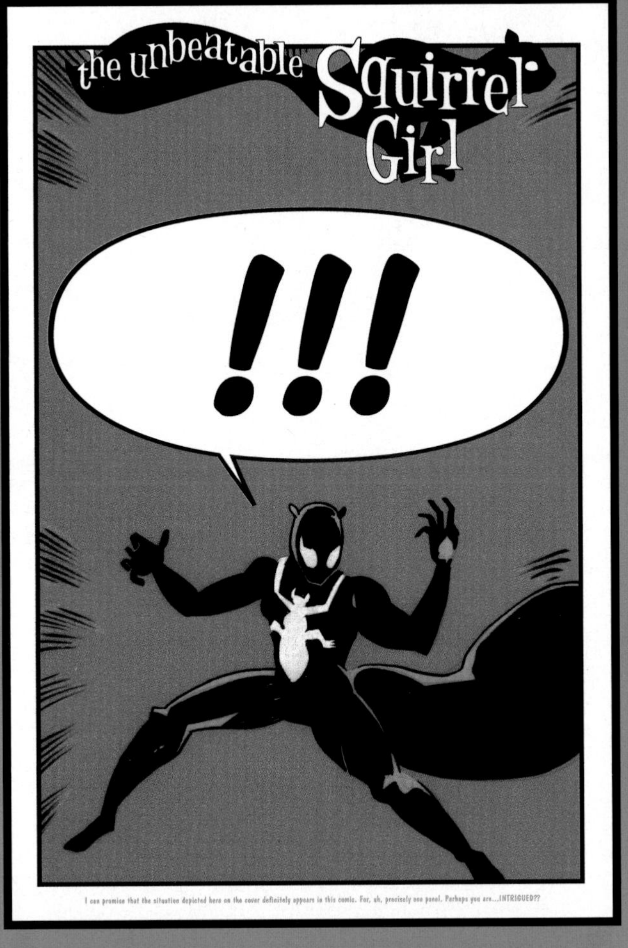
the unbeatable Squirrel Girl
!!!
I can promise that the situation depicted here on the cover definitely appears in this comic. For, uh, precisely one panel. Perhaps you are...INTRIGUED??

TOP ROW, FROM LEFT: ISSUE #1 3RD-PRINTING VARIANT COVER, ISSUE #2 3RD-PRINTING VARIANT COVER, ISSUE #3 2ND-PRINTING VARIANT COVER, ISSUE #4 2ND-PRINTING VARIANT COVER.
RIGHT: ISSUE #5 2ND-PRINTING VARIANT COVER

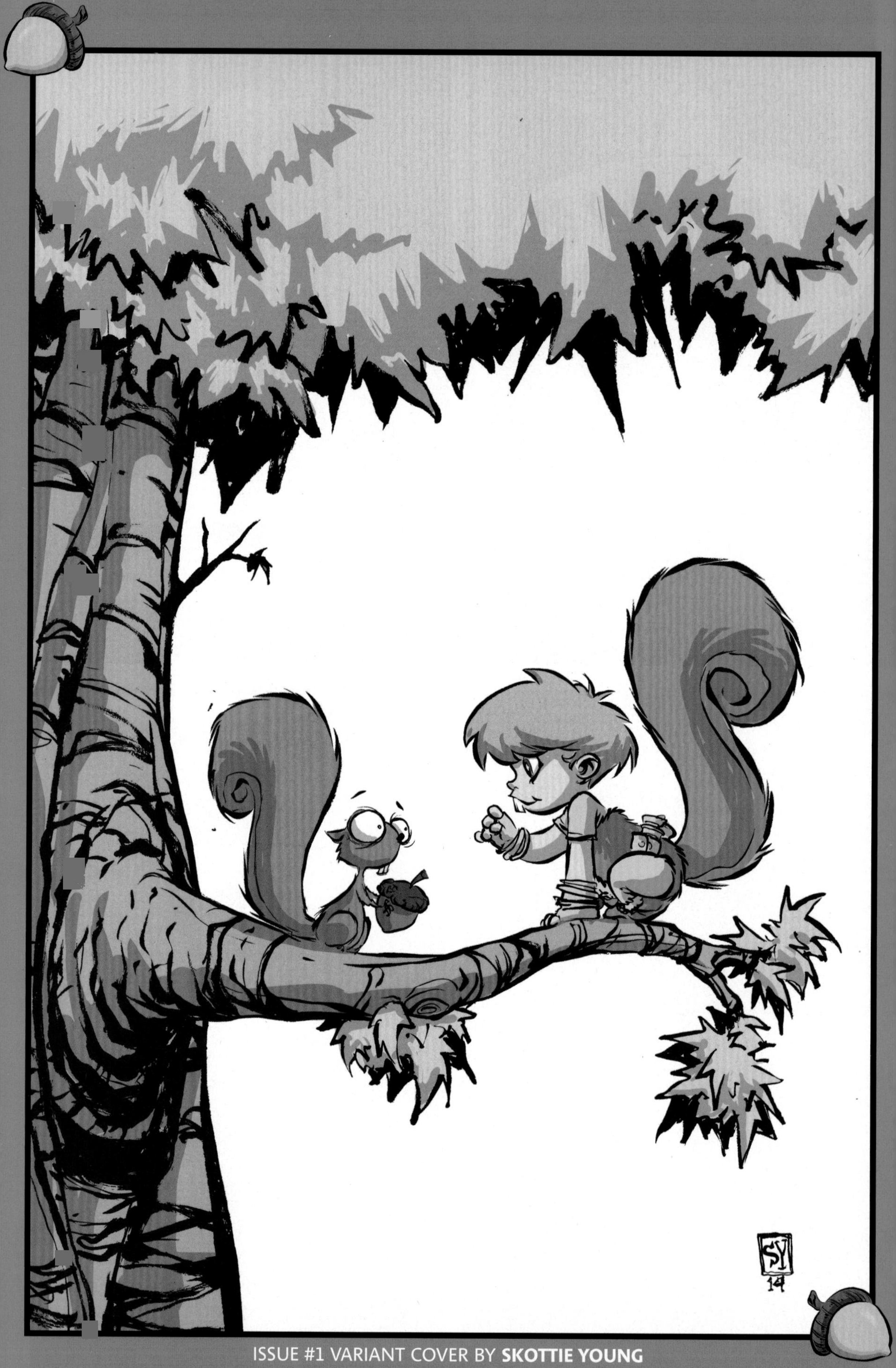
SY
14

ISSUE #1 VARIANT COVER BY **SKOTTIE YOUNG**

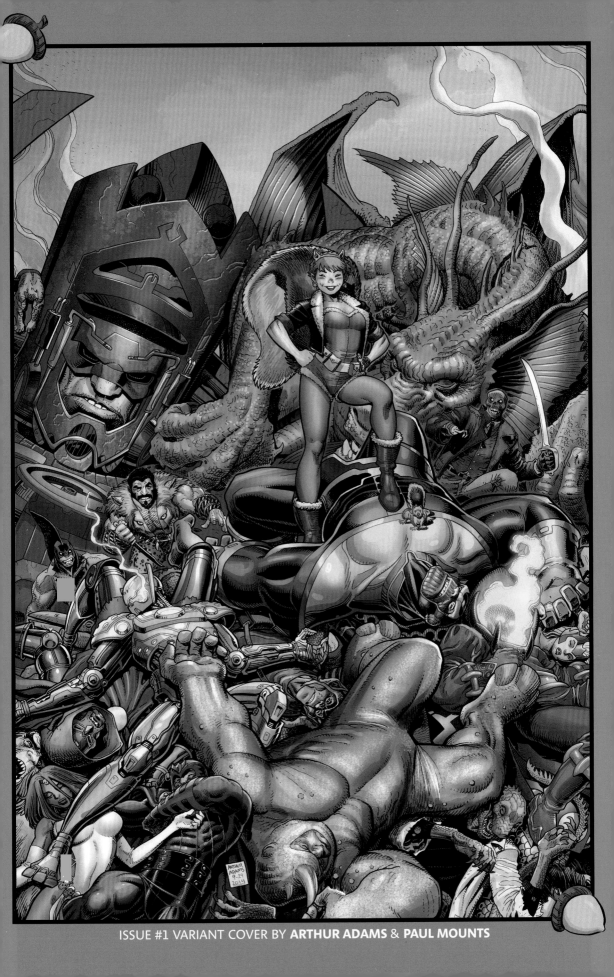

ISSUE #1 VARIANT COVER BY **ARTHUR ADAMS** & **PAUL MOUNTS**

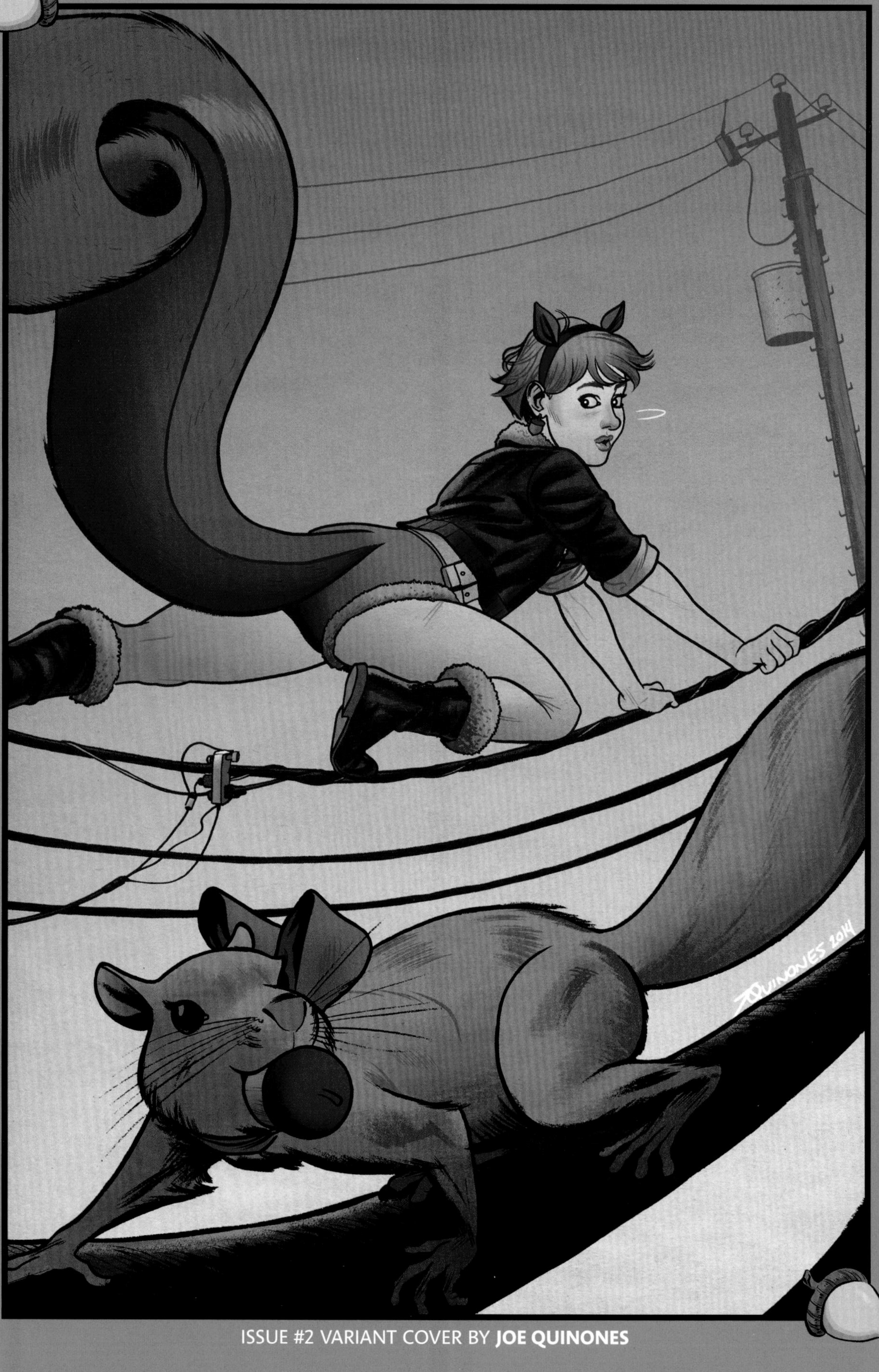
QUINONES 2014

ISSUE #2 VARIANT COVER BY **JOE QUINONES**

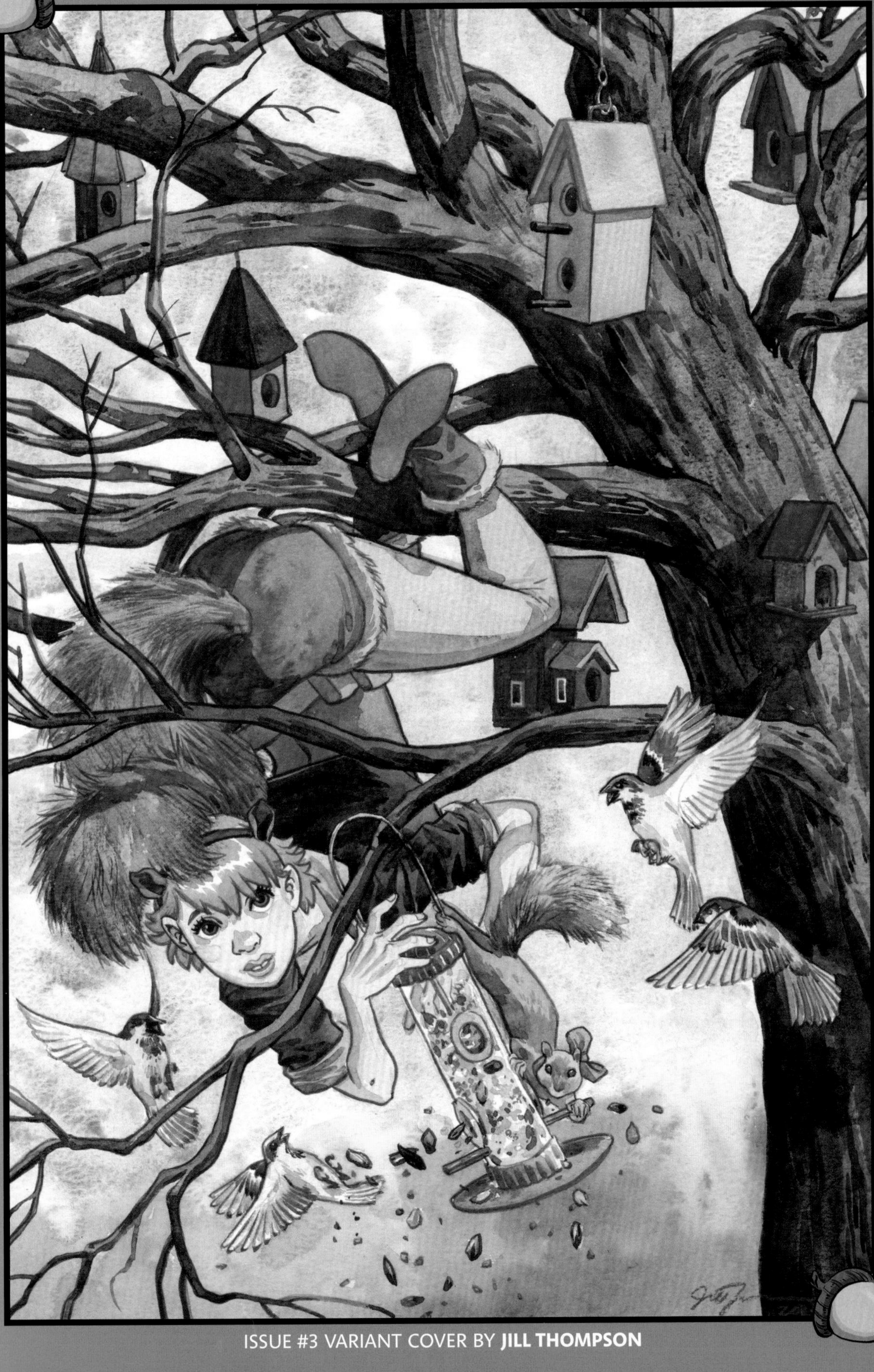

ISSUE #3 VARIANT COVER BY **JILL THOMPSON**

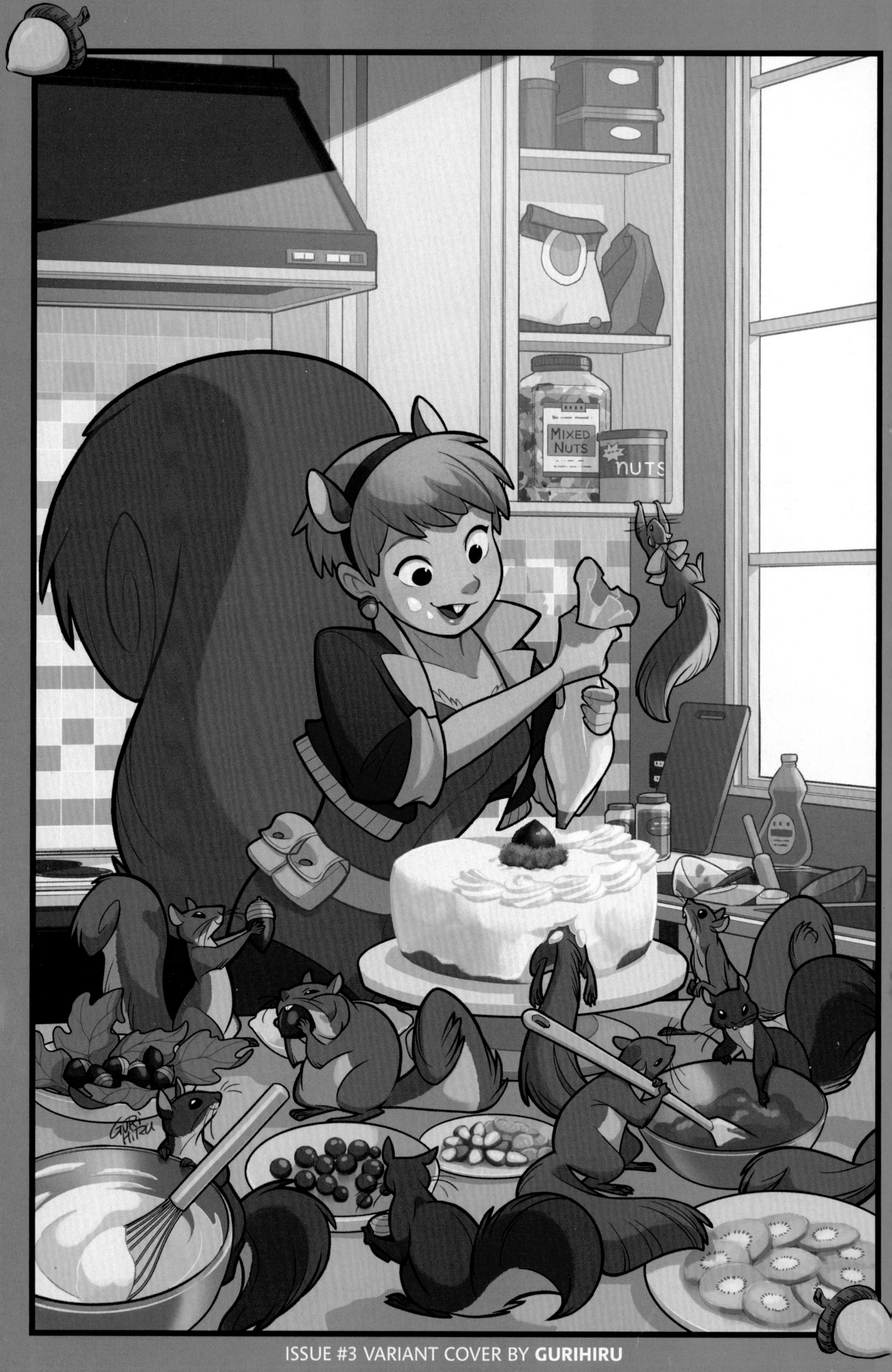
MIXED NUTS
NUTS
GURI HIRU

ISSUE #3 VARIANT COVER BY **GURIHIRU**